DATE DUE

MY 12 '99			

DEMCO 38-296

WEIRD WATER
& FUZZY LOGIC

WEIRD WATER
& FUZZY LOGIC

More Notes of a Fringe Watcher

Martin Gardner

Author of *Science: Good, Bad and Bogus*

 **Prometheus Books**

59 John Glenn Drive
Amherst, New York 14228-2197

Published 1996 by Prometheus Books

Weird Water and Fuzzy Logic: More Notes of a Fringe Watcher.
Copyright © 1996 by Martin Gardner

00 99 98 97 96   5 4 3 2 1

Library of Congress Cataloging-in-Publication Data

Gardner, Martin, 1914–
    Weird water and fuzzy logic : more notes of a fringe watcher / Martin Gardner.
        p.   cm.
    Includes bibliographical references.
    ISBN 1–57392–096–7 (cloth : alk. paper)
    I. Title.
AC8.G335   1996
081—dc20   96–31113
                                                                          CIP

Printed in the United States of America on acid-free paper.

CONTENTS

SKEPTICAL INQUIRER COLUMNS

1. Probability Paradoxes   11
2. Big Bang Is Alive and Well   23
3. Marianne Williamson and *A Course in Miracles*   29
4. Margaret Mead's Great Samoan Hoax   38
5. E-Prime: Getting Rid of Isness   51
6. RMT: Repressed Memory Therapy   63
7. Weird Water, or H_2Oh!   75
8. Pealeism and the Paranormal   83
9. The Cult of the Golden Ratio   90
10. Eyeless Vision and God   98
11. The Tragedies of False Memories   104
12. Literary Science Blunders   117
13. Science vs. Beauty?   131
14. Doug Henning and the Giggling Guru   140
15. Klingon and Other Artificial Languages   147
16. Fuzzy Logic   155

BOOK REVIEWS

17. From Here to Infinity   167
18. How Science Works and Fails   169
19. The Faith of Three Scientists   172

20. Speculations of Freeman Dyson — 175

21. Sheldon Glashow on Science and Superstrings — 178

22. Heinz Pagels on Minds and Computers — 181

23. Symmetry from A to Zee — 184

24. Mathematical Breakthroughs — 186

25. Technology's Awesome March — 193

26. To Pluto and Beyond — 195

27. Astronomers and God — 198

28. Reading the Mind of Nobody — 201

29. Is Western Culture Vanishing? — 203

30. Pencils — 206

31. Allan Sandage's Cosmology — 209

32. The Mystery of Consciousness — 212

33. Is There a God? — 216

34. The World of Stephen Jay Gould — 219

35. Incredible Ramanujan — 222

36. How to Make a PPO — 225

37. Archeological Crankery — 228

38. Joseph Campbell, "Racist" — 231

39. Information Theory and the Universe — 237

40. Mathematical Beauty and Certainty — 240

41. More Speculations of Freeman Dyson — 242

42. Richard Feynman, Magician — 245

43. Is the Second Coming Coming? — 248

44. Do Humans Spontaneously Combust? — 252

45. Will Science Discover Everything? — 255

46. Tunnels of the Mind — 258

If science were explained to the average person in a way that is accessible and exciting, there would be no room for pseudoscience. But there is a kind of Gresham's Law by which in popular culture the bad science drives out the good. And for this I think we have to blame, first, the scientific community ourselves for not doing a better job of popularizing science, and second, the media, which are in this respect almost uniformly dreadful. Every newspaper in America has a daily astrology column. How many have even a weekly astronomy column? And I believe it is also the fault of the educational system. We do not teach how to think. This is a very serious failure that may even, in a world rigged with 60,000 nuclear weapons, compromise the human future.

Carl Sagan, *Skeptical Inquirer* (Fall 1987)

SKEPTICAL INQUIRER
COLUMNS

CHAPTER ONE

PROBABILITY PARADOXES

The column that follows this prologue was written at the request of Ken Frazier, editor of the *Skeptical Inquirer*. In the Summer 1991 issue of the *Skeptical Inquirer* Frazier published a report by Gary Posner on an amusing flap generated by one of Marilyn vos Savant's columns in *Parade*. Ms. Savant had received more mail about her answer to a brain teaser than she had ever received about any topic in a previous column. Frazier in turn received more mail about Posner's article than he had received about any previous piece in the magazine.

It is truly astonishing how difficult it is for even professional mathematicians to comprehend the correct solution to the simple problem Ms. Savant posed. I myself, after devoting one of my *Skeptical Inquirer* columns to the problem, was besieged by letters and phone calls from readers who wanted to argue that the correct answer was in fact wrong.

Here is Posner's report, followed by Frazier's postscript, in turn followed by my column.

"NATION'S MATHEMATICIANS
GUILTY OF 'INNUMERACY,' "
BY GARY POSNER AND KENNETH FRAZIER

"When E. F. Hutton talks, people listen." Who can forget those indelible television commercials, in which the world came to a virtual standstill, focusing its sole attention upon that oracle of financial wisdom (that is, before Hutton went belly-up)? As a rule, when Marilyn vos Savant speaks in her weekly *Parade* magazine column, "Ask Marilyn" (her byline notes that she "is listed in the 'Guiness Book of World Records Hall of Fame' for Highest IQ"), people listen. In the instance discussed below, however, they may have been listening, but they weren't believing—although they should have been.

The following "brain teaser" was submitted to vos Savant last year by a reader:

Suppose you're on a game show, and you're given a choice of three doors. Behind one door is a car; behind the others, goats. You pick a door—say, No. 1—and the host, who knows what's behind the doors, opens another door—say, No. 3—which has a goat. He then says to you, "Do you want to pick door No. 2?" Is it to your advantage to switch your choice?

In her column, vos Savant answered, "Yes, you should switch." She explained that, obviously, there is a $\frac{1}{3}$ chance that the original choice, door No. 1, is the correct one. Therefore, there must be a $\frac{2}{3}$ chance that, since door No. 3 has now been eliminated as a possibility, the car is behind door No. 2. For those readers requiring further explanation, she illustrated the point with this example: "Suppose there are a *million* doors, and you pick door No. 1. Then the host, who knows what's behind the doors and will always avoid the one with the prize, opens them all except door No. 777,777. You'd switch to that door pretty fast, wouldn't you?

Apparently not, based upon the chastising letters vos Savant received from those who ought to know better—mathematicians who share CSI-COP's dismay over the nation's state of "innumeracy." In a follow-up column last December, vos Savant published some examples:

"I'm very concerned with the general public's lack of mathematical skills. Please help by confessing your error . . ."—Robert Sachs, Ph.D, George Mason University.

"You blew it, and you blew it big! . . . You seem to have difficulty grasping the basic principle at work here. . . . There is enough mathematical illiteracy in this country, and we don't need the world's highest IQ propagating more. Shame!"—Scott Smith, Ph.D, University of Florida.

"Your answer to the question is in error. But if it is any consolation, many of my colleagues have also been stumped by this problem." —Barry Pasternack, Ph.D, California Faculty Association.

In an effort to even more clearly illustrate the correctness of her original answer, vos Savant invoked the classic "shell game," in which a pea is placed beneath one of three shells. The gambler/victim is asked to place a finger on one shell, and the "house" then lifts away one of the others, leaving behind two shells, one of which covers the pea. As vos Savant explained, by removing one empty shell "we've learned nothing to allow us to revise the odds on the shell under your finger." She then presented a "probability grid" containing all possible permutations of the game, showing how "when you don't switch, you win one in three times and lose two in three. Try it yourself." (The "shell game" is illegal precisely because, despite the appearance of 50:50 odds, they actually favor the "house" 2 to 1.)

One might have thought, or at least hoped, that this second column would have settled the issue. But in her February 17, 1991, column, we were treated to the following:

"I am in shock that after being corrected by at least three mathematicians, you still do not see your mistake."—Kent Ford, Dickinson State University

". . . Albert Einstein earned a dearer place in the hearts of the people after he admitted his errors."—Frank Rose, Ph.D, University of Michigan

". . . Your answer is clearly at odds with the truth."—James Rauff, Ph.D, Millikin University

"May I suggest that you obtain and refer to a standard textbook on probability. . . ."—Charles Reid, Ph.D, University of Florida

". . . I am sure you will receive many letters from high school and college students. Perhaps you should keep a few addresses for help with future columns."—W. Robert Smith, Ph.D., Georgia State University

"You are utterly incorrect. . . . How many irate mathematicians are needed to get you to change your mind?"—E. Ray Bobo, Ph.D., Georgetown University

". . . If all those Ph.D.s were wrong, the country would be in very serious trouble."—Everett Harman, Ph.D., U.S. Army Research Institute

"Maybe women look at math problems differently than men."—Don Edwards, Sunriver, Oregon

"When reality clashes so violently with intuition," vos Savant responded, "people are shaken." In once again addressing the question "Should you switch?" she apparently decided this time to invoke a more universally accepted phenomenon. Suppose, she says, after choosing door No. 1, and having the host step in and "give a clue" by opening one of the two remaining doors, "at that point . . . a UFO settles down onto the stage. A little green woman emerges, and the host asks her to point to one of the two unopened doors. The chances that *she'll* randomly choose the one with the prize are $\frac{1}{2}$ (as opposed to $\frac{2}{3}$ chances of the original contestant winning by switching). But that's because she lacks the advantage the original contestant had—the help of the host. . . . If the prize is behind No. 2, the host shows you No. 3; and if the prize is behind No. 3, the host shows you No. 2. So when you switch, you win if the prize is behind No. 2 *or* No. 3. *You win either way!* But if you *don't* switch, you win only if the prize is behind door No. 1."

And if *that* isn't sufficiently clear, vos Savant asks the nation's math teachers to perform 400 trials of the "shell game" with their students, the first 200 with *no* "switching," followed by 200 "switches," with random selections to be made by rolling a die until a 1, 2, or 3 comes up. Even if no "little green woman" arrives in a UFO to supervise the trials, I predict a few red faces on those math instructors who will not see the light until the results of the trials are tallied.

–Gary P. Posner

(*Readers are also referred to* Innumeracy: Mathematical Illiteracy and Its Consequences, *by John Paulos [New York: Hill and Wang, 1988].*)

Dr. Posner, an internist in St. Petersburg, Florida, is a member of Mensa, and founder of the Tampa Bay Skeptics.

EDITOR'S POSTSCRIPT

Mathematicians at the Massachusetts Institute of Technology came to vos Savant's defense. "You are indeed correct," wrote Seth Kalson, Ph.D. "My colleagues at work had a ball with this problem, and I dare say that most of them—including me at first—thought you were wrong!" The same thing happened with mathematicians at the University of Oregon. After 92 percent of the letters vos Savant received expressed belief she was wrong, Frank Anderson, head of the University of Oregon's Mathematics Department, said, "Consensus is not the issue. She is 100 percent right."

Skeptical Inquirer reader Lenna Mahoney, an atmospheric scientist in Richland, Washington, writes that she too at first thought the answer was obvious. "It wasn't till I started writing a computer program to simulate the set of choices that I realized I was wrong. You have more information on the second choice because the emcee knew which curtain had the car and took that into account when he chose which curtain to open; after all, he couldn't show the car without prematurely ending the game." Mahoney says not one of the several technical professionals, including Ph.D. scientists, of her acquaintance who saw the thought problem got the right answer by immediate intuition. And several came up with "very fanciful ways of 'proving' that the odds were even." One "refused to accept the results of my computer program," arguing that "in short, if the program didn't agree with him it was wrong."

"This circular rationale illustrates what I find fascinating about the problem," says Mahoney. "Not even experts have the correct intuition, the incorrect answer is infinitely rationalizable using technical-type rhetoric, and everyone thinks the solution is obvious. The basic subtle fallacy seems to be the idea that because there is a choice of two unknowns and only one is right the odds must be even. The point that intuition ignores is that there were originally three choices, from which the two-choice set was derived. It is remarkable that so many technical Ph.D.s should miss that point."—K.F.

*   *   *

Now for my column:

The great controversy aroused by Marilyn vos Savant's several columns in *Parade* magazine about the problem posed by Monty Hall's three doors suggests that readers may like to see this and similar problems discussed in more detail.

The three-door problem, in the form of three prisoners and a warden, was floating around anonymously among mathematicians in the mid-fifties. It is possible that I was the first to write about it, in my October 1959 Mathematical Games column in *Scientific American.* The column was later reprinted in *The Second Scientific American Book of Mathematical Puzzles and Diversions* (1961), currently available as a University of Chicago Press paperback.

Here is how I described the problem:

Three men—A,B, and C—were in separate cells under sentence of death when the governor decided to pardon one of them. He wrote their names on three slips of paper, shook the slips in a hat, drew out one of them and telephoned the warden, requesting that the name of the lucky man be kept secret for several days. Rumor of this reached prisoner A. When the warden made his morning rounds, A tried to persuade the warden to tell him who had been pardoned. The warden refused.

"Then tell me," said A, "the name of one of the others who will be executed. If B is to be pardoned, give me C's name. If C is to be pardoned, give me B's name. And if I'm to be pardoned, flip a coin to decide whether to name B or C."

"But if you see me flip the coin," replied the wary warden, "you'll know that you're the one pardoned. And if you see that I don't flip a coin, you'll know it's either you or the person I don't name."

"Then don't tell me now," said A. "Tell me tomorrow morning."

The warden, who knew nothing about probability theory, thought it over that night and decided that if he followed the procedure suggested by A, it would give A no help whatever in estimating his survival chances. So next morning, he told A that B was going to be executed.

After the warden left, A smiled to himself at the warden's stupidity. There were now only two equally probable elements in what mathematicians like to call the "sample space" of the problem. Either C would be pardoned or himself, so by all the laws of conditional probability, his chances of survival had gone up from $\frac{1}{3}$ to $\frac{1}{2}$.

The warden did not know that A could communicate with C, in an adjacent cell, by tapping in code on a water pipe. This A proceeded to do, explaining to C exactly what he had said to the warden and what the warden had said to him. C was equally overjoyed with the news because he figured, by the same reasoning used by A, that his own survival chances had also risen to $\frac{1}{2}$.

Did the two men reason correctly? If not, how should each have calculated his chances of being pardoned?

The following month I answered like this:

The answer to the problem of the three prisoners is that A's chances of being pardoned are $\frac{1}{3}$, and that C's chances are $\frac{2}{3}$.

Regardless of who is pardoned, the warden can give A the name of a man, other than A, who will die. The warden's statement therefore has no influence on A's survival chances; they continue to be $\frac{1}{3}$.

The situation is analogous to the following card game. Two black cards (representing death) and a red card (the pardon) are shuffled and dealt to three men: A, B, C (the prisoners). If a fourth person (the warden) peeks at all three cards, then turns over a black card belonging to either B or C, what is the probability that A's card is red? There is a temptation to suppose it is $\frac{1}{2}$ because only two cards remain face-down, one of which is red. But since a black card can always be shown for B or C, turning it over provides no information of value in betting on the color of A's card.

This is easy to understand if we exaggerate the situation by letting death be represented by the ace of spades in a full deck. The deck is spread, and A draws a card. His chance of avoiding death is $\frac{51}{52}$. Suppose now that someone peeks at the cards, then turns face up 50 cards that do not include the ace of spades. Only two face-down cards are left, one of which must be the ace of spades, but this obviously does not lower A's chances to $\frac{1}{2}$. It doesn't because it is always possible, if one looks at the faces of the 51 cards, to find 50 that do not include the ace of spades. Finding them and turning them face up, therefore, has no effect on A's chances. Of course if 50 cards are turned over at random, and none prove to be the ace of spades, then the chance that A drew the death card *does* rise to $\frac{1}{2}$.

What about prisoner C? Since either A or C must die, their respective probabilities for survival must add up to 1. A's chances to live are $\frac{1}{3}$; therefore C's chances must be $\frac{2}{3}$. This can be confirmed by considering the four elements in our sample space, and their respective initial probabilities:

1. C is pardoned, warden names B (probability $\frac{1}{3}$).
2. B is pardoned, warden names C (probability $\frac{1}{3}$).
3. A is pardoned, warden names B (probability $\frac{1}{6}$).
4. A is pardoned, warden names C (probability $\frac{1}{6}$).

In cases 3 and 4, A lives, making his survival chances $\frac{1}{3}$. Only cases 1 and 3 apply when it becomes known that B will die. The chances that it is case 1 are $\frac{1}{3}$, or twice the chances ($\frac{1}{6}$) that it is case 3, so C's survival chances are two to one, or $\frac{2}{3}$. In the card-game model this means that there is a probability of $\frac{2}{3}$ that C's card is red.

It is obvious that this confusing problem is equivalent to Marilyn vos Savant's three-door puzzle. Let's model it as a three-shell game. You know that a pea is under just one shell, and you are told in advance—this is a crucial assumption—that after you choose a shell, the operator (who knows where the pea is) will turn over an empty shell. Because he can *always* do this, it provides no new information about the pea's whereabouts. The probability you chose correctly remains $\frac{1}{3}$ even though only two shells remain face down. The probability that the pea is under the other shell rises to $\frac{2}{3}$ because the two probabilities must add to 1 (certainty). Your chances are therefore doubled if you switch your choice to the other shell. Of course if someone approaches the table without knowing what has gone on before, and is told only that the pea is under one of the two shells, the probability *for this person* is 50-50 for each shell.

An even simpler probability brain teaser, equally counterintuitive, is one I introduced in an April 1957 column, but discussed more fully in October 1959. You find yourself sitting next to a stranger on a plane. The following dialogue occurs:

You: "How many children do you have?"
She: "Two."
You: "Is at least one of them a boy?"
She: "Yes."

What is the probability that both are boys? One is tempted to say $\frac{1}{2}$. If one child is a boy, it seems that the other child is either a boy or a girl with equal probability.

Surprisingly, this is incorrect. Assume that *if* there are two boys, they are not twins. Call the older boy B1 and the younger B2. There are three equally probable combinations that will meet the mother's statements: B1 and a girl, B2 and a girl, and B1 and B2. In only one case are both boys, so the chances both are boys is $\frac{1}{3}$, not $\frac{1}{2}$. If you now ask, "Is your *older* child a boy?" and she says yes, the equally probable cases reduce to B1 and a girl, and B1 and B2. The probability both children are boys then rises to $\frac{1}{2}$!

In my April 1957 column (reprinted in another University of Chicago Press paperback entitled *Hexaflexagons and Other Mathematical Diversions*) I gave a strongly counterintuitive problem that goes back at least to 1911. It is another marvelous example of how easily one's intuitions can be misled by seemingly trivial probability questions.

You are playing bridge. After the cards are dealt, you turn to Ms. Jones and ask, "Do you have at least one ace in your hand?" She truthfully answers yes. The probability she has at least one other ace is exactly 5359/14498, or .369+. This is a trifle more than $\frac{1}{3}$. You then ask, "Do you have the ace of spades in your hand?" Again the answer is yes. What is now the probability she has at least one other ace? Incredibly, it rises to 11686/20825, or .561+, which is better than $\frac{1}{2}$! How can naming an ace raise the probability of a second ace?

George Gamow and Marvin Stern, in their amusing little book *Puzzle-Math* (1958), showed how this can be understood by reducing the deck to just four cards: ace of spades, ace of hearts, two of clubs, and jack of diamonds. This "deck" is shuffled and dealt to two players. Ms. Jones's hand can be one of six that are equally possible:(AS, AH) (AS, JD) (AS, 2C) (AH, JD) (AH, 2C) (JD, 2C).

If you ask Ms. Jones if she has at least one ace, five of the hands allow her to say yes. Because only one has a second ace, the chances she holds two aces are $\frac{1}{5}$. If you now ask, "Do you have the ace of spades?" three hands permit her to say yes, one of which has two aces. The probability of a second ace rises from $\frac{1}{5}$ to $\frac{1}{3}$.

There are scores of other paradoxes involving probability that are just as mind-bending. I close with one that eminent philosophers and statisticians are still debating. It was introduced by philosopher of science Carl Hempel, and is known as "Hempel's paradox." Hempel invented it to show how unclear our understanding is of what is meant by a "confirming instance" of a theory.

Consider the conjecture "All crows are black." Everyone agrees that each time you find another black crow it counts as a confirming instance—that is, increases the probability—of the truth of the assertion "All crows are black." Finding a white crow would be a disconfirming instance that would make the conjecture false.

Now consider the fact that the statement "All crows are black" is logically identical with the statement "All not-black objects are not crows." So—you start looking at objects that are not black. You come upon a green necktie. It clearly is not a crow, therefore it confirms the statement,

"All not-black objects are not crows." But if it confirms *that* statement, it follows with iron logic that a green necktie must be a confirming instance of "All crows are black!" This of course seems absurd. It suggests that a scientist can do ornithological research simply by looking around a room.

As rhymester Armand T. Ringer once put it:

> I never saw a purple cow,
> But if I ever see one,
> Will the probability crows are black
> Have a better chance to be 1?

You will understand why I cannot discuss this paradox further when I tell you that in my *Hexaflexagons* book I have a bibliography for this paradox that lists more than sixty references in books and journals where widely different views about this paradox are defended.

The following two letters appeared in *Skeptical Inquirer* (Summer 1992), with my reply:

Martin Gardner's brainteasers are not really paradoxes, although they are certainly ingenious and amusing, as is everything Gardner writes. The air of paradox about his probability "paradoxes" evaporates upon reflecting that they arise from the subjectivist (personalist, Bayesian) interpretation of probability he adopts, which is inconsistent with the objectivist interpretation used in science. Let me explain.

In Gardner's probability problems, there is a question of ignorance or uncertainty, not of objective chance or randomness—which is when probability considerations are legitimate. Let us begin with the simplest problem, that of the woman who has two children, at least one of whom is known to be a boy. It makes no sense to ask what is the probability that the second child too is a boy, because he or she is already born with a definite sex. The question would have made sense only during the very short period of fertilization, because this is indeed a process of random gene shuffling, where each of the sexes has nearly the same chance, i.e., $\frac{1}{2}$. Once the ovum has been fertilized, one of the probabilities has expanded to 1 and the other has contracted to 0.

In the three-door problem the prisoners do not know who has been pardoned by the governor. During the random shuffling of three slips of paper with the names of the prisoners, each of these did have the same probability, namely $\frac{1}{3}$, of being pardoned. But when the shuffling came to an end and only one of the slips was picked, the probability of this one expanded to 1 whereas the probabilities of the other two contracted to 0. *Alea jacta est!* From here on the probability calculus has nothing to say because the random process has stopped. The circumstance that neither the prisoners nor their warden knew the outcome of the process does not authorize them to engage in probabilistic speculations. Probabilities can only be assigned to random events, and propositions are not among them. I have dealt with these problems in my paper "Four Concepts of Probability," *Applied Mathematical Modeling* 5:306–12 (1981).

Finally, Hempel's "paradox of confirmation," about the way to go about testing the proposition that all crows are black, is actually a fallacy. A zoologist intent on putting the generalization to the test begins by noting that it is about crows, so he will observe crows, not neckties, socks, or what have you. (And he will eventually come upon albino crows, which will refute the generalization in question.) The fallacy originates in the logician's exclusive attention to form and his neglect of content, in particular reference, as I have shown in my *Treatise on Basic Philosophy*, vol. 1, pp. 79–81 (Dordrecht: Reidel, 1974).

Mario Bunge, McGill University, Montreal, Canada

Probability applies only to the future. The probability of flipping heads in the future is $\frac{1}{2}$. The probability that an already-flipped coin is heads is either $\frac{1}{1}$ or $\frac{0}{1}$, not $\frac{1}{2}$. The result is fixed; we just don't know what the result is. In the example, once the governor decided whom to pardon, the probability of being executed for A and C is $\frac{1}{1}$ or $\frac{0}{1}$, not something in between. Knowing that B is to die does not change that fact. One might discuss the probability of A guessing the correct answer, but that is not the question posed.

In the example of the prisoners, A and C are said to have a large difference in probability of being executed. Why? How are these two people different? There is only one difference: A asked a question and was given an answer? What if C, not A, had asked and been given the same answer. Then C would have a probability of being executed of $\frac{1}{3}$, and A of $\frac{2}{3}$! Gardner's logic requires a belief that the act of asking the question and receiving the answer alters the probability of being executed. The *probability* of an outcome that has already been decided has been altered by the transfer of information. Now that's paranormal! What if C asked after A had asked? Would the probabilities now shift to $\frac{1}{2}$ for each or would each prisoner have simultaneous probabilities of $\frac{1}{3}$ and $\frac{2}{3}$?

Perhaps this is the long-sought application of quantum mechanics to the macroscopic world. Let's call this paradox "Schroedinger's Prisoner." We know there will be two dead prisoners eventually, but we won't know which the second will be until we examine the corpses. . . .

Frederick W. Gilkey, Takoma Park, Md.

Martin Gardner Replies

Bunge and Gilkey are quibbling over a choice of language that is universally used by ordinary people, gamblers, mathematicians, and scientists.

If I draw a card from a deck, it is perfectly proper for me to say, "The probability that this card is the Queen of Hearts is $\frac{1}{52}$." Everybody knows that the card either is the QH or is not the QH, and that what I mean is that I calculate the probability to be $\frac{1}{52}$ that it will be seen as the QH if I turn it over.

Consider the problem of the two children as modeled by a dime and a penny. I flip both coins and a person with his back turned to me asks, "Is at least one coin heads?" I say yes. No mathematician would hesitate to say that the man could not correctly declare, "The probability both coins are heads is $\frac{1}{3}$." Everybody understands that the coins either are or are not both heads. If he were to ask, "Is the penny heads?" and I answer yes, the probability rises to $\frac{1}{2}$.

The three problems discussed in my column obviously are not paradoxes in the sense of logical contradictions, but in the familiar sense of being surprising and counter-intuitive. For a good analysis of the three-door problem, and the second-ace problem, see "The Car and the Goats," by the distinguished mathematician Leonard Gillman in the *American Mathematical Monthly*, January 1992. (Note that he uses the same language I used.)

As for Bunge's quick dismissal of Hempel's notorious induction paradox, it seems to me he evades Hempel's subtle argument. To the many readers who wrote about this paradox, I urge them to look up my discussion in *Hexaflexagons and Other Mathematical Diversions,* a University of Chicago Press paperback, and check some of the papers listed in my four-page bibliography.

ADDENDUM

So great was the controversy generated by Marilyn vos Savant's column that the *New York Times* ran a front-page article about it: "Behind Monty Hall's Doors: Puzzle, Debate, and Answer?" by John Tierney (July 21, 1991). Letters about the article appeared in the August 11 issue. David Jacobson provided similar coverage in his article "Read This! It's Got Math and a Bit of Everything," in the *Hartford Courant* (March 1, 1991).

Professional mathematicians got into the act. The following papers appeared in mathematical journals:

"Monty's Dilemma: Should You Stick or Switch?" by J. Michael Shaughnessy and Thomas Dick, *Mathematics Teacher* (April 1991): 252–56. See also the Letters section in the January 1992 issue.

"Ask Marilyn: The Math Controversy in *Parade* Magazine," by Anthony Lo Bello, *Mathematical Gazette* (October 1991): 275–77.

"The Car and the Goats," by Leonard Gillman, *American Mathematical Monthly* (January 1992): 3–7.

For discussions of the problem preceding the *Parade* controversy see:

"The Problem of the Three Prisoners," by David Brown, *Mathematics Teacher* (February 1966): 131–32.

"A Paradox in Probability Theory," by Norton Starr, *Mathematics Teacher* (February 1973): 166–67.

"Intuitive Reasoning About Probability: Theoretical and Experimental Analysis of the 'Problem of the Three Prisoners,' " by Shinsuke Shimoto and Shin'ichi Ichikawa, *Cognition* 32 (1989): 1–24.

"Erroneous Beliefs in Estimating Posterior Probability," by Shin'ichi Ichikawa and Hiroshige Takeichi, *Behaviormetrica* 27 (1990): 59–73.

"Let's Make a Deal: The Player's Dilemma," by J. P. Morgan, N. R. Chaganty, R. C. Dahiya, and M. J. Doviak, *American Statistician* (November 1991): 284–89, 347–48.

The problem is included in Frederick Mosteller's *Fifty Challenging Problems in Probability with Solutions* (Addison Wesley, 1965).

CHAPTER TWO

BIG BANG IS ALIVE AND WELL

A few years ago astronomers discovered that the universe is much lumpier than they had supposed. Galaxies are not spread uniformly throughout space. They tend to cluster along the imaginary surfaces of enormous bubbles that surround monstrous voids, or along huge ribbons that twist through space. This lumpiness seems to contradict the uniform distribution of the microwave radiation believed to be the residual glow from a primordial fireball. If the universe is so clumpy, why is this background radiation so incredibly smooth?

Spurred on by a small group of scientists, the media have seized on these newly found large-scale structures as evidence that the big bang (BB) theory is mortally wounded. *Time* (September 2, 1991) headed a page "Big Bang Under Fire." Dozens of reports on the BB's demise have appeared in newspapers and such periodicals as *The Sciences* (January/February 1990) and England's *Nature* (August 10, 1989). Plasma physicist Eric J. Lerner has even written a book titled *The Big Bang Never Happened* (Times Books, 1991), which has been widely and favorably reviewed.

One might think that all conservative Christians would welcome BB theory. Because no one has any clear idea of how a "quantum fluctuation" can occur all by itself in nothing, the BB offers a convenient moment for a Creator to start the process of cosmic evolution. (Of course empty space is not pure nothing; it has to contain quantum fields capable of fluctuating). Indeed, many liberal Christians and philosophical theists have viewed the BB in this light. But among fundamentalists still clinging to the notion that God created the universe some ten thousand years ago, the BB is anathema. To accept it would require accepting an evolving cosmos billions of years old. Creationists are now all in a dither over prospects that the BB may be overturned. It only shows, they say, how shaky modern science is—maybe, just maybe, evidence for a young earth will soon be forthcoming.

"Notes of a Fringe Watcher," *Skeptical Inquirer* (Summer 1992).

It will not be forthcoming. Although BB theory may have to be modified, or even replaced by a new model, evidence that the universe is billions of years old is overwhelming. Not only that, but rumors of the BB's death are enormously exaggerated.

The term *big bang* was coined by British astronomer Fred Hoyle to poke fun at the BB conjecture of physicist George Gamow. At that time Hoyle favored an expanding steady-state model with no beginning and no end. To keep the infinite universe always in the same overall state while it balloons, new matter is constantly being created in the form of hydrogen atoms—though where those atoms come from was never explained. Hoyle's theory met its death when the cosmic background radiation was detected.

At the moment, the BB's chief rival is a theory proposed twenty years ago by Hannes Alfvén, a Swedish physicist and holder of a 1970 Nobel Prize, now eighty-four years old. Alfvén has a reputation as a maverick whose proposals have been a mix of successful hits and unfortunate misses. One of his controversial conjectures was the basis for his *Worlds-Antiworlds* (Freeman, 1966). The book defended the view that half the galaxies in the universe contain stars made of matter and that the other half contain stars made of antimatter. Almost all astrophysicists now agree that the universe is entirely matter.

In Alfvén's model, gravity is not alone in shaping galaxies. They are formed mainly by the electromagnetism of titanic helical vortices in plasma, an ionized (electrically charged) gas, often called a "fourth state of matter," that permeates the universe. Indeed, 99 percent of the universe is plasma. Suns are made of plasma. Their winds are plasma. Plasma surrounds the larger planets, including Earth. It is plasma that produces the polar auroral lights. Fluorescent lights contain a form of plasma.

Only a few plasma physicists favor Alfvén's view that plasma shapes the galaxies. If gravity was acting alone, they maintain, the large-scale galactic clumping would have required at least a hundred billion years, far exceeding the amount of time permitted by BB theory. The plasma theory, they say, not only allows sufficient time for clumping, it also predicted just such clumping.

Although Alfvén's universe is infinite in time and space, it is not a steady-state model like some of its rivals. Drawing on the views of Belgian chemist Ilya Prigogine, it is a universe that began in chaos and is steadily evolving more and more complex forms of order. At the beginning was a uniform hydrogen plasma that had always existed. Over trillions of years it began to develop vortices and gravitational instabilities that finally, after hundreds more billions of years, formed galaxies, stars, and planets. Unlike the BB model, Alfvén's universe is not running down as its entropy increases, but is being continually wound up in ways that Prigogine seeks to explain. Its future is unlimited and unpredictable.

Now, the greatest obstacles to this infinitely evolving cosmos are the red shifts of distant galaxies, which are best explained by a uniformly expanding, finite model. If you run the expansion backward, you reach a time, 10 to 20 billion years ago, when the universe had to be an infinitely dense singularity that exploded.

How does Alfvén evade this evidence? His conjecture is that the primeval plasma first produced a thin mixture of matter and antimatter that gathered into huge clouds. Gravity caused each cloud to start to collapse until the collisions of matter and antimatter produced an explosion that covered a space hundreds of millions of light-years across and lasted millions of years. Portions of each original cloud blew apart to form smaller clouds of matter and antimatter that in turn exploded in myriads of smaller bangs. Alfvén calls this his "fireworks model."

We live in what Alfvén calls a "metagalaxy." It arose from a little bang that occurred 10 to 20 billion years ago, as indicated by the red shifts. In infinite space an infinity of other metagalaxies is forming. Half our galaxies are made of matter; the other half, of antimatter. Stars are so far apart that when galaxies of opposite matter collide, they pass through one another without mutual annihilation. The microwave background comes not from the BB of a singularity. It is radiation from nearby stars, smoothed by intergalactic plasma.

Eric Lerner acknowledges that there are grave difficulties with this scenario, even though he is certain that BB theory has been refuted by the universe's large-scale structures and that something like Alfvén's model will have to be substituted. Another alternative to BB cosmology is the possibility that red shifts are not measures of receding velocities, but the result of other, as-yet-unknown causes. If this is true, then of course our metagalaxy is not expanding at all. Few cosmologists believe that any other explanation of red shifting will be found, or that there is any evidence to support Alfvén's fireworks.

Lerner's battering of the BB theory would be more effective if he would soften his rhetoric, which is like that so often used to support fringe science. Not content with giving data and arguments against the BB, and sketching alternative models, Lerner bashes the scientific establishment for its stubborn inability to accept new ideas. If BB theory is discredited, he warns, would not the careers of hundreds of researchers be threatened?

Although evidence against the BB remains far from persuasive, Lerner's enthusiasm is boundless. He likens the coming rejection of BB theory to the Copernican revolution. Just as astronomers tried vainly to patch up the Ptolemaic model with mystical epicycles, so (Lerner claims) BB buffs keep patching their dying model with such "epicycles" as a sudden inflation of the universe immediately after the BB, mammoth cosmic strings to sculpt the galaxies, yet undiscovered "dark matter" to keep whirling galaxies intact, black holes, gut theories, superstrings, and other improbable ad-hoc devices.

Lerner correctly perceives that if certain popular versions of the BB go, a drastic revision of modern particle physics will be needed, perhaps even a refinement of quantum mechanics. This is a tall order, especially since Lerner has nothing to offer in the way of a better theory of particles.

The most surprising aspect of Lerner's book is his plunge into a dubious sociology of science. He actually believes that the BB's popularity rests not on sound evidence but on an obsession with a free-market economy that allows the rich to get richer and the poor to get poorer. He thinks the dream of working for a brighter future has been forgotten as greed takes over. Along with the greed comes a pessimism about the future of humanity, which in turn generates a pessimism about the future of the universe. He subscribes to the view that if our universe is destined to die from an overdose of entropy, or from a big crunch at the end of a contracting phase, then the universe does seem, as in a much-quoted passage from a book by Steven Weinberg, to be "pointless."

Presumably, if we could only get rid of unfettered capitalism and substitute a more humane democracy, economic woes would be diminished, hope for humanity's future would revive, and scientists would replace the pessimistic BB theory with an optimistic plasma model. The dying universe of BB theory would give way to a universe in which humanity would flourish forever, evolving into higher and higher forms of intelligence as it colonizes the stars. It is hard to believe, but Lerner goes out of his way to point out that Alan Guth developed his inflationary model of the BB at the very time that our nation was experiencing its worst monetary inflation of the century!

Here is a sample of Lerner's sociological speculations:

> Obviously, the small-scale speculators of cosmology did not, in any conscious way, imitate the large-scale speculators of Wall Street. Yet, as in every other epoch, society's dominant ideas permeated cosmology. If the wealthiest members of society earned billions by mere manipulation of numbers, without building a single factory or mill, it didn't seem too strange that scientific reputations could be made with theories that have no more relation to reality. If a tower of financial speculation could be built on debt—the promise of future payment—then, similarly, a tower of cosmological speculation could be built on promises of future experimental confirmation.

Because science is always corrigible, there is indeed a possibility that as more evidence accumulates the BB model will blow up with a bang, or fade slowly with whimpers, or what seems most likely at the moment, be steadily refined. It is true that astronomers change their models of the universe about every fifty years. As someone has said, cosmologists are always wrong but seldom uncertain.

Unfortunately, the dogmatism of big-bangers is exceeded by the dogmatism of their detractors. "The Big Bang is a myth," Alfvén has declared, "a wonderful myth maybe, which deserves a place of honor in the columbarium which already contains the Indian myth of a cyclic universe, the Chinese cosmic egg, the biblical myth of creation in six days, the Ptolemaic cosmological myth, and many others." Writing in *Sky and Telescope* (February 1992), Lerner likens BB theory to the emperor's nonexistent clothes.

Lerner seems to think that we mortals, knowing we will soon die, are less concerned about our own fate than about the fate of our universe hundreds of billions of years from now! Here is his book's stirring next-to-last paragraph:

> Do we live in a finite universe doomed to decay, where humans are insignificant transitory specks on a tiny planet? Or are we instead the furthest advance of an infinite progress in a universe that has neither beginning nor end? Will our actions today have no meaning in the end of all things, and are we now being swept into that inevitable decay? Or does what we do here and now permanently change the cosmos, a change that will echo through a limitless future?

If Lerner's sociology is right, we may have to get rid of capitalist greed before our scientists will open their minds to Alfvén's optimistic cosmology. Lerner is confident that as new evidence against the BB is forthcoming, the pendulum will start swinging the other way and cosmologists will abandon armchair theorizing for a model based more firmly on hard empirical data. It is not clear whether he thinks such a change in cosmology will help eliminate economic greed, or whether the greed will have to go before the cosmology changes.

Although the BB is still favored by the vast majority of cosmologists, who knows what big surprises our new telescopes and particle accelerators have in store? We must wait and see.

ADDENDUM

As the *Skeptical Inquirer's* Summer 1992 issue was on its way to press, the startling news broke that NASA's Cosmic Background Explorer (COBE), peering back some 15 billion years into the past, found that the microwave radiation was far from uniform. Fluctuations in the radiation showed that soon after the big bang there were nonuniform patterns in the radio waves sufficient to account for a rapid congealing of primeval gas into large-scale structures.

The discovery was hailed as the most important in cosmology for the past two decades. "If you're religious, it's like looking at God," said George Smoot, an astrophysicist at the University of California, Berkeley, who led the research team. "The big bang," exclaimed astrophysicist Edward Wright, a member of Smoot's team, "is alive and well, very well!"

Still a mystery is the nature of the "dark matter" required by big-bang theory to account for the galactic structure. As I write, there is yet no word from Alfvén or Lerner about their reaction to the news. My guess is they are not likely to toss in their towels, but will be proposing an explanation for the COBE results that is consistent with their plasma model.

CHAPTER THREE

MARIANNE WILLIAMSON AND
A COURSE IN MIRACLES

Shirley MacLaine, top New Age showbiz guru, has been shoved aside by a new woman on the block, Marianne Williamson. For several years now Williamson has been preaching up a storm about a massive *Course in Miracles,* said to have been dictated by none other than Jesus himself. Let's start at the beginning.

Helen Cohen Schucman (1909–1981) was a psychologist on the staff of the psychiatry department of Columbia University's College of Physicians and Surgeons. In the same department was William N. Thetford. In her middle years Schucman became Thetford's assistant at New York City's Presbyterian Hospital, where he headed the psychology department.

They were an unlikely pair. Thetford, a tall, handsome bachelor, was fourteen years younger that Schucman. She was short, slight, and a professed atheist. Suddenly in 1965 a strange thing happened. A silent "inner voice" commanded her to take notes for a "course in miracles." For almost eight years (1965 to 1973) the Voice dictated at intervals. It was not automatic writing, because Helen was always wide awake. If a phone call interrupted the channeling, the Voice would stop and later take up where it had left off.

Totally stunned, Schucman did not even believe the statements she was scribbling in her shorthand notebooks. When she finally confided to her boss what was happening, he advised her to keep scribbling. Her husband, Louis Schucman, who ran a bookstore in Manhattan, seems also to have been sympathetic. Thetford, previously an agnostic, became so intrigued that he began an intensive study of mysticism and world religions.

Schucman would read her notes aloud and Thetford would type them. There is some dispute over how much the channeled material was edited. Thetford claimed such changes were minor. From time to time they would ask the Voice questions. Eventually a three-part manuscript was produced. Until her death at seventy-one, Helen refused to be identified as the channeler. Since then Thetford has also died.

"Notes of a Fringe Watcher," *Skeptical Inquirer* (Fall 1992).

Enter Judith Skutch, then the wife of Robert Skutch, a New York stock-broker and former writer of television commercials. Born in Brooklyn of Jewish parents, Judy Skutch became extremely active in psychic circles. Her Foundation for Parapsychology Investigation helped fund Stanford Research Institute's research on Uri Geller. She became known as "para-psychology's den mother." When she began to read Helen Schucman's channeled manuscript she was floored, like Paul on the road to Damascus. Abandoning her activities in parapsychology (she had taught the topic at New York University) Skutch decided to devote all her energies to getting *A Course In Miracles* into print. Her organization was renamed the Foun-dation For Inner Peace, now located in Tiburon, California.

Reed Erickson, an American industrialist living in Mexico, shelled out $60,000 for the *Course's* first printing of 300 copies—a photocopy of the typescript published in 1975 under the imprint of Freeperson Press, San Francisco. The next year Judy's foundation printed 5,000 copies in a hardcover set of three blue-bound volumes, a total of 1,188 pages. Vol-ume 1, 622 pages, is the *Course*. Volume 2, *Workbook for Students*, is 478 pages and describes an exercise for each day of the year. Volume 3, *Man-ual for Teachers*, 88 pages, further explicates the *Course*. The set has now sold hundreds of thousands of copies.

The *Course* quickly acquired ardent disciples. Psychologist Kenneth A. Wapnick, a Jewish convert to Roman Catholicism, has dedicated his life to spreading the new revelation. His Foundation for a Course in Mir-acles, in Roscoe, New York, has published six books in which he strug-gles to harmonize the *Course* with Christian doctrine.

The *Course* has spawned a dozen other books and more than a thou-sand study groups here and abroad. Thetford coedited *Choose Once Again*, a book of selections from the *Course*. Robert Skutch's *Journey Without Distance* is a history of the *Course*. His *Messages from My Higher Self* was, he claims, produced by automatic writing while meditating.

Centerlink issued a disk version of the *Course*. Steven Halpern, a New Age pianist, set passages from the *Course* to music. Miracle Distri-bution Center put Halpern's songs on audiotape, and Beverly Hutchinson, who also lectures on the *Course*, is the vocalist. An ad says the songs are "like jewels set in a background of velvet." A wag named Michael Still-water wrote a small handbook for gardeners titled *A Course in Marigolds*, published by the Foundation for Dinner Peas.

Like Mary Baker Eddy, Helen Schucman produced reams of forget-table verse. Judy Skutch issued a posthumous selection of Shuchman's poems in a book titled *The Gifts of God*. The poems read as if they were written by the author of *A Course in Miracles*.

Before their divorce, the Skutches had four children. A daughter, who is now Tamara ("Tammy") Cohen, had exhibited as a child what her parents took to be strong psy powers. In 1985, Cohen and her mother collaborated on *Double Vision*, a book in which each gives an account of her psychic adventures. Judy Skutch now lives in Belvedere, California, with her new husband, retired Army officer William Whitsun.

The *Course* had a profound impact on many notables in psi circles. Willis Harman, who heads the Institute of Noetics, called it "the most important book in the English language." Glen Olds, former president of Kent State University, was similarly smitten. A raft of top parapsychologists praised the book and testified that its exercises had cured their ulcers and other ailments. Other prominent New Agers were not so impressed. The Esalen Institute's cofounder, Michael Murphy, had this to say:

> But there's much more of Helen in the *Course* than I first thought. She was brought up mystically inclined. At four she used to stand out on the balcony and say that God would give her a sign of miracles to let her know that he was there. Many ideas from the *Course* came from the new thought or metaphysical schools she had been influenced by.

Psychiatrist Gerald Jampolsky was a distinguished convert. The *Course* banished his agony after a divorce and cured his alcoholism and back pain. Well known for his work with terminally ill children, Jampolsky has written about the *Course* in books with such titles as *There Is a Rainbow Behind Every Cloud, Love is Letting Go of Fear, Teach Only Love, Goodbye to Guilt*, and *Children as Teachers of Peace*.

It is hard to believe that intelligent people could take seriously a work that is little more than a crude rehash of ideas from the old New Thought movement, which generated a vast literature about a century ago. Initiated by an amusing quack, Phineas Parkhurst Quimby, the movement sprouted into a variety of religions, of which the most successful were Christian Science and Unity.

Like New Thought, which rang all the changes of today's New Age, including psi phenomena and reincarnation, the *Course* swarms with Christian terminology, but uses it in Pickwickian ways. "Atonement," for example, is not the blood atonement of Jesus. It means "at-one-ment," the unity of each of us with everyone else and with God. Acceptance of this "at-one-ment" is the equivalent of Christian conversion and rebirth.

Central to the *Course* is the Hindu notion that time and the physical world are maya, or illusions. The sole reality is Love, which is the same as God. Here is how the *Course* sums itself up in its brief introduction: "Nothing real can be threatened. Nothing unreal exists. Herein lies the peace of God."

The opposite of love, we are told, is not hate but fear. All our major decisions are choices between those two emotions. We can't fear if we love. We can't love if we fear. What everyone else calls sin and guilt do not exist. The course puts it bluntly: "There is no sin," and "evil does not exist." Sin is merely false thinking and perception. We can be mistaken, but in God's eyes we are all guiltless. Even Judas did not sin, Schucman was told. Sin, evil, sickness, even death, are illusions arising from an absence of love, as darkness is the absence of light.

Here is how Mary Eddy Baker said the same thing in her book *Retrospection and Introspection*:

> [Christian] Science saith to Fear: "You are the cause of all sickness; but you are a self-constituted falsity,—you are darkness, nothingness. . . . You do not exist, and have no right to exist, for 'perfect love casteth out fear.' " . . . A demonstration of the unreality of evil destroys evil.

Like so many other New Agers, Thetford likened the unreality of the world to the solipsism that tinges quantum mechanics. "Somehow," he said in an interview, "we are perceiving something that isn't there, and it is our perception of it which gives it reality." As Shirley MacLaine likes to say, we create our own reality.

Forgiveness is another basic concept of the *Course*. Once we experience atonement, cast out fear, and love one another and God, we automatically forgive ourselves and others. Well, not really, because there is nothing to forgive!

The *Course's* "miracles" are not miracles in the biblical sense of violations of natural laws. They are simply "shifts in perception" that cast out fear. However, a disturbing line in the *Course* reads: "Miracles enable you to heal the sick and raise the dead because you made sickness and death yourself, and can therefore abolish both." I'm not sure just what that means. Like Christian Science, the *Course* abolishes evil only by redefining it. As an illusion, pain still remains. An old limerick puts it crisply:

> There was a faith-healer named Neil
> Who said, "Although pain isn't real
>   When I sit on a pin
>   And it punctures my skin
> I dislike what I fancy I feel."

As did New Thought, the *Course* places enormous stress on right thinking—eliminating the negative, accentuating the positive. Its admonitions, however, are expressed in such vapid clichés that they make Norman Vincent Peale and Robert Schuller seem like profound philosophers.

Enter Marianne Williamson. Like Schucman, she comes from a Jewish background. She is thirty-nine, a small, fragile brunette, who was born in Houston, where her father is a wealthy lawyer. A college dropout, she became mired in a series of unhappy love affairs, alcohol and drug abuse, a nervous breakdown, and endless sessions with therapists. She speaks candidly of her "wild" youth and "angry left-wing" opinions. Reading the *Course*, she says, was her "path out of hell."

Williamson's fervent preaching—she has the rapid-fire delivery of a televangelist—soon attracted so many followers that *Time* (July 29, 1991) and *Newsweek* (March 30, 1992) each devoted a full page to her growing fame. In 1992 HarperCollins published her book *A Return to Love: Reflections on the Principles of A Course in Miracles*. After Oprah Winfrey said she had given away a thousand copies, the book jumped to the top of the *New York Times* "How-to" best-seller list.

Williamson lives in West Hollywood as a single mother with her baby daughter India Emmaline. In addition to lecturing regularly in Los Angeles and Manhattan, she has founded a Center for Living in both cities to help victims of AIDS and other serious diseases. A project of the Los Angeles Center, called "Angel Food," provides meals for victims of AIDS. It is supported by such Hollywood luminaries as Shirley MacLaine, Bette Midler, Richard Gere, and Meryl Streep. Although not an ordained minister, Williamson likes to "officiate" at marriages and funerals. It was she who officiated at Elizabeth Taylor's recent marriage to Larry Fortensky.

Williamson's theme song is "What the world needs now is love, sweet love." The word *love* must appear in her book more than a thousand times, in such sentences as "We are all part of a vast sea of love. . . . Love is a win-mode. . . . Only love is real. Nothing else actually exists. . . . Love is to people what water is to plants."

Here are some more gems of Marianne's mushy metaphysics: "We are pregnant with possibilities. . . . Nothing occurs outside our minds. . . . If God is seen as electricity, then we are his lamps. . . . Gray clouds never last forever. The blue sky does. . . . Time does not exist. . . . We're always perfect. We can't not be. . . . Sickness is an illusion and does not actually exist."

"Jesus saves," Williamson tells us, does not mean he rescues us from perdition. It means "Love heals the mind. The leper was healed by Jesus because 'Jesus did not *believe* in leprosy.' "

Some converts to the *Course* are loath to admit that the Voice was the voice of Jesus, but passages in the *Course* make this clear, and Helen Schucman was openly frank about it. She spoke of how disturbed she had been when the Voice first identified itself "in no uncertain terms." One reason she gave for remaining anonymous was so "the true author, Jesus," would always be the *Course's* "sole inspirational figure."

Williamson also assumes that the Voice came from Jesus, but she adds that "Jesus" is merely a metaphor for the love inside us, not a "person." When *Time* and *Newsweek* ran their articles about Williamson, neither had the courage to name Jesus as the *Course's* author. I sent Time a letter asking why. It was not published; but I received a surprising letter from an editor saying that, although they were aware that Schucman claimed Jesus as the author, "space limitations" prevented them from mentioning it.

More amusing is the fact that no article I've yet seen about the *Course* reveals that Jesus once dictated instructions to Schucman on how to construct an electronic machine that would heal sickness. Because only love can heal, I assume the machine would heal through the love of those who manufactured it. Robert Skutch, in his history of the *Course*, says that the description of the device was shown to several "eminent scientists." Unfortunately, none was able to understand it.

What about reincarnation? Like the *Course*, Williamson waffles. Death is unreal because when our bodies die, our spirit indeed lives on. It is like removing an old suit of clothes, she writes, or like a book that never ends. "The end of our physical incarnation is like the end of a chapter, on some level setting up the beginning of another."

Again: "We have been alive forever. We will be alive forever more."

Does this mean previous and future lives on earth? Williamson is vague. She quotes the *Course* as saying, "Reincarnation cannot, then, be true in any real sense." Why? "Because there is no linear time. If we have past lives, or future lives, then they're all happening at once." This is mystifying. Physicists like to define time as that which keeps everything from happening at once. Can you imagine "living" in a timeless world where everything happens at once?

"Heaven is here," says the *Course*. "There is nowhere else. Here is now. There is no other time." Again: "Heaven is not a place. . . . It is merely the awareness of perfect oneness, and the knowledge that there is nothing else; nothing outside this awareness, and nothing within."

On the other hand, Williamson can write, "Angels are the thoughts of God and in Heaven you will think like angels."* Can you conceive of "thinking" without time, and in a place that is not a place?

One can be a deep student of the *Course*, Williamson says, and either

---

*In her mystifying "glossary" at the close of *Science and Health,* Mary Baker Eddy defined "Angels" as "God's thoughts passing to man."

believe or not believe in reincarnation. Whether she believes it the way Shirley MacLaine does is hard to know. At any rate, we are mercifully spared details about Williamson's previous incarnations.

However, like MacLaine, Williamson is aware of her good looks, humor, and charisma. Like MacLaine, she enjoys tossing around four-letter words. Like MacLaine, she is self-absorbed and relishing her glitzy fame. Like MacLaine, she is forever recalling episodes in her past, as if (for instance) anyone cares to know she was once strongly attracted to a gay man.

In recent months she seems to have forgotten the *Course's* lessons. The *New York Post* (February 25, 1992) headed its "Page Six" column: "Top-Selling Guru Trashed as Tyrant." The column pictures Williamson as "becoming a power sponge: abusing subordinates, throwing temper tantrums, and forcing out highly connected board members who've brought in celebrities and millions of dollars to her work."

At one party, says the *Post*, Williamson "pitched a hissy" because the host asked Shirley MacLaine to give the fundraising speech instead of her. Also according to the *Post*, she told a talent manager "to go f—— himself because she wasn't properly introduced to Dolly Parton. She seems to be on a major power trip. She's gotten rid of everyone who disagrees with her."

Williamson is quoted as saying: "I should be allowed those reactions. I'm not perfect." Not perfect? Doesn't the *Course* say everyone is perfect?

Williamson has called herself "a bitch for God." Powerful Hollywood people, reports "Page Six," "are saying the description is two words too long."

Will the attractive guru rediscover love, sweet love? And will her followers, along with other disciples of the *Course*, ever succeed in plugging the holes in their heads?

On May 22, 1992, the *New York Post* reported that Random House, offering an advance in the millions, had signed Williamson for two more books: *On Women** and *The Healing of America*. Jacqueline Onassis, a Doubleday senior editor, wined and dined Williamson, but Random House got the contract.

ADDENDUM

Several readers, including a rabbi, were disturbed by my identifying several true believers in the *Course* as Jewish. I did this because I find it

---

*Random House published Williamson's book on women in 1993 under the title *A Woman's Worth*.

amazing that anyone with a Jewish background would relish a book written by Jesus. When I spoke on the phone with Helen Schucman's husband, I asked him if he believed that Jesus had dictated the *Course*. His
immediate response was, "How could I? I'm Jewish."

I also went out of my way to mention Helen's professed atheism, and
the Catholic background of one prominent promoter of the *Course*. I did
this because the *Course* so obviously contradicts both atheism and
Catholicism. If I were to write about Christian converts to, say, Islam,
would it not be relevant to mention that they were former Christians?

That the Voice claimed to be the voice of Jesus there is not the slightest doubt. Here are two passages from the *Course*: "If the Apostles had
not felt guilty, they never could have quoted me as saying, 'I come not to
bring peace but a sword.' This is clearly the opposite of everything I
taught" (p. 87). "I raised the dead by knowing that life is an eternal
attribute of everything that the living God created" (p. 59).

In 1991 Kenneth Wapnick published a 521-page biography of Helen
titled *Absence from Felicity: The Story of Helen Schucman and Her Scrib-
ing of A Course in Miracles*. I have not read this work, but D. Patrick
Miller, a journalist and admirer of the *Course*, sent me a copy of his review
of Wapnick's book from *Gnosis* magazine (Fall 1992). As Miller tells us,
Wapnick reveals a lot of dialogue between Helen and the Voice "that was
too personal to be published." For example, on one occasion Jesus
explained to Helen why he had sent her shopping to a certain bargain basement. It was because a salesman there needed her advice! Miller adds:

> Despite such intimate guidance, Schucman never warmed to the volu-
> minous message of spiritual healing and brotherhood that she transmit-
> ted, and it failed to heal her troubled relationship with Thetford. "By the
> time I met them in late fall of 1972, right after the *Course* was com-
> pleted," Wapnick writes, "their relationship was at an all-time low, and
> it only seemed to worsen from there. It was almost as if Helen were
> determined to prove that the *Course* was ineffective at least, and dele-
> terious at worst, enabling her to feel more justifiably bitter about her
> life." She died of pancreatic cancer in 1981, her conflicts with Thetford,
> Jesus, and the *Course* still apparently unresolved.

Miller is harsh on Williamson's book for its "flat, artless prose style."
He attributes this to the fact that several ghostwriters had a hand in shaping the text.

Miller also sent me a copy of his article "A Course in Miracles: A Balanced View," which appeared in Brooklyn's New Age magazine *Free
Spirit* (December/January 1990–91). Miller had spoken to everyone
closely connected with the *Course*, and was the last to interview Thetford

before he died in 1988. The article bristles with revealing material. Helen's mother, Miller tells us, "dabbled both in theosophy and Christian Science." The influence of Christian Science on the *Course,* as I pointed out in my column, is pervasive, especially in its denial that the physical world is "real," and its pretense of being Christian while abandoning such basic Christian doctrines as original sin and the atonement. Three times in *Science and Health* Mary Baker Eddy explains "atonement" as meaning "at-one-ment" with God.

According to Miller, the major religious influences on young Helen came from her Roman Catholic governess and a Baptist cook. In her later years she was fascinated by the writings of Edgar Cayce, and became a member of the Cayce Foundation in Florida.

Miller shares Wapnick's belief that Helen's professed atheism was a sham:

> "Helen's atheism makes a good story," Ken Wapnick told me, "but it's not really true. You can't be that militant against something unless you believe in it at some level. There were periods of Helen's life when she went to Mass every day; she was attracted to it without believing in it. She had two purses full of Catholic rosaries and medals, accumulated prior to the *Course.* She had a deep knowledge of the Bible. Helen really adopted a pose, because she was a psychologist who *had* to be an atheist."

Wapnick, who abandoned plans to enter a Catholic monastery after reading a rough manuscript of the *Course,* became its principal editor. He and Helen worked for a year on shaping the text. It was not easy, because at times Helen would burst into laughter and say she couldn't understand a word of what a sentence meant. Wapnick would then have to interpret it for her and put it into clearer English.

Thetford told Miller that Helen always exhibited a split personality with respect to the *Course.* Willis Harman, in his foreword to Robert Skutch's history, *Journey Without Distance,* recalls Helen saying, "I know the *Course* is true—but I don't believe it."

In their newsletter, *The Lighthouse* (September 1993), Kenneth and Gloria Wapnick revealed that they left out portions of the *Course* dictated by Jesus, but which he asked them to remove. . . . In an earlier issue (December 1992) the Wapnicks disclosed that is was Jesus who ordered them to copyright the *Course.* The Copyright Office told them the work could not be copyrighted as anonymous. On the other hand, the Lord had forbidden Helen to put her name on the *Course.* The Wapnicks compromised. The work's author was registered as "anonymous," followed by Helen's name in parentheses!

CHAPTER FOUR

MARGARET MEAD'S
GREAT SAMOAN HOAX

In an earlier column on Margaret Mead, reprinted in my book *The New Age*, I focused mainly on Mead's occult beliefs and her conviction that the earth is being observed by extraterrestrials in flying saucers. Only a brief mention was made of Derek Freeman's *Margaret Mead and Samoa: The Making and Unmaking of an Anthropological Myth* (Harvard University Press, 1983). This explosive book roundly trounced Mead for flagrant errors in her most famous work, *Coming of Age in Samoa: A Psychological Study of Primitive Youth for Western Civilization* (Morrow, 1928).

Since I wrote that column, new and irrefutable evidence has come to light proving that young Mead was indeed the gullible victim of a playful hoax. Her book, until recently considered a classic, is now known to be of minimal value—an amusing skeleton in anthropology's closet.

Mead was twenty-three in 1925 when she went to Samoa as a Columbia University graduate student working under Franz Boas, then the nation's most eminent anthropologist. At that time cultural anthropology was in the grip of extreme environmentalism, understandable as a reaction against earlier ethnocentric anthropologists who faulted alien cultures for failing to conform to the values of the anthropologists' own society. Boas could not accept the notion of a biologically determined human nature that would provide the basis for ranking cultures in terms of how well they met human needs. Genetic elements, Boas wrote in *The Encyclopedia of the Social Sciences*, are "altogether irrelevant as compared with the powerful influence of environment."

For Boas and his protégée Mead, human nature consisted entirely of such body needs as food, water, and sex. How a culture copes with those needs was seen as enormously varied in ways that could not be evaluated across cultural boundaries. In brief, for Boas there were no universal human values.

This extreme view, known as "cultural relativism" or "cultural determinism," poses obvious difficulties. How, for example, can a relativist

---

"Notes of a Fringe Watcher," *Skeptical Inquirer* (Winter 1993).

condemn slavery, seeing that slavery was integral to so many great cultures from ancient Greece to our own nation's South before the Civil War? How can a relativist object to the racism of Hitler's Germany, the torturing of heretics by the Inquisition, or the burning and hanging of witches? However, this is not the place to discuss the defects of cultural determinism. Instead, I shall stress the fresh evidence that Mead was shamelessly hoodwinked by two Samoan pranksters.

Derek Freeman, an Australian anthropologist, summarizes this new evidence in three papers: "Fa'apua'a Fa'amu and Margaret Mead," in *American Anthropology* (December 1989); "There's Tricks i' thi' World" (a quote from Hamlet), in *Visual Anthropology Reviews* (Spring 1991) and "Paradigms in Collision," in *Academic Questions* (July 1992). It is from these articles that I take what follows.

When Mead visited Samoa she was under the impression, based solely on hearsay, that Polynesians were as sexually promiscuous as anthropology graduate students. Because she thought their sex lives were unrestrained, Mead was convinced that Samoan adolescents never suffered the anxieties and torments of Western teenagers.* Her mentor, Boas, sent her to Samoa for the express purpose of confirming this view, thereby providing strong support for his radical cultural determinism.

Because Mead spoke very little Samoan, she conducted most of her interviews through interpreters. Her principal informants were two native "girls" (as Mead herself called them), Fa'apua'a Fa'amu, who spoke English, and her friend Fofoa, who did not. All three "girls" were about the same age. In a letter, Mead called the other two her "merry companions."

Embarrassed and offended by Mead's constant questions about sex, a taboo topic in Samoa, the two merry companions decided to play on Mead what they thought would be a harmless joke. Such pranks on outsiders were and are a common form of Samoan fun. The two girls had no inkling that Mead was an anthropologist who would go home and write a book about what they told her. To them she was just a young, naive, meddlesome tourist.

With sidelong glances at each other, and lots of giggling, the two merry companions told Mead everything she wanted to hear. Yes, adolescents had complete sexual freedom, moving stress-free from childhood to adultery. Samoans were a happy, free-love people. Poor Mead bought it all. Samoa, she wrote in her book, is "a casual, problem-free society" in which the ambition of every adolescent girl is "to live with as many

---

*The classic work on the storms and stresses of the "coming of age" of American children was the two-volume work *Adolescence*, by psychologist G. Stanley Hall, published in 1904.

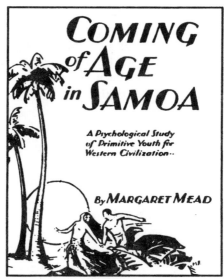

The jacket of the first edition of Mead's book shows two young Samoans, bare above the waist, romping under a full moon toward a tryst under the palm trees.

lovers as possible" before she marries. Even after wedlock sexual freedoms are permitted. Not only was the book avidly read by our nation's "flaming youth," eager for sex without commitment, but anthropologists praised it to the skies. In his foreword to the book Boas called it a "painstaking investigation" of a "culture so entirely different from our own." Bertrand Russell, Havelock Ellis, H. L. Mencken, and other famous writers joined in the chorus of adulation.

After Mead's book appeared, disturbing news began to emerge from more qualified investigators of Samoan life. Unanimously they concluded that Samoan Society was exactly the opposite of what Mead had portrayed. It was a culture of strict parental controls and unbending sex taboos. Female virginity was so highly prized that brides were tested for virginity before they were allowed to marry! Adolescents had the same difficulties in coming of age as they had in Western lands. But so great was Mead's growing reputation as the nation's top female anthropologist, and so firmly entrenched was cultural relativism among anthropologists and sociologists, that Mead's book remained an admired work for more than half a century. It is still in print in both hardcover and paperback editions.

Freeman's book, the first to accuse Mead of having been flim-flammed, aroused his colleagues to unbelievable fury and vindictiveness. Freeman was called "crazy," "fueled by academic venom," a person who "threw nothing but spitballs." He was accused of bribing Samoans to support his bizarre opinions and of having "attacked a missionary with an axe." Melvin Embler attacked Freeman in "Evidence and Science in Ethnography: Reflections on the Freeman-Mead Controversy," in *American Anthropologist* (vol. 87, 1985, pp. 906–909).

At the 1983 meeting of the American Anthropological Association, in Chicago, a special session was devoted to vilifying Freeman. Later that day a motion was passed denouncing his book as "unscientific." Here is how British philosopher Karl Popper reacted in a letter to Freeman:

> Many sociologists and almost all sociologists of science, believe in a relativist theory of truth. That is, truth is what the experts believe, or what the majority of the participants in a culture believe. Holding a view like this your opponents could not admit that you were right. How could you be, when all their colleagues thought like they did? In fact, they could *prove* that you were wrong simply by taking a vote at a meeting of experts. That clearly settled it. And your facts? They meant nothing if sufficiently many experts ignored them, or distorted them, or misinterpreted them.

Not until 1987 was Freeman completely vindicated. Fofoa had died in 1936, and Fa'apua'a was presumed also dead. To Freeman's surprise she was very much alive and eager to talk. For decades, she said, she had been burdened with guilt over the huge success of Mead's book, and now was relieved at last to be able to tell her story. A lifelong Christian, she swore to the truth of her account with a hand on a Samoan Bible.

When Mead intimated that Fa'apua'a was promiscuous, Fa'apua'a was shocked. At that time she was what in Samoa is called a *laupou*, or ceremonial virgin. After comprehending what Mead wanted them to say, the two girls decided to play a typical Samoan prank on this curious young woman from America. They never dreamed that Mead would base an entire book on their lies.

When Larry Gertenstein interviewed Fa'apua'a for his article "Sex, Lies, Margaret Mead, and Samoa," in the Australian magazine *Geo* (June-August 1991), the elderly woman, now a grandmother and nearing ninety, said that when Mead asked where she and Fofoa went at night they would pinch each other and say, "We spent our nights with boys, yes, with boys!" Samoan girls, Fa'apua'a added, "are terrific liars when it comes to joking. But Margaret accepted our trumped-up stories as though they were true. Yes, we just fibbed and fibbed to her."

Had Mead ever pressed her two merry friends for verification of their lies, Fa'apua'a said, they would have at once confessed, but Mead never challenged anything. She just scribbled it all down avidly in her note-books. There was a rumor that Mead had an affair with a young Samoan. It is not known if this is true, but Fa'apua'a said she and Fofoa firmly believed it, and this made them feel less hesitant in hoaxing their visitor.

On three occasions Mead was made a "ceremonial virgin" of Samoa. These honors, which she greatly enjoyed, would never have been con-ferred on her if she had revealed that she was married at the time! It was said that Mead, during one of the ceremonies, danced about bare-chested.

Cultural relativism may be dying a slow death as more and more anthropologists and sociologists rediscover what they could have learned decades ago from John Dewey, a strong believer in a common human nature as a foundation for a naturalistic ethics. Here are some passages from Dewey's essay "Does Human Nature Change?" in *Problems of Men* (Philosophical Library, 1946):

> The existence of almost every conceivable kind of social institution at some time and place in the history of the world is evidence of the plas-ticity of human nature. This fact does not prove that all these different social systems are of equal value materially, morally, and culturally. The slightest observation shows that such is not the case.
>
> ... By "needs" I mean the inherent demands that men make because of their constitution. Needs for food and drink and for moving about, for example, are so much a part of our being that we cannot imagine any condition under which they would cease to be. There are other things not so directly physical that seem to me equally engrained in human nature. I would mention as examples the need for some kind of companionship; the need for exhibiting energy, for bringing one's powers to bear upon surrounding conditions; the need for both cooper-ation with and emulation of one's fellows for mutual aid and combat alike; the need for some sort of aesthetic expression and satisfaction; the need to lead and to follow, etc.
>
> Whether my particular examples are well chosen or not does not matter so much as does a recognition of the fact that there are some ten-dencies so integral a part of human nature that the latter would not be human nature if they changed. These tendencies used to be called instincts. Psychologists are now more chary of using that word than they used to be. But the word by which the tendencies are called does not matter much in comparison to the fact that human nature has its own constitution.

Freeman points out that back in 1945 anthropologist G. P. Murdock provided a long list of universals common to all known cultures. A simi-lar case for them was made by Donald Brown in *Human Universals*

(1991). Still another defense can be found in Irenaus Eibl-Eibesfeldt's massive *Human Ethology* (1989).

Freeman quotes an anthropologist as saying, "There is no such thing as human nature independent of culture." Obviously true, Freeman agrees, but the same truth can be put the other way around: "There is no such thing as culture independent of human nature."

Freeman believes that what he calls an "interactionist paradigm shift" is now taking place in anthropology. A crude, outdated relativism is slowly giving way to the sensible view that cultures arise from an interplay of genetics and environment. Perhaps the time is approaching when cultural anthropologists will have the courage to declare, without shame, that evils such as slavery, racism, infanticide, genocide, and tobacco smoking are not value-free customs comparable to such folkways as traffic regulations and fashions in dress, but behavior that can be condemned on the basis of values common to humans everywhere.

ADDENDUM

My column on Mead provoked a large number of letters both favorable and unfavorable. The *Skeptical Inquirer* (Summer 1993) published letters from three anthropologists, followed by my rejoinder.

John R. Cole

I was surprised by Martin Gardner's article for a couple of reasons. I believe he may rely too strongly on the case made against Margaret Mead by Derek Freeman with Mead now dead and unable to reply. More important, I question his rather extreme and puzzling definition of the "cultural relativism" taught by anthropologist Franz Boas and Gardner's assertion that this idea was at great odds with John Dewey's philosophy.

In fact, Franz Boas and philosopher John Dewey co-taught courses at Columbia University on the nature of culture and the relationship between education and biological determinism. Both were adamant cultural determinists in the "nature-nurture" argument. Both men are widely regarded as founders of the modern "humanist" movement, which emphasized human behavioral plasticity and the possibility of improving society through education, defining morality without recourse to divine or biological absolutes, and by learning from diverse cultures rather than condemning the "other." Boas was one of the leading spokespersons for racial and religious tolerance until his death in 1943; like Dewey (and unlike most professional scholars) he devoted huge amounts of time and energy to public writing, radio interviews, advising popular movements, and so forth, on the need to respect cultural differences without assuming the superiority of white, Western European mores—*while at the same time tirelessly campaigning against racism, sexism, culturally imposed inequality, imperialistic warfare, and many other "progressive" issues; he worked extensively with Dewey and others on these matters.* Boas in fact died at a luncheon he was helping to sponsor to support Paul Rivet and the French Resistance.

I once asked Boas's daughter Franziska about the possible conflict between her father's relativism and his political activism. She replied, in essence, that her father taught his students what he taught his family: not to judge people harshly because they differ from your culture, but to defend human dignity and oppose suffering—by taking the lead in your own society, showing that doing "right" does not get defined as just doing things the way "normal, middle-class Europeans do them," one gains the authority to criticize harmful cultural practices in other cultures as well.

Cultural relativism is such a cornerstone of the skeptical, humanistic movement that I do not like to see it portrayed otherwise. It certainly has its problems, and at worst it can be used by a Jerry Falwell to slander any form of respect for other peoples' beliefs, but that certainly was not Boas's approach or goal. It was not the "moral relativism" Gardner implies.

Margaret Mead, did, in fact, say some oversimplified things in public about the absoluteness of cultural relativism. I challenged her on this a couple of times when I was in one of her classes and was not satisfied with her "public," pat answer, which seemed to imply that "all behaviors are equal." But this was not her view in serious conversation or in her long life of work for specific goals, such as opposing war, sexism, and inequality.

Some—maybe a lot—of the critique of her book *Coming of Age in Samoa* is accurate. Mead was indeed looking for evidence that there were people a lot different from her own, happier with their sexuality, and proof that "normal" was not limited to the supposed Victorian ideal. Boas did send her in search of evidence to demonstrate that the Euro-American middle class was not the only viable way of life, and she was undoubtedly too uncritical of informant information.

Without defending everything in *Coming of Age in Samoa*, in her last years Mead and some of her allies in fact made some serious counterarguments. (Freeman's complaints and others like them were in the wind long before he published them.) Sadly, she confided possibly important information to friends while maintaining that it was important not to "stoop to reply." The result, of course, leaves her reputation tarnished probably more than it should be. At least one of her long-time assistants told me of her frustration at living up to her promise not to "hit back."

Gardner is correct that this was unscientific conduct, but silence is not quite the same thing as agreement with charges or the inability to reply.

Incidentally, Gardner does not mention that one of the factors that led anthropologists to defend Mead so strongly was Freeman's seeming to save his attack until after her death when he had been nursing it long before. Also, there was resentment that he seemed to break the story sensationalistically via press conferences and press releases with comments along the lines of how his book was going to put an end to Mead's reputation once and for all. Many thought his success on the talk-show circuit made his claims look less scientific (although Mead was a champion on that route). Instead of "adding to an earlier ethnography," or "revising" it, or correcting errors (not everything in it was wrong), Freeman made it his mission to destroy the reputation of the book's recently deceased author.

In any case, I'm troubled to see this blanket denunciation of cultural relativism. Boas and Mead and others have used the concept to advocate tolerance of diversity without defending human suffering, which is, of course, a widespread human norm.

John R. Cole is an anthropologist at the University of Massachusetts, Amherst.

Theodore Schwartz

Such is my great respect for Martin Gardner, whom I identify with skepticism, that I was grieved to see the lapse in his own skepticism in "The Great Samoan Hoax." The article shows what happens when skepticism is applied to only one side of a polemic. I do not see evidence of close *critical* reading of Derek Freeman's (1983) book and certainly not of Margaret Mead's (1928; 1930) two books on Samoa. I wrote one of the many reviews (Schwartz 1983) of the Freeman book (together with Mead's), striving to be objective and balanced (an aim that I thought needed no apology in this journal). Mead's second field trip was to Manus, in what is now Papua New Guinea, a few years after her work in Samoa. When she returned to Manus twenty-five years later (1953), I worked with her as a field assistant while doing my own doctoral research. I was neither her student nor an acolyte; we both agreed and disagreed on many things, but I observed her work at firsthand and was able to check her earlier work in Manus. I do not find it credible that she was so mistaken or taken in as Freeman argues and Gardner swallows.

One could write Freeman's book by negating every sentence in Mead's. I will not repeat here what I wrote in my review. There is much more in her book than the tales of trysts to which Gardner refers, which were to some degree institutionalized as a part of Samoan and Polynesian culture. The idea that the anthropologists' informants (now correctly referred to as "associates" and "collaborators") systematically lie to the gullible anthropologist over an extended period is a story that I have heard quite often, not just with respect to Mead. We are aware that people often tell us what they think we are eager to hear, although of course this doesn't apply to Freeman and those who interviewed Mead's informants fifty years later.

What we study disappears before our eyes over a few decades. I have made a dozen field trips to Manus over the past forty years. There is much that I was once told and can document that would now be denied, as people construct a past suited to present beliefs and values. What is remarkable is that some of pre- or early colonial native culture survives, although often underground or under a deep reluctance to speak of past customs so thoroughly condemned by Christian modernity. Freeman's own book is not without contradictory indications with respect to Samoan sexual morality. Mead's other book on Samoa, like her second book on Manus, is a scholarly monograph on kinship and social organization. I am sure that there are both errors and omissions, as there are in her Manus works. They are nevertheless remarkable for the time in which they were done.

That Mead was highly intelligent, quick, perceptive, and phenomenally energetic cannot be taken from her. Gardner's inclusion of mere gossip, which followed her wherever she went, that she took native lovers, that she danced bare-breasted, does him no credit. Freeman convinces me that Mead gave a one-sided picture of Samoan culture and temperament (as does he). She was partly mistaken. Having labored for decades to prove this, it seems odd that Freeman could now offer, and Gardner accept, the idea that she was the "hoaxee" rather than the "hoaxer." I believe that she was neither, but rather that she was partly in error, biased by a wish to prove her point and dramatize it as was her wont. So, for example, she failed to give a full account of Samoan aggressivity. She discounted the Samoan cult of virginity. (I argue it is likely that Freeman has done the opposite.)

As for the elementary discourse on human nature, spare us! Freeman's and Gardner's "interactionism" is at a level that no sane person denies—and when it gets more specific, as in some of the claims of sociobiology, Freeman also balks. The "biology" that Boas (a person of towering stature in the founding of anthropology) combated was *not* that of a generic biological substrate to human behavior and culture, but rather that of racism and eugenics that would explain the differences among cultures (and individuals) by biological difference. Freeman and Mead, were it not for his quest to redeem the Samoan people from her depiction of a relaxed sexuality, would fully agree in rejecting the idea that differences between Samoan and American behavior and culture were biological.

Further, Boas and Mead believed that when any universalistic characterization of human nature was offered, it was subject to what Mead called the "yes, but the Eskimo . . ." test. The issue that Mead addressed was not whether puberty was a universal biological event, but whether adolescence inevitably had the characteristics of "storm and stress" attributed to it by psychologists like G. Stanley Hall. Puberty here is the near-genotype; adolescence is phenotypic, what particular cultures make of puberty. Even if Mead were wrong about Samoa, the point is solidly established by many other studies in Polynesia and elsewhere that the concomitants of puberty are variable, that cultures run the gamut from sexual permissiveness to repressiveness, as has our own Amer-European culture in different subcultures and historical periods. The only biological determinism that this would offend would be a straw man as phony as the cultural determinism that Freeman and, alas, Gardner choose to engage.

Any sensible formulation of cultural relativism and cultural determinism would see it for what it then was, a well-founded antidote to racism and ethnocentrism. Gardner suggests that the values by which we condemn genocide or infanticide must be grounded in the biological base of human nature. I would suggest that these values are emergent, and as yet incompletely so, from cultural evolution.

REFERENCES

Freeman, Derek. 1983. *Margaret Mead and Samoa: The Making and Unmaking of an Anthropological Myth.* Cambridge, Mass.: Harvard University Press.
Mead, Margaret. 1928. *Coming of Age in Samoa: A Psychological Study of Primitive Youth for Western Civilization.* New York: William Morrow.
———. 1969 (orig. 1930). *Social Organization in Manu'a.* Honolulu: Bishop Museum.
Schwartz, Theodore. 1983. "Anthropology: A Quaint Science." *American Anthropologist* 85, no. 4 (December): 919–29.

Theodore Schwartz is a professor of anthropology at the University of California at San Diego, LaJolla.

Frank Lee Earley

I greatly appreciated Martin Gardner's article. As Karl Popper said, "The habit of calling its own findings into question and attempting to disprove them is the core of scientific work." From that perspective, Gardner has done notable service on the Margaret Mead issue and on many previous occasions.

There is, however, one troublesome aspect of the article: Gardner's treatment of cultural relativity. He takes the most extreme possible view in citing Boas ("there were no universal human values"), erroneously equates that position with cultural determinism, and then implies that anthropology adopted the whole package.

In fact, the anthropological approach to cultural relativity is quite different. Cultural relativity begins with the recognition that there are many ways of solving human problems; and it is the task of anthropology to research and understand all of them. If the task is to understand, then adopting a priori judgments about what is good or bad becomes an impediment to the study. We can understand any cultural behavior only if we find the assumptions on which it is based. If an American anthropologist begins a study by expecting that the target population ought to behave like Americans, and that other behaviors are bad, savage, primitive, child-like, or ignorant, then what chance would the researcher have of learning why Aztecs sacrificed their best warriors or why Americans ask their best athletes to maim themselves in football games?

From the understanding about cultural assumptions and the systems of logic that drive human behavior, anthropologists can define not only the limits of human behavior (the cultural universals specified by Franz Boas, Clark Wissler, and others in the 1930s and since), but the beneficial or harmful consequences that stem from various systems or elements of culture. From these definitions and insights comes the large, growing, and very useful practice of applied anthropology.

Applied anthropology, as Gardner is probably aware, is one of only a few disciplines that attempt to make improvements in the human condition by blending academic research and practical application of social knowledge. The Society for Applied Anthropology (SAA) in 1948 adopted an elaborate and very useful statement on ethics. The ethics statement has been revised several times since then and has never assumed, as Gardner blithely asserts, that there are no universal values. The statement deals specifically with the anthropologist's obligations to science, to human dignity and rights, and to the communication of knowledge and research.

This ethical and universalist approach to cultural studies, and the very vigorous debate in anthropology over the Mead-Freeman controversy, indicates that Gardner has misunderstood the anthropological use of cultural relativity.

Frank Lee Earley is an anthropologist and Social Science Department Chair at Arapahoe Community College, Littleton, Colorado.

Martin Gardner Responds

Several times John Cole faults Freeman for publishing his book on Mead after she died. This seems unfair. Holding the book until after her death was an act of kindness. Had he published it earlier, Mead admirers would have accused him of bashing a sick, elderly woman, perhaps contributing to her demise.

Rather than continue to defend Freeman, or to repeat criticisms of Mead I have made elsewhere (especially in my book *The New Age*, where I focus on her lifelong beliefs in psychic phenomena and her late in life conviction that we are being observed by aliens in flying saucers), let me try to erase some ambiguity about the term "cultural relativism."

Terms with a strong meaning at one time often grow weak over the years. If cultural relativism is taken today to mean only that cultures vary enormously and that one must not judge an alien culture by the standards of one's own, then of course everyone should be a cultural relativist. However, when young Mead wrote about Samoa, the term had a more controversial, philosophical meaning. It denied the existence of "cultural universals"—metabiological needs that were common to humans everywhere.

In his essay "What Is Human Nature?" the Polish anthropologist Bronislaw Kaspar Malinowski answered by defining it as a set of such needs as breathing, eating, drinking, sex, rest, activity, sleep, micturition, defecation, escape from danger, and avoidance of pain. As I pointed out in an early essay "Beyond Cultural Relativism" (reprinted in my *Order and Surprise*), the amusing thing about this list is that it gives human nature to a cow.

It was an easy step from such a narrow concept of human nature to the notion that the task of cultural anthropology is not to decide what is good or bad about cultures, but merely to study their multifarious patterns. In actual practice, however, cultural relativists constantly issued value judgments that crossed cultural boundaries. Boas and Dewey were indeed friends who shared lofty ideals about tolerance, democracy, and world progress, but these ideals rested on different philosophical foundations. Consider racism, such an integral part of our Southern culture. When Boas attacked it, on what podium did he stand? Pinned down, he would have been forced to say that his opinions and actions emerged from his own cultural background, not from values that could be defended objectively.

Melville Herskovits once defined cultural relativism as "a philosophy which, in recognizing the values set up by every society to guide its own life, lays stress on the dignity inherent in every body of custom and on the need for tolerance." Admirable words, but as one reviewer commented, dignity and tolerance are not accepted values even in American culture.

Similar contradictions can be found in the writings of dozens of anthropologists of Boas's day. Ruth Benedict's *Patterns of Culture*, for instance, includes a vitriolic attack on the mores of American business tycoons. She considered them worse than hardened criminals. True, their behavior is the product of a business subculture, but it never occurred to Benedict that her attack ran counter to her book's main theme.

When Clyde Kluckholn attacked cultural relativism in his paper "Ethical Relativism: Sic Et Non," he was roundly chastised by colleagues. There are, he said, common human needs and motives "so deep and so generic that they are beyond the reach of argument." Calling attention, he continued, to the diversity of cultural behavior is an excellent way to combat ethnocentrism, but the more important task now for cultural anthropology is to search for common elements within the diversity—elements that can become the basis of a worldwide naturalistic ethics.

This was Dewey's view. It is Karl Popper's view. I suspect it is the view of all three letter writers. If so, it would be a clearer use of language if they would stop redefining cultural relativism and instead recognize it as an extreme philosophical view that long ago had its day.

*   *   *

After writing the above, a reader called my attention to page 412 of Jane Howard's *Margaret Mead: A Life* (1984). Mead claimed that wherever she went to do field work she was always accompanied by two "spirit guides." The sad fact is that Mead was enormously gullible, with very little comprehension of how to conduct controlled investigations of an alien culture.

In April 1996 a play titled *Heretic,* by Australia's leading dramatist David Williamson, opened at the Sydney Opera House to an enthusiastic sell-out crowd. Based on Freeman's critique of Mead, the play purports to be an LSD dream inside Freeman's head. Mead appears on stage disguised at times as Marilyn Monroe, Jackie Onassis, and Barbra Streisand. Boas wears a pink suit, red bowtie, and black cowboy boots.

Freeman's 1983 book, retitled *Franz Boas and the Flower of Heaven: "Coming of Age in Samoa" and the Fateful Hoaxing of Margaret Mead,* was published down under. The 1996 edition is dedicated to Williamson. For a review of the play, see "Fantasy Island," by Peter Monaghan, in *Lingua Franca* (July/August 1996, pp. 7–8).

"The Debate, at Heart, Is About Evolution," a recent paper by Freeman defending his efforts to combat anthropology's overemphasis on environment, can be found in *The Certainty of Doubt: Tributes to Peter Munz,* edited by M. Fairburn and W. H. Oliver (New Zealand: Victoria University Press, 1996).

CHAPTER FIVE

E-PRIME: GETTING RID OF ISNESS

A man who shouts "Your house is on fire" may not be able to define exactly what he means by *your* and *house* and *is* and *on* and *fire*, but he might still be saying something quite important.

—J. B. Priestley

From time to time, individuals become smitten with a strong urge to reform the English language. Improving spelling has been the most popular impulse. George Bernard Shaw was a prominent champion of such a cause. The philosopher-critic I. A. Richards developed Basic English, a simplified subset of English that he hoped would become a unifying world language. Today's writers and editors seek to replace masculine-loaded words like *mankind* and *chairman* with gender-neutral words like *humanity* and *chairperson*. The philosopher John Dewey wanted to drop the word *truth* from philosophical discourse, substituting for it "warranted assertability."

In recent years, the most curious proposal for a subset of English has come from the ranks of General Semantics, a movement started in the United States some sixty years ago by the Polish-born Count Alfred Habdank Skarbek Korzybski. The new language is called "E-Prime." Few outside the movement were aware of it until Cullen Murphy wrote about it in " 'To Be' in Their Bonnets: A Matter of Semantics," in the February 1992 issue of the *Atlantic Monthly*. The article aroused a great surge of interest among the magazine's readers.

Count Korzybski was far from the first to be concerned with semantics, the study of how signs, especially words, relate to things. An enormous literature on the topic existed long before the Count even heard of the term. Philosophers going back to Plato and Aristotle had, of course, been much concerned with analyzing the meanings of words. The American philosopher Charles Peirce pioneered the modern study of signs, and more recent philosophers, such as Charles Morris, Alfred Tarski, Rudolf

---

"Notes of a Fringe Watcher," *Skeptical Inquirer* (Spring 1993).

Carnap, and W. V. Quine, wrote extensively about semantics. (See the long article, "Semantics, History of," in *The Encyclopedia of Philosophy*.)

However, it was Korzybski's massive work *Science and Sanity* (1933). and popularly written books by Stuart Chase and other enthusiasts, that brought the word *semantics* into public use. Let me expose my bias at once by quoting what I said about *Science and Sanity* in my 1952 book *Fads and Fallacies in the Name of Science*:

> It is a poorly organized, verbose, philosophically naive, repetitious mish-mash of sound ideas borrowed from abler scientists and philosophers, mixed with neologisms, confused ideas, unconscious metaphysics, and highly dubious speculations about neurology and psychiatric therapy.

It was not that Korzybski said anything wrong about semantics but that what he said was trivial. Everybody knows, to use one of Korzybski's best-known slogans, that "the map is not the territory." Everybody knows, to quote another slogan, that "the word is not the thing."

Except in formal logic and mathematics, all words have fuzzy definitions. Fuzzy logic, a flourishing new approach to formal logic, has been designed to handle fuzzy sets. (See this book's chapter 16.) Chairs fade off in many directions, along continua, into things no one calls a chair. No sharp lines divide day from night, tall from short, beautiful from ugly, or the front of your head from the back of it. (Are your ears in front or in back?) Moreover, everything changes in time. You are not the person you were many years ago. The universe was once the size of a pinpoint.

Korzybski was down on Aristotelian logic for its emphasis on identity in such syllogistic statements as "All men are mortal." ("Men" obviously includes women, but does it include our apelike ancestors?) To emphasize nonidentity the Count distinguished between chair 1, chair 2, chair 3, et cetera. This is called indexing. Changes in time are indicated by dating: chair 1920, chair 1992, et cetera. "Et cetera" symbolizes the many, sometimes infinite, referents a noun can have. *ETC.* is the title of the general semantics movement's leading journal, a quarterly founded by the late (he died in 1992) Samuel Ichiye Hayakawa. He edited *ETC.* for twenty-six years, before becoming a controversial Republican senator from California. Many introductions to general semantics have been written, but Hayakawa's *Language in Action* (1941) has been by far the most popular.

Science and Sanity, the 800-page bible of general semantics, was published in 1933 by the Count himself. When I was a philosophy student at the University of Chicago, I used to attend lectures at his Institute of General Semantics. It was said that he chose the building for the Institute,

Cover of the Summer 1992 *ETC.*, showing forms of "to be" slashed out of English. Note the symbolic bee at upper right.

1234 East Fifty-sixth Street, because its address had the first six digits in numerical order. The Count was a stocky man who shaved his head and liked to wear ar.ny-type clothing. He frequently interrupted his talks by shouting, "Bah; I speak baby stuff." A man of enormous ego, he fancied himself one of the world's greatest philosophers. Charles Morris told me that when the university's philosophy department sponsored a symposium on semantics, Korzybski was invited to speak. He refused because he was not allowed to deliver the main address.

As the word *general* implies, Korzybski broadened the meaning of semantics to include all the ways that living things interact with the outside world. The turning of a sunflower toward the sun is a "semantic reaction." A baby vomiting to get a second nursing, the Count wrote, is her "semantic way of controlling 'reality.' " The most debatable aspect of *Science and Sanity* is its great emphasis on how learning to evaluate words properly can raise one's intelligence, increase one's health and happiness, and cure all sorts of neuroses, psychoses, and psychosomatic ills. Korzybski coined the word *unsane* for people who are not far enough gone to be in mental institutions, but whose neurotic behavior springs from an inability to distinguish their mental maps from the outside territory.

The Count strongly disliked the overuse of "is" and all other forms of "to be." Such words, he argued, are a primary source of semantic mis-

Count Korzybski as "General Semantics."

chief. We naively assume that all apples are red, forgetting that some are green and some are yellow. Race prejudice arises from such notions as "all blacks are mentally inferior." "Isness," the Count declared, "is insanity." Incidentally, a vast philosophical literature preceding general semantics deals with identity. A famous paper by George Santayana, first published in 1915, is titled "Some Meanings of the Word Is."

Almost all philosophers consider *Science and Sanity* a crankish work. "It is my considered opinion that *Science and Sanity* has no merit whatever," wrote the distinguished philosopher of science Ernest Nagel in a letter to the *New Republic* (December 26, 1934), replying to readers who objected to his earlier (October 24) hatchet review of the book.

Bertrand Russell was the modern philosopher Korzybski most admired. The feeling was not mutual. In a letter to be found in *Dear Bertrand Russell* (1969, p. 103), a collection of Russell's correspondence, he wrote: "I have never admired the work of Korzybski and I do not, in any degree, endorse the supposed connection of Aristotelian logic with mental illness."

For the American philosopher W. V. Quine's low opinion of the Count, see his autobiography, *The Time of My Life* (1985, p. 140), where he calls him "Wayward Waywode" (*waywode* is a Polish term for an army general). In *Quiddities* (1989, p. 232), Quine chastises Korzybski for going to such absurd extremes in his attacks on identity—the Count wrote in *Science and Sanity* (p. 194) that "1 = 1" is false because one 1 is on the left, the other on the right. As Quine puts it, "He confused the ink spots with the number, abstract and invisible."

Alfred Tarski, the great Polish mathematician and logician, had this to say about Korzybski in his classic paper "The Semantic Conception of Truth" (1944):

> It is perhaps worthwhile saying that semantics as it is conceived in this paper (and in former papers of the author) is a sober and modest discipline which has no pretensions of being a universal patent-medicine for all the ills and diseases of mankind, whether imaginary or real. You will not find in semantics any remedy for decayed teeth or illusions of grandeur or class conflicts. Nor is semantics a device for establishing that everyone except the speaker and his friends is speaking nonsense.

Note that when the Count said "Isness is insanity," he used the word "is." Was this really necessary? He could have said, "Constant use of 'is' tends to damage one's perception of reality." Would it not be helpful, therefore, to develop a subset of English in which all forms of "to be"— *is, are, am, was, were, been,* et cetera—are verboten?

In the late 1940s, this thought occurred to general semanticist D. David Bourland, Jr. He called such a purified language "E-Prime." The term comes from the formula $E' = E - e$, where E is ordinary English from which e (all forms of "to be") is subtracted. He first explained his proposal in "Introduction to a Structural Calculus: A Postulational Statement of Alfred Korzybski's Non-Aristotelian Linguistic System" (*General Semantics Bulletin,* nos. 8 and 9, 1952). In the same journal (nos. 32 and 33, 1965/66), he followed with "A Linguistic Note: Writing in E-Prime."

The idea of writing and speaking E-Prime caught on quickly among a small group of dedicated Korzybskians. Papers written entirely in E-Prime began to appear. E. W. Kellogg III, after many years of arduous training, actually mastered the ability to talk fluently, without hesitations, in E-Prime! He is on record as saying he even dreams in E-Prime, and that learning to speak it greatly improved his mental and physical health. Writing E-Prime is less difficult, though still not easy. Cullen Murphy struggled so hard to put his *Atlantic Monthly* article into E-Prime that he said it gave him a headache that lasted a week.

Korzybskians are now divided over E-Prime into three factions. Purists insist that the language is of little value unless all forms of "to be" are excised. Moderate E-Primers object to total exclusion. They prefer a language called E-Choice (after a grade of meat), in which "to be" forms are used sparingly. Anti-E-Primers grant that learning to write or speak E-Prime may be a useful teaching device to impress on students the need for careful thinking about words, but that E-Prime should not be used otherwise.

Literature arguing the merits and demerits of E-Prime is growing in the books and journals of general semantics. An anthology defending E-Prime, *To Be or Not*, was published by the International Society for General Semantics in 1991. The book's back cover crisply summarizes the volume's content:

> Some of the benefits: lively, concise writing and speaking; clearer, more critical thinking; better communication, evaluation, and decision making. In E-Prime, you can't say "*I am*," and this results in a different and healthier way of evaluating yourself and others. The use of E-Prime can transform how you relate to the world and to yourself—for the better! Try it.

The entire Summer 1992 issue of *ETC.* was devoted to the E-Prime controversy, with twenty-one papers for or against the language. It is filled with examples of how to translate common speech into E-Prime. If a stranger asks, "What's your name?" you can't answer, "My name is John Smith." You must say something like "People call me John Smith." If a child points to something red and asks, "What color is this?" you should reply, "I call it red," or "Everyone calls it red." You must not tell a child, "That animal you see over there is an elephant." In E-Prime you say, "People call that animal an elephant." To be more precise you should say, "People who speak English call that animal you see an elephant." Note that even this sentence implies that the object seen is an animal, but getting rid of all implied forms of "to be" is impossible.

Was Keats a greater poet than Eddie Guest? You can't say "he was" in E-Prime. The correct statement is: "I consider Keats a greater poet than Eddie Guest." This implies that Keats and Guest *were* poets, but we let that pass. Is it raining? Your correct reply is: "I see rain falling." Is Bill Clinton president of the United States? Your E-Prime answer: "American voters have elected him president." You can't just say "Yes," because that endorses the identity in the question. Even Korzybski's famous statement that the map is not the territory violates E-Prime. Correctly rephrased it says, "The map and the territory do not share identical properties."

Although it is possible to eliminate from English all explicit forms of "to be," is it worth all the trouble? Critics of E-Prime, many within the ranks of general semantics, point out that it takes months, sometimes years, to master the art of writing and speaking E-Prime. It is quixotic to expect anyone outside the ranks to go to all this trouble. If we did not constantly use fuzzy words we couldn't talk at all. The fact that no two cows are alike doesn't make the word *cow* useless in such sentences as "All cows have udders." If you want to tell a neighbor his house is on fire, you don't stop to think that *your, house, fire, on,* and *is* lack precise definitions. Even if you warned him in E-Prime by saying, "I see flames on your roof," you are using fuzzy words.

Critics also remind enthusiastic E-Primers that there is no empirical evidence that persons who speak the language have become healthier or happier or have learned to think more clearly. As one contributor to the E-Prime issue of *ETC.* said, the language seems so preposterous to outsiders that stressing it may be bad public relations. It suggests to outsiders that general semantics is an eccentric cult.

Translating ordinary language into E-Prime may well be good training for someone just learning the kindergarten levels of semantics, but it strikes me as almost as useless an exercise as translating English into words that avoid the letter E. Because E is the alphabet's most common letter, it is not easy to write good English without using it. Nevertheless, entire novels without the letter E have been published. The best specimen in English is *Gadsby*, by Ernest Vincent Wright, printed by the author in Los Angeles in 1939. Wright said he had to tie down his typewriter's E-bar to keep him from typing an E. In 1969 the famous French novelist Georges Perec published *La Disparition* (The Disappearance), a novel in which E had totally disappeared. It is said that some French critics praised the novel without realizing a letter was missing. Here we have a different kind of E-Prime, E (English) from which e is subtracted. The language might even have some slight value in impressing on students of cryptography how much E is overused in English and French spelling.

Korzybskians have written poetry in E-Prime. If their enthusiasm for it continues, I wouldn't be surprised if someone wrote a novel in E-Prime. In 1993 E. W. Kellogg hoped to publish a workbook for high school English classes that would be written in E-Prime. I considered composing this column in E-Prime, but when a headache developed after the first few paragraphs, I gave it up and went back to common English.

ADDENDUM

My column on E-Prime provoked the following letters, all printed in the *Skeptical Inquirer* (Fall 1993):

> When Shirley Temple, after a magnificent career as a child star followed by a graceful adolescence, married and gave birth to a daughter, the *New York Daily News* headline read: "Now Shirley Has a Real Live

Dolly All Her Own." From which I concluded that Shirley Temple had grown up, but the headline writer hadn't.

I got somewhat the same feeling when I read Martin Gardner's 1952 animadversions on general-semantics (g-s), which he injected into his piece on E-Prime, English without the verb "to be" (*SI*, Spring 1993). The discipline founded by Alfred Korzybski in 1933 continues to grow and develop, but Gardner seems stuck in the time-track.

I appreciate that Gardner does recognize clearly that E-Prime is not a necessary practice of general-semanticists, whose reactions may be enthusiasm, indifference, or to use it just as a training device. But those differences are hardly likely to result in the "bloody reprisals" feared by Cullen Murphy; general-semantics finds no virtue in enforcing dogmas. Instead, with its basic notions of consciousness of abstracting, and of the uncertainty and incompleteness of all statements, it encourages good-humored striving for agreement. Small wonder philosophers who want "The Truth" to stand still until they can engrave it in stone find g-s "crankish."

G-s had numerous successful offshoots, like Gerard Nierenberg's Art of Negotiation, or Albert Ellis's Rational-Emotive Therapy (Ellis even translated some of his books into E-Prime), or the many researches listed in Kenneth Johnson's compilation *Graduate Research in General Semantics*.

But what might interest Gardner are our resolutions of semantical paradoxes that have plagued philosopher-mathematicians most of this century. James D. French and I have demolished four famous ones: Frege's "Village Barber"; Berry's Paradox; Russell's "Class of Non-self-including Classes"; and Grelling's "Heterological Terms."

Stuart A. Mayper, Editor, General Semantics Bulletin,
Ridgefield, Conn.

As a director of the International Society for General Semantics, I have some comments on Martin Gardner's essay on Alfred Korzybski.

Gardner quotes Bertrand Russell's negative reactions to Korzybski's work; but early in the 1930s, Russell sent the following cable to Korzybski from London: "Your work is impressive and your erudition extraordinary. Have not had time for thorough reading but think well of parts read. Undoubtedly your theories demand serious consideration."

That telegram is cited in *Science and Sanity*, in the back of the book, along with seven pages of strongly favorable quotations from twenty-one other men of great attainment, representing fifteen different fields.

Russell Meyers, chief of neurology and chairman of the Division of Neurosurgery at the University of Iowa, 1946–1963, once described *Science and Sanity* as "the most profound, insightful, and globally significant book I have ever read." I would infer from that statement that

Meyers, who also held academic positions in psychology, neuropsychology, and speech pathology, found nothing too terribly amiss with Korzybski's extensive discussions of the nervous system, conditional reactions, and mental illness.

Gardner reports that Korzybski said "1 = 1" is false, on page 194 of his book. Of course, Korzybski said nothing of the sort, on page 194 or anywhere else. We know that he accepted mathematical statements of equality as true, because he described them as being "always correct in mathematics" (p. 195).

With regard to the *symbolic expression* "1 = 1" Korzybski denied *absolute* sameness in *all aspects* (identity). He did not discuss 1 as a *number* (which was W. V. Quine's mistaken interpretation), but as a *symbol*. Every symbol has its physical aspect. Even internal words are the result of electrochemical reactions in the brain. Hence, "not identical in *all* aspects."

James D. French, Albany, Calif.

The dogmatism, name-calling, inaccurate quotes, repetition of rumors, insulting and misrepresentative cartooning, etc., in Gardner's "E-Prime and Isness" hardly serve the skeptical cause. Gardner's "map" only vaguely resembles the "territory" of general-semantics.

While indicating some of the controversy within the general-semantics community surrounding E-Prime, which eliminates all forms of the verb "to be," Gardner absolutistically rejects any significant usefulness for E-Prime, or for general-semantics for that matter.

Neither Korzybski nor all general-semanticists have suggested eliminating all uses of the verb "to be." However, Korzybski's applied neurolinguistic focus and denial of identity (defined as " 'absolute sameness' in 'all' aspects") does lead to, among other things, an emphasis on avoiding the " 'is' of identity," which connects a noun to a noun, and the " 'is' of predication," which connects a noun to an adjective.

Someone may say, "General semantics is a cult" or "General semanticists are eccentric." Such statements may reflect an absolutistic and dogmatic way of evaluating, which, through neurolinguistic mechanisms, may tend to reinforce such dogmatism in oneself and others.

If anything, the development of E-Prime and the debate surrounding it indicate that general semantics remains a growing and healthily diverse discipline that has much to contribute to the development of a nonabsolutistic, nondogmatic skepticism.

Bruce I. Kodish, Baltimore, Md.

Martin Gardner's forty-year-long antipathy for Alfred Korzybski and general semantics flared up again in his "E-Prime: Getting Rid of Isness." From the title, one might think the article was about E-Prime, the use of English without any form of "to be." But most of it consists of a rehash of tired old stories about Korzybski's eccentricities and ego-tism, and putdowns of him from various old sources. None of this had much to do with E-Prime, which others developed long after Korzyb-ski's death. The article devoted only a few paragraphs to a rather thin critique of E-Prime.

As near as I can understand it, Gardner's main (if not only) point is that he feels the benefits of E-Prime are not worth the alleged trouble of using that language.

However:

1. Albert Ellis, the founder/guru of Rational Emotive Therapy, has written his books in E-Prime, and considers E-Prime important in that system of therapy.

2. An increasing number of teachers of English composition are having their students write in E-Prime, to help them develop greater accuracy, clarity, and readability.

The *Skeptical Inquirer* does a fine job challenging and exposing the illogical, the irrational, and the unreasonable. But I think you've chosen an inappropriate target here.

Robert Wanderer, San Francisco, Calif.

Thank you for Martin Gardner's article on E-Prime.

I began teaching in 1961, and—together with a colleague, Fred Smith—was told to emphasize critical thinking. How to proceed?

We began by using Chase's *Guides to Straight Thinking* (1954). We were careful about generalizations made. We tried to avoid words like *always* and *never*, which allow for no exceptions. We made efforts to complete comparisons ("Bigger than what?") and discussed impressions given. On writing projects students used words in dictionary ways and tried to avoid "self-evident truths." We developed an awareness of "Black/White Thinking" and singular causations.

The focus continues. We emphasize distinctions between com-monly agreed-upon "facts" and the values and interpretations loaded onto these facts. On term projects each student "focuses on a perceived social injustice" and selects an "expert in the area." Then each: (1) sum-marizes the expert's facts, (2) summarizes his or her prescriptions, and (3) judges reliability by analyzing credentials and logic.

Gardner says that "translating ordinary language into E-Prime may well be good training for someone just learning the kindergarten level of semantics." In high school, we are on the "kindergarten level of semantics"! I don't tell students to get rid of "isness" or to write in "E-Prime," but apparently I have been influenced by Korzybski's ideas. As used in the ways described, understandings derived from general semantics have been one of the continuing bright spots in my teaching career.

Brant Abrahamson, Riverside-Brookfield H.S., Riverside, Ill.

Martin Gardner says: "I wouldn't be surprised if someone wrote a novel in E-Prime." And, in fact, someone has, at least in part. Veteran science-fiction readers will be familiar with the name of Alfred Elton van Vogt, author of such novels as *The Weapon Shops of Isher and Slan*, and the short story "Black Destroyer," which owed a great debt to John Campbell's "Who Goes There?"

In late December 1971, van Vogt received a phone call from a senior editor of *Saturday Review—The Sciences* asking him for an article on general semantics. Van Vogt wrote the article, titled "The Semantics of Twenty-First Century Science," but policy changes within the *Saturday Review* organization made its publication impossible. It eventually appeared in an anthology called *The Best of A. E. van Vogt*, published in 1976 by Pocket Books. In the introduction to the article, van Vogt wrote: "What does this [general semantics] have to do with reality? General semantics is a systematic approach to reality, that's what."

In the article's afterword, van Vogt concludes: "But we may certainly deduce from the foregoing arguments that reality is not yet available in literature except intuitively, and then only in the works of a few geniuses." Link this statement to the article's third paragraph, where van Vogt writes: "Some years ago I wrote two science-fiction novels, *The World of Null-A* and *The Players of Null-A*, in which, in thousands and thousands of paragraphs, I employed the various GS recommended usages for rectifying *what might be called* the shortcomings of English. . . . For my second semantics-oriented novel, *The Players of Null-A*, I wrote a twenty-two-paragraph explanation of GS, and used one paragraph as the heading of each chapter. The summation took three weeks to do. When it was out of the way, I had *essentially* completed my eight-year study of general semantics."

Andrew Dagilis, Verdun, Quebec, Canada

I'd like to point out that there is an entire language that doesn't use the verb "to be": the Klingon tongue created for the *Star Trek* movies and television series. This feature later caused its inventor headaches when he was asked to translate Hamlet's "To be or not to be" for *Star Trek VI: The Undiscovered Country*.

Klingon may be a fictitious tongue, but it has its own dictionary and I've met people at science-fiction conventions who speak it for fun. [See this book's chapter 15.]

Zen Faulkes, Department of Biology,
University of Victoria, Victoria, B.C., Canada

Aha! I thought so! It wasn't I. A. Richards who devised Basic English, but C. K. Ogden.

John Brunner, South Petherton, Somerset, U.K.

Martin Gardner Responds

Bertrand Russell's polite thank-you note was written before he carefully read *Science and Sanity*. The statement I quoted was his considered opinion, as well as the opinion of all other leading philosophers of science.

Readers are urged to check the final chapter of Max Black's *Language and Philosophy*. The Count's misunderstandings of Aristotelian logic, Black writes, led him into countless absurdities. "Very little remains of Korzybski's theory of abstractions except some hypothetical neurology fortified with dogmatic metaphysics." Ernest Nagel, reviewing Black's book, said: "Black's restrained but nonetheless devastating critique of the basic ideas on which Korzybski rests his pretentious claim is alone worth the price of the book." For Rudolf Carnap's low opinion of the Count, see the index of *Dear Carnap, Dear Van* (1990), a collection of letters between Carnap and Quine.

The eminent semiotician Thomas Sebeok found my column amusing and accurate. Like me, he attended the Count's lectures in Chicago, finding him "arrogant and unpleasant." He recalls the enormous ill feelings that arose between the Count and Hayakawa before the Count's Japanese disciple founded *ETC*.

I did not say Richards "invented" Basic English. I said he "developed" it, albeit an ambiguous verb easily misinterpreted. Ogden was indeed the inventor, but for forty years Richards was its chief developer and promoter. Basic's famous list of 850 words was the collaborated effort of the two friends.

Yes, Van Vogt was fascinated by general semantics. He was even more fascinated by Scientology, actually working for years as one of its therapists. I didn't know about the Klingon tongue, which proves I'm not a Trekkie.

*   *   *

Interest in E-Prime seems not to have diminished among Korzybskians. A second anthology, *More E-Prime: To Be or Not II*, was published in 1994, edited by Paul Dennithorne Johnston, David Bourland, Jr., and Jeremy Klein. Albert Ellis, psychiatrist, wrote the Foreword. "This volume," so reads an ad, "offers the inquisitive reader unique vistas of a fascinating linguistic territory, whose exploration has just begun."

CHAPTER SIX

RMT: REPRESSED MEMORY THERAPY

In March 1992, a group of distinguished psychologists and psychiatrists banded together to form the False Memory Syndrome (FMS) Foundation. The organization is headquartered in Philadelphia under the direction of educator Pamela Freyd. Its purpose: to combat a fast-growing epidemic of dubious therapy that is ripping thousands of families apart, scarring patients for life, and breaking the hearts of innocent parents and other relatives. It is, in fact, the mental-health crisis of the 1990s.

The tragic story begins with Freud. Early in his career, when he made extensive use of hypnotism, Freud was amazed by the number of mesmerized women who dredged up childhood memories of being raped by their fathers. It was years before he became convinced that most of these women were fantasizing. Other analysts and psychiatrists agreed. For more than half a century the extent of incestuous child abuse was minimized. Not until about 1980 did the pendulum start to swing the other way as more solid evidence of child sexual abuse began to surface. There is now no longer any doubt that such incest is much more prevalent than the older Freud or the general public realized.

Then in the late 1980s a bizarre therapeutic fad began to emerge in the United States. Hundreds of poorly trained therapists, calling themselves "traumatists," began to practice the very techniques Freud had discarded. All over the land they are putting patients under hypnosis, or using other techniques, to subtly prod them into recalling childhood sexual traumas, memories of which presumably have been totally obliterated for decades. Decades Delayed Disclosure, or DDD, it has been called. Eighty percent of the patients who are claimed to experience DDD are women from twenty-five to forty-five years old. Sixty percent of their parents are college graduates, 25 percent with advanced degrees. More than 80 percent of their parents are married to their first spouse.

Here is a typical scenario. A woman in her thirties seeks therapy for symptoms ranging from mild depression, anxiety, headaches, or the

---

"Notes of a Fringe Watcher," *Skeptical Inquirer* (Summer 1993).

inability to lose weight, to more severe symptoms like anorexia. Her therapist, having succumbed to the latest mental-health fad, decides almost at once that the symptoms are caused by repressed memories of childhood abuse. Profoundly shocked by this suggestion, the woman vigorously denies that such a thing could be possible. The stronger her denial, the more the therapist believes she is repressing painful memories.

The patient may be hypnotized, or given sodium amytal, or placed into a relaxed, trancelike state. Convinced that a childhood trauma is at the root of the patient's ills, the therapist repeatedly urges the woman to try to remember the trauma. If she is highly suggestible and eager to please the therapist, she begins to respond to leading questions and to less obvious signs of the therapist's expectations.

After months, or even years, images begin to form in the patient's mind. Shadowy figures threaten her sexually. Under continual urging, these memories grow more vivid. She begins to recognize the molester as her father, or grandfather, or uncle. The more detailed the visions, the more convinced both she and the therapist become that the terrible truth is finally being brought to consciousness. To better-trained psychiatrists, these details indicate just the opposite. Childhood memories are notoriously vague. Recalling minute details is a strong sign of fantasizing.

As the false memories become more convincing, the patient's anger toward a once-loved relative grows. The therapist urges her to vent this rage, to confront the perpetrator, even to sue for psychic damage. Stunned by their daughter's accusations, the parents vigorously deny everything. Of course they will deny it, says the therapist, perhaps even suppress their own memories of what happened. The family is devastated. A loving daughter has inexplicably been transformed into a bitter enemy. She may join an "incest survivor" group, where her beliefs are reinforced by hearing similar tales. She may wear a sweatshirt saying, "I survived."

No one doubts that childhood sexual assaults occur, but in almost every case the event is never forgotten. Indeed, it festers as a lifelong source of shame and anger. Studies show that among children who witnessed the murder of a parent, not a single one repressed the terrible memory. Not only do victims of child incest not repress such painful memories (to repress a memory means to completely forget the experience without any conscious effort to do so); they try unsuccessfully to forget them. That traumas experienced as a child can be totally forgotten for decades is the great mental-health myth of our time—a myth that is not only devastating innocent families but doing enormous damage to psychiatry.

In the past, when juries found a parent guilty of child incest, there has been corroborating evidence: photos, diaries, letters, testimony by others, a history of sexual misconduct, or even open admission of guilt. Juries today are increasingly more often judging a parent guilty without any confirming evidence other than the therapy-induced memories of the "victim."

Patients as well as their families can be scarred for life. They are led to believe that bringing suppressed memories to light will banish their symptoms. On the contrary, the symptoms usually get worse because of traumatic breaks with loved ones. Moreover, this treatment can also cause a patient to refuse needed therapy from psychiatrists who have not fallen prey to the FMS epidemic. Pamela Freyd has likened the traumatists to surgeons doing brain surgery with a knife and fork. Others see the epidemic as similar in many ways to the great witch-hunts of the past, when disturbed women were made to believe they were in Satan's grip. The Devil has been replaced by the evil parent.

FMS takes many forms other than parental sexual abuse. Thousands of victims are being induced by traumatists to recall childhood participation in satanic cults that murder babies, eat their flesh, and practice even more revolting rituals. Although there is widespread fascination with the occult, and an amusing upsurge in the number of persons who fancy themselves benevolent witches or warlocks, police have yet to uncover any compelling evidence that satanic cults exist. Yet under hypnosis and soporific drugs, memories of witnessing such rituals can become as vivid as memories of sexual abuse.

Thousands of other patients, highly suggestible while half asleep, are now "remembering" how they were abducted, and sometimes sexually abused, by aliens in spaceships from faraway planets. Every year or so victims of this form of FMS (assuming they are not charlatans) will write persuasive books about their adventures with extraterrestrials. The books will be heavily advertised and promoted on talk shows, and millions of dollars will flow into the pockets of the authors and the books' uncaring publishers. Still another popular form of FMS, sparked by the New Age obsession with reincarnation, is the recovering of memories of past lives.

Pop-psychology books touting the myth that memories of childhood molestations can be suppressed for decades are becoming as plentiful as books about reincarnation, satanic cults, and flying saucers. Far and away the worst offender is a best-seller titled *Courage to Heal* (Harper & Row, 1988), by Ellen Bass and Laura Davis. Although neither author has had any training in psychiatry, the book has become a bible for women convinced they are incest survivors. Davis thinks she herself is a survivor, having recalled under therapy being attacked by her grandfather. A survey of several hundred accused parents revealed that in almost every case their daughters had been strongly influenced by *Courage to Heal*. (See box for some of the book's more outrageous passages.)

From the growing literature of FMS cases I cite a few typical horrors.

Passages from Courage to Heal, the "Bible" of Incest Survivors

"You may think you don't have memories, but often as you begin to talk about what you do remember, there emerges a constellation of feelings, reactions, and recollections that add up to substantial information. To say, 'I was abused,' you don't need the kind of recall that would stand up in a court of law. Often the knowledge that you were abused starts with a tiny feeling, an intuition. . . . Assume your feelings are valid. . . . If you think you were abused and your life shows the symptoms, then you were."

"If you don't remember your abuse you are not alone. Many women don't have memories, and some never get memories. This doesn't mean they weren't abused."

"If you maintained the fantasy that your childhood was 'happy,' then you have to grieve for the childhood you thought you had. . . . You must give up the idea that your parents had your best interest at heart. . . . If you have any loving feelings toward your abuser, you must reconcile that love with the fact that he abused you. . . . You may have to grieve over the fact that you don't have an extended family for your children, that you'll never receive an inheritance, that you don't have family roots."

"If your memories of the abuse are still fuzzy, it is important to realize that you may be grilled for details. . . . Of course such demands for proof are unreasonable. You are not responsible for proving that you were abused."

"If you're willing to get angry and the anger just doesn't seem to come, there are many ways to get in touch with it. A little like priming the pump, you can do things that will get your anger started. Then once you get the hang of it, it'll begin to flow on its own."

"You may dream of murder or castration. It can be pleasurable to fantasize such scenes in vivid detail. . . . Let yourself imagine it to your heart's content."

A twenty-eight-year-old woman accuses her father of molesting her when she was six months old. "I recall my father put his penis near my face and rubbed it on my face and mouth." There is not the slightest evidence that a child of six months can acquire lasting memories of *any* event.

Betsy Petersen, in *Dancing with Daddy* (Bantam, 1991), tells of being convinced by her therapist that she had been raped by her father when she was three. "I don't know if I made it up or not," she told the therapist. "It feels like a story," he replied, "because when something like that happens, everyone acts like it didn't."

In 1986 Patti Barton sued her father for sexually abusing her when she was seven to fifteen months old. She did not remember this until her thirty-second therapy session. She recalls trying to tell her mother what happened by saying, "Ma, ma, ma, ma!" and "Da, da, da, da!"

Geraldo Rivera, in 1991, had three trauma survivors on his television show. One woman insisted she had murdered forty children while she was in a satanic cult but had totally forgotten about it until her memories were aroused in therapy. Well-known entertainers have boosted the FMS epidemic by openly discussing their traumas on similar sensational talk shows. Comedienne Roseanne recently learned for the first time, while in therapy, that she had been repeatedly molested by her parents, starting when she was three months old! Her story made the cover of *People* magazine. Her parents and sisters deny it and have threatened legal action. A former Miss America, Marilyn Van Derbur, has been in the news proclaiming her decades-delayed recollection of abuse by her father, now deceased.

It is an alarming trend that a dozen states have revised their statute-of-limitations laws and now permit legal action against parents within three years of the time the abuse was *remembered*! In 1990 the first conviction based on "repressed memory" occurred. George Franklin was given a life sentence for murdering an eight-year-old in 1969 almost entirely on the basis of his daughter's memory, allegedly repressed for twenty years, of having witnessed his murdering her friend.* A year later a Pennsylvania man was convicted of murder on the basis of a man's detailed account of what he had seen when he was five, but had totally forgotten for sixteen years.

Although therapists usually deny asking leading questions, tapes of their sessions often prove otherwise. If no memories surface they will prod a patient to make up a story. After many repetitions and elaborations of the invented scenario, the patient starts to believe the story is true. One therapist, who claims to have treated fifteen hundred incest victims, explained her approach. She would say to a patient: "You know, in my experience, a lot of people who are struggling with many of the same problems you are have often had some kind of really painful things happen to them as kids—maybe they were beaten or molested. And I wonder if anything like that ever happened to you?" Another traumatist says: "You sound to me like the sort of person who must have been sexually abused. Tell me what that bastard did to you."

The FMS epidemic would not be so bad if such therapists were frauds interested only in money, but the sad truth is that they are sincere. So were

---

*Franklin's conviction was recently reversed, his daughter's testimony being called unreliable.

the doctors who once tried to cure patients by bleeding, and the church-men who "cured" witches by torture, hanging, and burning.

Better-trained, older psychiatrists do not believe that childhood mem-ories of traumas can be repressed for any length of time, except in rare cases of actual brain damage. Nor is there any evidence that hypnosis improves memory. It may increase certitude, but not accuracy. And there is abundant evidence that totally false memories are easily aroused in the mind of a suggestible patient.

A two-part article by Lawrence Wright, "Remembering Satan" (*New Yorker*, May 17 and 24, 1993), tells the tragic story of Paul Ingram, a respected police officer in Olympia, Washington, who was accused by his two adult daughters of sexually abusing them as children. Ingram's fam-ily are devout Pentecostals who believe that Satan can wipe out all mem-ories of such crimes. Ingram remembered nothing, but after five months of intensive questioning, he came to believe himself guilty. Psychologist Richard Ofshe, writing on "Inadvertent Hypnosis During Interrogation" (*International Journal of Clinical and Experimental Hypnosis* 11 [1992]: 125–55), tells how he fabricated an imaginary incident of Ingram's sex-ual abuse of a son and daughter. After repeated suggestions that he try to "see" this happening, Ingram produced a written confession!

Jean Piaget, the Swiss psychologist, tells of his vivid memory of an attempted kidnapping when he was two. The thief had been foiled by Piaget's nurse, who bravely fought off the man. When Piaget was in his teens the nurse confessed that she made up the story to win admiration, even scratching herself to prove there had been a struggle. Piaget had heard the story so often that it seeped into his consciousness as a detailed memory.

Paul McHugh, a psychiatrist at Johns Hopkins University, in "Psy-chiatric Misadventures" (*American Scholar*, Fall 1992), writes about a woman who under therapy came to believe she had been sexually assaulted by an uncle. She recalled the exact date. Her disbelieving mother discovered that at that time her brother was in military service in Korea. Did this alter the woman's belief? Not much, "I see, Mother," she said, "Yes. Well let me think, if your dates are right, I suppose it must have been Dad."

Although the incest-recall industry is likely to grow in coming years, as it spreads around the world, there are some hopeful signs. Here and there women are beginning to discover how cruelly they have been deceived and are suing therapists for inducing false memories that caused them and their parents great suffering. They are known as "recanters" or "retractors."

Another welcome trend is that distinguished psychologists and psy-chiatrists are now writing papers about the FMS epidemic. I particularly recommend the book *Confabulations* (Social Issues Research Series, Boca Raton, Fla., 1992) by Eleanor Goldstein, and the following three articles: "Beware the Incest-Survivor Machine," by psychologist Carol Tavris, in the *New York Times Book Review* (January 3, 1993); "The Reality of Repressed Memories," by Elizabeth Loftus (psychologist, University of Washington), *American Psychologist* 48 (May 1993, pp. 518–37); and "Making Monsters," by Richard Ofshe and Ethan Watters, in *Society* (March 1993). Most of this column is based on material in those articles. Copies can be obtained, along with other literature, from the FMS Foundation, 3401 Market Street, Philadelphia, PA 19104. The phone number is 215-387-1865, Fax: 215-387-1917.

The FMS Foundation is a nonprofit organization whose purpose is to seek reasons for the FMS epidemic, to work for the prevention of new cases, and to aid victims. By the end of 1992, only ten months after its founding, more than two thousand distressed parents had contacted the Foundation for advice on how to cope with sudden attacks by angry daughters who had accused them of horrible crimes.

I trust that no one reading this column will get the impression that either I or members of the FMS Foundation are not fully aware that many women are indeed sexually abused as children and that their abusers should be punished. In its newsletter of January 8, 1993, the Foundation responded to criticism that somehow its efforts are a backlash against feminism. Their reply: Is it not "harmful to feminism to portray women as having minds closed to scientific information and as being satisfied with sloppy, inaccurate statistics? Could it be viewed as a profound insult to women to give them slogans rather than accurate information about how memory works?"

The point is not to deny that hideous sexual abuse of children occurs, but that when it does, it is not forgotten and only "remembered" decades later under hypnosis. Something is radically amiss when therapist E. Sue Blume, in her book *Secret Survivors*, can maintain: "Incest is easily the greatest underlying reason why women seek therapy. . . . It is my experience that fewer than half of the women who experience this trauma later remember or identify it as abuse. Therefore it is not unreasonable that *more than half of all women* are survivors of childhood sexual trauma."

As Carol Tavris, author of *Mismeasure of Women*, comments in her article cited above: "Not one of these assertions is supported by empirical evidence."

ADDENDUM

It was no surprise that many defenders of RMT (Repressed Memory Therapy) would send letters blasting my column. Two such letters, and one favorable letter, appeared in the Winter 1994 issue of the *Skeptical Inquirer*:

> Re Martin Gardner's "The False Memory Syndrome" (*SI*, Summer 1993): Some traumas for some people clearly are repressed; other traumas for other people are clearly not repressed. Repressions may last for years.
>
> In World War II, there were hundreds of documented cases of battlefield trauma-induced neuroses, characterized by symptoms appearing after the trauma and an inability to remember the trauma. Among helpful treatments used by the military and VA was a brief psychotherapy utilizing hypnosis or sodium pentothal interviews with the aim of quickly restoring a pre-traumatic level of functioning. Heightened suggestibility of the patients was not a problem, since other people knew what had happened.
>
> Patients usually do try to get external confirmation of what they uncover insofar as it deals with externally observable events. With incest, however, the people best able to confirm or deny have a strong motive to lie if it is true.
>
> Patients who accept false events as "real" memories (during badly conducted psychotherapy) do badly in their subsequent life. In psychoanalytic therapy this is not so much a problem; eventually the truth will be discovered as patient and therapist investigate and consider all possibilities. An honest psychotherapist may not know the truth for a long time; it is therapeutic for patients to learn to tolerate uncertainty and to consider that the reconstructed memory might or might not be true. But courts want the "truth" immediately.
>
> Because of the social importance of memories the American Psychological Association has formed a task force to survey all we know about memory from both experimentation and clinical observations.
>
> Bertram P. Karon, Professor, Department of Psychology,
> Michigan State University, East Lansing, Mich.

For a journal purportedly devoted to "scientific investigation of the paranormal," the inclusion of "The False Memory Syndrome" by Martin Gardner in your summer issue is disturbing, to say the least. This is an area in which I can speak from some knowledge: I am one of those "better trained" (will Harvard do?), "older" therapists, a writer of one book (*Second Childhood*, Norton, 1989) and many journal articles, and a teacher (of memory, among other subjects) on the postgraduate level. More important, however, I keep up with the literature: I would say, off-hand, that I have read carefully at least ten full-length professional books and two hundred or more professional articles, as well as lay articles on the subject of delayed memory, including all of those cited in Gardner's contribution. In addition, just this year I have, in the interests of skepticism, curiosity, and open-mindedness, attended a lecture by John Mack, M.D. (surely an "older" Harvard psychiatrist, he of the UFOs), and a conference in which Pamela Freyd (she of the False Memory Syndrome Foundation) played a major part. I was greatly unimpressed—in fact, horrified—by both of them, each with an axe to grind that blinded them to consideration of real data. Unfortunately, I feel the same way about Gardner.

In the interests of brevity, I will focus on a fundamental point made by Gardner: "No one doubts that childhood sexual assaults occur, *but in almost every case the event is never forgotten*" (italics mine). This statement is in direct contradiction to evidence established in myriad serious studies. Let me refer him to just one small journal article that summarizes a retrospective study of two hundred admissions to an emergency room in which the admission records recorded sexual assault of female children under the age of twelve (Linda Meyer Williams, "Adult Memories of Childhood Abuse: Preliminary Findings from a Longitudinal Study," *The Advisor*, Summer 1992): 38 percent of a hundred of those interviewed seventeen years later did not remember the abuse or the hospitalization, which had been objectively documented. I have, myself, had clients who remembered childhood sexual abuse for the first time as adults, in or out of therapy, and, upon talking to the accused, were actually supported in their allegations by confessions and, sometimes, apologies. Still others located witnesses, or other unimpeachable evidence, such as records of a forgotten childbirth (due to forgotten incest) at a home for unwed mothers. Similar findings of corroborated accusations are documented in Herman's recent scholarly book, *Trauma and Recovery*. So, surely Gardner's assertion here is blatantly incorrect. In addition, his spurious comparison of delayed memory of sexual abuse to claims of "past lives" and UFO abductions puts a poor light on his intentions to be objective and fair-minded.

Marian Kaplun Shapiro, Ed.D.,
Licensed Psychologist, Lexington, Mass.

Martin Gardner's column about the false memory syndrome (*SI*, Summer 1993) is an outstanding expose of a pseudoscientific practice with devastating consequences for patients and their families. I commend Gardner for writing it and *Skeptical Inquirer* for publishing it.

Forrest M. Mims III, Seguin, Texas

Martin Gardner Replies

I have no objection to anything said by Bertram P. Karon. No one denies that traumatic memories can be repressed. The question is whether the thousands of such memories now being elicited by zealous, untrained, self-deceived therapists are genuine or are the product of dubious techniques abetted by sensational books read by the patients.

There are many ways memories of child abuse can be substantiated. A father capable of raping his four-year-old daughter betrays such psychotic behavior that it is almost impossible for there to be no other records of his mental illness. Wives, siblings, and other relatives seldom have reason to maintain a state of "denial." There can be confirming diaries and letters, or at times a full confession. When there is no evidence at all, coupled with vigorous denials by relatives and a history of the alleged victim's love and admiration for the alleged perpetrators, incalculable harm can be done both to parents and to their innocent families by therapy-induced false memories.

Marian Kaplun Shapiro's doctorate is in education. This does not qualify her to practice psychiatry. She is a self-proclaimed hypnotherapist.

Her praise of Judith Herman's book is misplaced. Herman did indeed find that in fifty-three cases of incest survivors, thirty-nine found corroborative evidence. This seems impressive until you learn that thirty-nine survivors had no loss of memory to begin with. "It wouldn't be surprising," said University of Arizona psychologist John Kihlstrom in a recent lecture, "if these individuals were able to validate their memories. Confirmation of abuse is not the same as confirmation of repressed memories."

In Herman's study, patients with nonrepressed memories reported sex abuse when they were eight or older. Those who recalled abuse only after prolonged therapy reported an average abuse age of four to five years. Why were these memories pushed so far back? Because, Kihlstrom suggests, they had to push them back to a time when they couldn't remember anything else.

Shapiro objects to my comparing repressed memories of child sex abuse with similar memories of Satanic rituals, UFO abductions, and past incarnations. But techniques for evoking such memories are exactly the same in all four areas. In the case of Satanic cult memories, the therapy is just as widespread.

I urge readers to check the sensational two-part article "Remembering Satan," by Lawrence Wright, in the *New Yorker* (May 17 and 24, 1993), Leslie Bennetts' article in *Vanity Fair* (June 1993), Gayle Hanson's article in *Insight* (May 24, 1993), and Claire Safran's piece in *McCall's* (June 1993). Better still, write for literature to the False Mem-

©Jim Ryan. Reprinted by permission.

ory Syndrome Foundation, 3401 Market Street, Philadelphia, PA 19104. This rapidly growing organization, supported by eminent psychiatrists, was formed in 1993 to combat the greatest witch hunt and mental health scandal of this half-century.

Ms. Shapiro fired back in the Summer 1994 issue:

> I could respond at great length about the content of Martin Gardner's "reply" to my letter regarding False Memory Syndrome. However, in this letter I will, with difficulty, restrict myself to a response to his inaccurate references to me, as these are potentially injurious to my professional reputation.
>
> It is telling that Gardner needs to bolster his arguments with an artful but deceptive end run on my credentials. First, he says that my doctorate does not qualify me "to practice psychiatry"; however, it is only he who looks foolish here, since I clearly identified myself not as a psychiatrist, but as a licensed psychologist. Next, and far worse, he employs character assassination by labeling me a "self-proclaimed hypnotherapist," which is tantamount to being called an unethical clinician, practicing a specialty without appropriate training. I cannot allow that statement to go uncorrected: After about two hundred hours of postdoctoral training in hypnotherapy, I have been certified as a hypnotherapist by the American Society of Clinical Hypnosis (ASCH), a well-estab-

lished training organization recognized by the American Psychological Association and the American Psychiatric Association. In addition, I have been certified at the ASCH's highest level, that of consultant qualified to train and supervise other licensed clinicians in hypnotherapy. Had Gardner taken the time as a "scientific inquirer" to ask me, before publishing his derogatory and incorrect characterization, I would have been glad to furnish any relevant documents in relation to my qualifications. Surely a basic of responsible journalism is to check the accuracy of one's assertions—especially potentially defamatory ones—before publishing them.

Marian Kaplun Shapiro,
Licensed Psychologist, Lexington, Mass.

Martin Gardner Responds

Freud began his career as a hypnotherapist, but soon abandoned hypnotism as a worthless technique, an opinion shared by most psychiatrists today. Nevertheless, I apologize to Marian Kaplun Shapiro, who has a doctorate in education, for using the adjective "self-proclaimed." She has indeed been thoroughly trained in the use of hypnotism for treating the mentally ill.

CHAPTER SEVEN

WEIRD WATER, OR H$_2$OH!

> How sweet from the green mossy brim to receive it,
> As poised on the curb it inclined to my lips!
> Not a full blushing goblet would tempt me to leave it,
> The brightest that beauty or revelry sips.
> —Samuel Woodworth, "The Old Oaken Bucket"

We are so familiar with ordinary water that we forget how magical it is. Cool it and it turns into a solid. Heat it and it vanishes into thin air. Under certain weather conditions it becomes snow, with its beautiful crystals. Salt water covers most of the earth's surface, from which it rises as invisible vapor to make clouds. The clouds condense to produce salt-free rain, which in turn fills rivers and lakes. The rivers flow into the sea, and the awesome cycle repeats endlessly. Clearly, life as we know it could not exist without water.

"Be careful with water!" reads one of Ashleigh Brilliant's aphorisms. "It's full of hydrogen and oxygen." Is it not amazing that, when those two gases combine, something emerges, seemingly from nowhere, with totally different properties? "Water-lover" Bloom, in Joyce's *Ulysses* (pp. 442–43), fills almost two pages with poetic musings on the wonders of water.

In view of water's omnipresence, it is hardly surprising that it would be involved, throughout history, with all sorts of preposterous claims. In recent decades there have been two outstanding instances, neither of which turned out to hold water. In 1968 a top Soviet chemist startled the scientific world by revealing tests showing that distilled water, when it condensed in hairlike capillary tubes, turned into "polywater," so called because it acquired a polymeric molecular structure with fantastic properties. Federal agencies squandered millions on polywater research. Hundreds of reports were published in scientific journals before it was shown that polywater doesn't exist. It was nothing more than ordinary water contaminated by human perspiration and silica from glass and quartz containers.

"Notes of a Fringe Watcher," *Skeptical Inquirer* (Fall 1993).

Another much-publicized flap over a peculiar kind of water occurred in 1988, when a French biochemist, funded by a firm that made homeopathic medicines, announced a dramatic confirmation of homeopathic theory. Homeopathic doctors maintain that when one of their drugs is diluted in water to such a degree that no molecule of the substance remains, the dose somehow becomes extremely potent. The French laboratory claimed that when all the molecules of a certain antibody are removed by repeated dilutions, the water, owing to some unknown process, manages to "remember" the antibody's properties. "Water with a memory" it was called. This watery claim, too, quickly evaporated when serious flaws were found in the French experiments. (See my article on this in the Winter 1989 *Skeptical Inquirer*, reprinted with an Addendum in *On the Wild Side* [Prometheus Books, 1992].)

A book would be needed to cover all the spurious claims made in the past for water's curative properties. We all know the medieval legend about the Fountain of Youth, and how it spurred Ponce de León to search for it in Florida. The New Testament (John 5:2–9) tells of a pool at Bethesda where an angel periodically "troubled the water," giving it the power to cause miraculous cures. Since recorded history, all over the world, certain pools, wells, and springs have been thought to have great healing powers.

During the previous century and the first half of this century, health-giving bottled "mineral water," said to come from natural sources, was widely advertised and sold. Mineral springs, especially those with hot water, were visited by millions of eager bathers. In recent decades companies have made enormous profits selling bottled water to customers who assumed it was free of the chemicals in tap water. In some cases, inspections showed that the bottled water actually came from taps.

The British philosopher Bishop George Berkeley, for whom Berkeley, California, is named, wrote an entire book extolling the healing powers of water contaminated by tar. Holy water, blessed by pagan and Christian priests, has for centuries been taken by believers to have healing properties. Oral Roberts once mailed to his financial contributors tiny vials of water that he and his son Richard had blessed.

Belief in the curative power of ordinary water reached its apex in the 1850s, when *hydropathy,* or water cure, became a mania in America and Europe. All over the land, especially in New England, water-cure resorts sprang up, charging rates only the wealthy could afford. They were patronized by millions of the ill, including such famous men and women as William James and Harriet Beecher Stowe. Stowe spent ten months at a water-cure resort, and her husband was there later for a year. Hundreds of books promoted hydropathy. There were several impressive journals, notably the popular *Water-Cure Journal*, published by the Fowler brothers, the nation's best-known phrenologists.

A classic crank work, *Rational Hydropathy* (1900), was written by the Seventh-day Adventist (before he was excommunicated) John Harvey Kellogg. The inventor of breakfast cereal, he was founder and head of the famous Battle Creek Sanitarium, in Michigan. My copy, a 1906 third revised edition, is three inches thick, has 1,217 pages, weighs five pounds, and contains 293 illustrations, some in full color. Every known ailment, according to the doctor, can be cured or helped by proper applications of cold, hot, or tepid water. Here is what Kellogg has to say about the sitz bath (bathing in a sitting position with water above the hips):

> The sitz bath is useful for chronic congestions of the abdominal and pelvic viscera, diarrhea, piles, dysentery, constipation, uterine diseases, and genital and urinary disorders. In treating female diseases it is an indispensable remedy. It is very valuable in various nervous affections, especially those which immediately involve the brain.

Kellogg defined a "douche" as a stream of water aimed at any part of the body. More than thirty different kinds of douches are discussed, with photographs. The soles of the feet, Kellogg wrote, are connected by nerves to the bowels, genitals, and brain. "A short, very cold douche to the feet, combined with strong pressure . . . dilates the vesicles of the uterus, and is hence useful in amenorrhea."

Bathing feet, we are informed, alleviates "headaches, neuralgia, toothache, catarrh, congestion of the abdominal and pelvic organs, colds, and cold feet." How good to know that hot water will warm cold feet! A wet towel wrapped around the body "is a very efficient remedy for constipation, chronic diarrhea, and most other intestinal disorders. It is equally valuable in dyspepsia, torpid liver, enlarged spleen, and uterine derangements."

I am indebted to reader Ben Carlton for sending me recent literature promoting what it calls "Catalyst Water." In July 1980, Harry Reasoner, on CBS's "60 Minutes" television show, interviewed John Wesley Willard, the elderly inventor of Catalyst Water, and many of his enthusiastic patients in Rapid City, South Dakota. Ingredients in the water's secret formula, Willard said, act as a catalyst, transforming the water into a powerful curative agent. Several people in Rapid City told Reasoner how rapidly Willard's water cured their severe ailments. A farmer insisted his wheat crop greatly increased after he soaked the seeds in Catalyst Water. Giant fruits and plants were shown, allegedly produced by spraying buds with Catalyst Water.

A recent advertising brochure from Lyke and Associates, in Hoffman Estates, Illinois, says that in ten years it has sold more than two million bottles of the water. The price listed is $24.95 per bottle, plus $4.00 for UPS shipping. Dan Vasil, a chiropractor, is quoted in the brochure as saying the "catalyst" alters the water's molecular structure, "making its molecules smaller." This allows them to "penetrate the cell's walls at a much greater rate and carry nutrient to where it needs to be."

Catalyst Water can be imbibed or applied locally to the skin. You can add it to bath water and brush your teeth with it. The Lyke brochure prints stirring testimonials of cures. No addresses are supplied, and a note reveals that "names have been changed to protect privacy." This of course makes it impossible to check authenticity. The testimonials tell how the water cured sinusitis, skin ulcers, liver spots, arthritis, irregular heartbeats, warts, constipation, sore throats, and insomnia. It stopped cataract growth, allowed a diabetic to decrease his insulin, and made a woman's face look younger. Literature from other firms selling the water claims that it grows hair, preserves food, cures cancer in cows, cleans walls and paintbrushes, and unclogs drains.

A phone call to William Jarvis, CSICOP's medical-claims expert, turned up the bizarre history of Catalyst Water. It was originally called "Willard's Water," after its discoverer, who was then a chemistry professor at the South Dakota School of Mines and Technology, in Rapid City. In the 1930s Willard patented a detergent used to clean passenger trains. Later he discovered it had marvelous curative properties for both humans and beasts. He attributed this to the fact that it decreases surface tension, allowing water to permeate cell membranes more readily.

For many years "Doc" Willard sold his water through CAW Industries. CAW being the initials of "Catalyst Altered Water." His son, William J. Willard, eventually took over the firm. After the great boost provided by "60 Minutes," several other firms acquired distribution rights for the water. Domino Chemicals, in New York, called it "biowater." Solvent, Inc., in Kansas City, Kansas, advertised "Willard's Water as seen on CBS '60 Minutes.' " In Fort Lauderdale, Florida, Russ Michael, president of the Fountain of Youth International Trust, published a book about the water called *Miracle Cures*. He puts "Dr." in front of his name because he holds a doctor of divinity degree from the Church of Humanity, which he himself founded.

In 1982, the U.S. Food and Drug Administration (FDA) threw cold water on Willard and his son by refusing to approve their water as medicine. The Willards agreed to stop promoting it as a curative agent. FDA laboratories found that the water, in spite of claims that it used no "chemicals," contained varying combinations of rock salt, lignite, sodium metasilicate, sulfated castor oil, calcium chloride, and magnesium sulfate. The amounts are so small, however, that drinking the water apparently has no baleful effects.

Another type of weird water, designed to replace gasoline in cars, periodically enters the news. A Portuguese immigrant named John Andrews, who settled in McKeesport, Pennsylvania, early in the century, was such a claimant. He said he had discovered a mysterious green powder which added to tap water would run engines more efficiently than gas. Successful tests of his powder in 1916 generated considerable press coverage. The Navy was said to have offered him $2 million if he would disclose his formula and train ten naval officers on how to make the powder. Andrews insisted he be paid first. The Navy refused, and Andrews vanished for many years. Interest in his powder was revived in 1942 by Drew Pearson's favorable report (May 22, 1942) on his popular radio show "Washington Merry-Go-Round."

Andrews was finally located on a farm in Elizabethtown, Pennsylvania. Now in his sixties, he denied ever being offered large sums for his secret. It was said that Andrews had been a Canadian seaman in his youth, and that he was mysteriously murdered in his final home in Liberty, Pennsylvania. I have not been able to verify either of these claims. His death gave rise to the rumor that big car and oil firms did him in to keep his great discovery off the market.

The best source on Andrews is *The Wilson Era* by Josephus Daniels (1946), chapter 15. As Secretary of the Navy, it was he who had been interested in Andrews's claims. See also chapter 3, on suppressed inventions, in George O. Smith's *Scientists' Nightmares* (1972), and John Toland's "The Truth About Suppressed Inventions," in *Cavalier* (May 1955). Toland also covers the inventions of Charles Pogue and Jess Ritchie, mentioned later in this chapter.

In 1973, Guido Franch claimed to transform water into what he called "mota" fuel ("atom" backward), also by using a green powder. Occult journalist Tom Valentine interviewed him for the *National Exchange* tabloid (January 1977). Franch said he learned his secret formula from a German scientist, but at other times he claimed he got it from spacemen who lived on Neptune. He wanted $250,000 up front to disclose his secret, $10 million in escrow, and one cent per gallon royalty on all fuel sold.

In 1976, Jean Chambrin, in Rouen, France, claimed he could run engines on a mixture of 60 percent water and 40 percent alcohol (*Atlas World Press Review*, December 1975 and February 1976). Archie Blue, in London, extracted $17,000 from three businessmen for a similar scheme (*Toronto Star*, October 12, 1977).

Inventions designed to obtain cheap energy by extracting hydrogen from tap water turn up every few years around the world, but invariably prove to be as worthless as perpetual motion machines. The most recent major flap of this sort in the United States was in 1976. It involved a hydrogen converter a bit larger than a trunk, invented by sixty-one-year-old Sam Leach of Southern California. He called it the SLX, the SL being his initials. The machine was said to separate water's hydrogen from oxygen in a self-sustaining reaction that required almost no energy input. If it worked, it obviously would change world economics by providing unlimited cheap energy to heat homes, run cars, and so on, without even polluting the air.

Leach was so convincing, and his prototype models worked so well, that he actually sold rights to two companies: The Presley Company, and MJM Hydrotech. Both sales were widely publicized in 1976 (see the *New York Times* [March 29, April 23]; *Newsweek* [April 19]; and *Science News* [April 24]). Presley's stock quadrupled in value in just three months, causing the SEC to suspend trading on April 3.

Physicists were unanimous in calling the machine a fraud. They pointed out that laws of thermodynamics make it impossible to obtain an energy output greater than the input. Leach accused the physicists of "tunnel vision." Of course nothing ever came of the SLX, and I've been too lazy to find out what finally happened to it or to Mr. Leach.

In 1990 a firm called the Water Fuel Cell, in Grace City, Ohio, issued a sales manual of several hundred pages about their method of powering engines with tap water. Its manual swarms with biblical quotations foretelling this great breakthrough. In 1992, the *Reno Gazette-Journal* (May 18) reported that physicist Rudolf Gunnerman could run car engines with a 50-50 mix of water and gasoline. What he called "catalytic poles" split the water into hydrogen and oxygen. Plasma physicist Milton Rothman exploded Gunnerman's claims in "Running on H_2O," an article in CSICOP's *Skeptical Briefs* newsletter (September 1992).

The notion that mammoth corporations, fiercely competitive, suppress such inventions is, of course, baloney. It is regrettable enough when the media, ever eager to sensationalize science, publicize miracle-water inventors. It is more tragic when honest but ignorant investors stubbornly refuse advice from knowledgeable physicists, only to find themselves in hot water as their funds dribble down the drain.

ADDENDUM

The danger of relying on hydrotherapy and other forms of fringe medicine is that one can die. The enormous popularity of water cures led to many such tragedies. I will cite only one. John Roebling, the engineer who designed Brooklyn Bridge, had a foot amputated after an accident. His faith in hydrotherapy was so unshakable that he refused medical treatment and promptly died of preventable tetanus. See *The Great Bridge* by David McCullough (1983) for details.

Richard Metcalf's *Rise and Progress of Hydrotherapy* (1906) is a well-documented history of the water-cure craze. For information on the history of Seventh-day Adventist health reform and the commanding role of Sister Ellen White, see Ronald Numbers's *Prophetess of Health: A Study of Ellen G. White* (1976). On hydrotherapy in the United States, two good references are *The Great American Water-Cure Craze* by Harry Weiss and Howard Kemble (1967), and *Wash and Be Healed* by Susan Caylett (1987).

Engineering consultant Thomas A. Hunter sent me a memo he had prepared for Homelight Corporation in 1974. It stated that Guido Franch, through a firm called Cyclomatic Engineering, in Des Moines, Iowa, offered to reveal his formula for a nonreturnable payment of $10,000, with $990,000 to be placed in escrow for 120 days until Homelight satisfied itself that the green powder worked, plus a minimum royalty of $1 million per year for five years. Nothing came of the offer.

Hunter also sent two other articles by Tom Valentine that appeared in a tabloid called *The National Tattler*. In "Man Who Turns Water into Gasoline Can Still Do It: Spurns Financing," Valentine reports on numerous offers rejected by Franch because he could not get a nonreturnable cash advance. Another article by Valentine titled "*Tattler* Investigation Shows How Big Business Suppressed Inventions That Could Aid Mankind" is about three magic carburetors said to get more than a hundred miles per gallon of gas. (Unfortunately neither article is dated.) All three inventions, Valentine claims, were suppressed by car manufacturers and oil companies who feared the carburetors would damage their profits.

One of these marvelous carburetors was patented in 1936 by a Toronto mechanic named Charles Nelson Pogue. The famous radio commentator Frank Edwards created flurries of excitement in 1953 by claiming that the device gave two hundred miles to a gallon. The patent expired in 1953, but no car company picked it up. Another magic carburetor by an unnamed inventor is said to be locked away by General Motors to keep it off the market. The third carburetor had been invented four decades earlier by John Robert Fish. He set up his own firm in Agawam, Massachusetts, to peddle his device by mail. The Post Office eventually charged him with fraud and closed down his business. He died in 1958, Valentine writes, convinced that the Post Office had been pressured by big oil companies to destroy him.

A more successful swindler was Louis Enricht, a German immigrant who settled in Farmingdale, New York. In 1916 he succeeded in bamboozling both Henry Ford and Hiram Percy Maxim, inventor of the Maxim Silencer, and head of Maxim Munitions. According to Alan Hynd, in a chapter about Enricht in *The Confidence Game* (1970), Enricht's substitute for gasoline was water into which he poured a small amount of a green liquid. (Why so many gas-substitution mountebanks preferred green beats me.) Hundreds of persons wanted to invest in the liquid, but as usual, Enricht refused to disclose his formula until he was paid a vast sum.

The green liquid smelled like almonds. Enricht admitted it contained prussic acid, but insisted he put it there only to hide the smell of two other chemicals. An investigation by the *New York Herald Tribune* revealed that Enricht had been arrested in the past over other shady deals. Henry Ford believed his excuses that these were merely careless mistakes, and reportedly gave him a ten-thousand-dollar advance. Mention of this in the press prompted Hiram Maxim to approach Enricht with a contract offering $1 million for his secret, and a $100,000 advance to build a laboratory. Enricht returned Ford's check. Maxim lost $100,000 without learning the formula.

Enter the next pigeon, a wealthy financier named Benjamin Franklin Yoakum. In 1916 he gave Enricht $100,000 for the formula. Enricht wrote it down, stuck it in an envelope, and placed it in his Farmingdale safety deposit box to be opened only after his death. The box was said to require two keys, one kept by Enricht, the other by Yoakum. Yoakum became suspicious that Enricht was a German spy. (The United States was then at war with Germany.) Yoakum forced an opening of the safety deposit box. It held nothing but some government bonds.

After Yoakum died a few years later, Enricht began looking for fresh suckers. After milking thousands of dollars from stupid investors, he was finally arrested in 1921, tried for fraud, and sentenced to seven years in prison. Then in his late seventies, he obtained parole a year later. If we can trust Hynd's account, Thomas Edison and others later concluded that the green liquid was a mixture containing acetylene. It would run motors all right, but not only did it cost more than gasoline, it would quickly wear out a motor. Hynd's main sources were some twenty reports than ran in the *New York Times* from 1915 through 1917.

An account of mysterious additives said to greatly increase gasoline mileage is also a long story. I will cite only the much publicized case of AD-X2, an additive that caused great excitement when Jess M. Ritchie introduced it in 1953. It was said to consist mainly of sodium and magnesium sulphates. An investigation by the National Academy of Sciences proved it worthless. Ritchie's education turned out to be a degree from the College of Universal Truth, located in a three-room Chicago office.

CHAPTER EIGHT

PEALEISM AND THE PARANORMAL

> Pray Big! Believe Big! Act Big!
> —Norman Vincent Peale

Norman Vincent Peale, the "minister to millions" who burst into prominence in 1952 with his block-busting best-seller *The Power of Positive Thinking,* is the subject of an excellent unauthorized biography by Carol V. R. George, professor of history at Hobart and William Smith Colleges. Titled *God's Salesman,* and published in 1993 by Oxford University Press, it is the first detailed, objective account of Peale's life and his influence on American Protestantism.

Throughout her book George refers to her subject's views as "Pealeism," a term he intensely dislikes. Actually, his central themes are not a new ism. They repeat over and over again, with endless anecdotes, in sermon after sermon and book after book, the basic ideas of New Thought. This was a religious movement that flourished in the decades before and after 1900 and is still being preached in some hundred off-beat churches around the nation. With roots in the transcendentalism of Emerson, and sparked by the teachings of a Maine faith-healer named Phineas Quimby, New Thought generated an enormous number of books and periodicals, of which the most influential was Ralph Waldo Trine's *In Tune with the Infinite.* You'll find a history of New Thought, with emphasis on its promotion by the poet Ella Wheeler Wilcox, in the last chapter of my biography of Mary Baker Eddy, *The Healing Revelations of Mary Baker Eddy* (Prometheus Books, 1994).

Christian Science and Unity were the two most successful spin-offs from New Thought, both with elements that are major aspects of Pealeism. "I think Christianity is truly a science," Peale said in a 1971 sermon, "and I believe the church is a laboratory in which the science is demonstrated." Mrs. Eddy couldn't have said it better.

The essence of Pealeism is this: If you accentuate the positive, elim-

---

"Notes of a Fringe Watcher," *Skeptical Inquirer* (Winter 1994).

inate the negative, pray fervently to a personal God, and "picturize" in your mind your goals (one of Peale's books is titled *Imaging*), miracles will occur in your life. You will be healthier, happier, and make lots more money. Indeed, *The Power of Positive Thinking* made Peale an instant millionaire. It is easy to understand its appeal to businessmen and sales personnel. George quotes Peale as saying that if he hadn't become a preacher, he would have been a salesman.

George skillfully explains why Peale's "feel good" Christianity aroused so much ire among both conservative and liberal christians. Liberals were especially annoyed by Peale's far-right political opinions, and especially by his energetic efforts to block John Kennedy's nomination. Peale actually thought that Kennedy's election would mean Vatican control of our politics. He later apologized for this. "I've never been too bright, anyhow," he told his congregation when he offered to resign as pastor.

Liberals were also annoyed by Peale's lifelong friendship and admiration for Richard Nixon. The Nixons attended Peale's church whenever they were in New York, and it was Peale who married Julie Nixon to Eisenhower's grandson. "I think Kennedy is a jerk," Peale wrote in a letter that George cites. In 1984 President Reagan pinned on Peale the Presidential Medal of Freedom. "Dr. Peale and I disagree on everything, religiously and politically," Reinhold Niebuhr told *Time* (September 19, 1960). During Peale's campaigning for Eisenhower's election, Adlai Stevenson, speaking in St. Paul, said he found Paul appealing and Peale appalling.

Born-again Christians were equally appalled by Peale's refusal ever to mention such doctrines as the Virgin Birth, the bodily Resurrection of Jesus, the Incarnation, and the blood atonement. As to what Peale actually believes about such dogmas it is impossible to tell. It is this theological fogginess that so infuriates both liberal and conservative Christians, even though the fogginess has enabled Peale to keep one foot in and one foot out of both camps. George quotes a marvelous answer that Peale gave to an inquiry about his theological beliefs:

> "I'm a conservative, and I will tell you exactly what I mean by that. I mean that I have accepted the Lord Jesus Christ as my personal Savior. I mean that I believe my sins are forgiven by the atoning work of grace on the cross." Then he added, "Now I'll tell you something else. . . . I personally love and understand this way of stating the Christian gospel. But I am absolutely and thoroughly convinced that it is my mission never to use this language in trying to communicate with the audience that has been given me."

Here is how Peale answered a similar question about his debt to New Thought: "They think I am one of them, but I am not. Actually, I am not opposed to it."

This is not the place to discuss Peale's vague theology. Instead I shall focus on a little-known aspect of his beliefs that receives only the following paragraph in *God's Salesman*:

> To those who claimed that the power of unconscious mind was a form of "clairvoyance," he explained it as "spiritual telepathy" accomplished by "the passage of God's thoughts through the mind." It was rather like Emerson's transparent eyeball. Peale studied the literature of psychic research and was familiar with J. B. Rhine's experiments at Duke University. With neither embarrassment nor hesitation, he revealed in sermons and speeches his personal experiences with psychic phenomena. Most of his references were to encounters with intimates who had died, such as the time he felt the touch of his mother's hand on his head after her death, or when he saw his father's vigorous image approaching him on the platform at Marble Church, or when he recognized his deceased brother Bob smiling at him and greeting him through a brick wall at the Foundation for Christian Living. And there were many others to which he bore witness, at least one of which was picked up and headlined by the sensational *National Enquirer*. Within his Easter sermons orthodox and alternate perceptions of death often competed, with a traditional view of the resurrection sharing place with a metaphysical understanding of death as movement to another level of existence.

Peale's book *The Amazing Results of Positive Thinking* has a chapter on extrasensory perception titled "How to Live with the Spiritual Forces Around You."

In "Why I Believe in Life After Death," an article in Peale's monthly magazine *Guideposts* (April 1977), he described the visitation by his dead father:

> And just last year, when I was preaching at a Methodist gathering in Georgia, I had the most startling experience of all. At the end of the final session, the presiding bishop asked all the ministers in the audience to come forward, form a choir and sing an old, familiar hymn.
>
> I was sitting on the speakers' platform, watching them come down the aisles. And suddenly, among them I saw my father. I saw him as plainly as I ever saw him when he was alive. He seemed about 40, vital and handsome. He was singing with the others. When he smiled at me and put up his hand in an old familiar gesture, for several unforgettable seconds it was as if my father and I were alone in that big auditorium. Then he was gone, but in my heart the certainty of his presence was

indisputable. He was there, and I know that some day, somewhere, I'll meet him again.

We don't try to prove immortality so that we can believe in it; we try to prove it because we cannot help believing in it. Instinct whispers to us that death is not the end; reason supports it; psychic phenomena uphold it.

Interviewed by the *National Enquirer* (July 5, 1983), Peale described another ghostly visitation in 1970. He was addressing a group in Pawling, New York, where he lives, when he distinctly saw his dead brother Bob walking outside the building. The apparition appeared behind "two solid walls. . . . I had seen him right through those walls."

In a 1957 interview with the *American Weekly*, reprinted in Martin Ebon's anthology *The Psychic Reader* (1969), Peale recalled a visitation by the spirit of his departed mother. The day after she died a badly shaken Peale put his hands on his Bible, hoping to gain strength. "Suddenly I felt two cupped hands laid on the top and back of my head." He did not turn to look, but he knew telepathically that his mother was saying, "Everything is all right, Norman. I am happy. This is a wonderful place. Do not grieve for me."

Recalling this incident in his *Guideposts* article cited above, Peale wrote: "An illusion? A hallucination caused by grief? I don't think so. I think my mother was permitted to reach across the gulf of death to touch and reassure me."

Peale told the *American Weekly* about a later visitation by his mother that took place outside a New Jersey restaurant. He was feeling guilty about having paid $400 for two hurricane lamps to give his wife as a surprise. Peale had left the restaurant ahead of Ruth when he heard in his mind his mother say: "Norman, don't worry about the lamps. They will please Ruth. She deserves them, she is so wonderful."

Peale began sobbing uncontrollably. He and Ruth drove several miles on their way to New York before he could tell her what had happened:

Why did my mother come through to me at such a time and place, about so relatively trivial a matter? I don't know. I do not think I am unstable or neurotic. I believe I have my feet on earth. It wasn't grief that sent me out of control, it was an amazed feeling of being in the presence of an overwhelming force.

My feelings of the reality and importance of these experiences have grown ever since my mother's death. Just now I am waiting, with a sense of expectancy, for a communication from a friend of mine, a very tough-minded, skeptical nurse, who had often told me of extrasensory demonstrations she had witnessed in line of duty and with whom I had an agreement that the first of us to die would try to communicate with the other. She died last Saturday. So, I am waiting—not too confidently. But still I wouldn't be surprised.

Peale has always been a firm believer in the reality of near-death experiences, or what are now called NDEs. As he wrote in *Guideposts*:

> Time and again it has been reported of people on the brink of death that they seem to become aware of a great radiance or hear beautiful music or see the faces of departed loved ones who are apparently waiting for them across the line. Are these just hallucinations? I don't think so. Several such episodes have happened within my own family.

Asked by *American Weekly* if he believed science would someday prove there is life after death, Peale answered, "Let us hope so. When it comes it will be the greatest scientific discovery ever made. But I don't have to wait. Mother told me all I need to know."

I am in debt to reader Chris Niemeyer for calling my attention to constant proclamations of paranormal events in the pages of *Guideposts*. They strongly resemble the testimonies at the back of Mrs. Eddy's *Science and Health*, but go even deeper into the miraculous.

Niemeyer began his letter by recalling testimonies he had read in *Guideposts* at a time when he believed them. One told of a woman who experienced the stigmata—one of her hands miraculously began oozing blood. . . . In another testimony, a woman described her visit with a friend to a beautiful garden at a religious retreat, tended by a nun. Later she learned that the retreat had no such garden, and no nun in residence. Her friend confirmed their visit to the garden.

Has *Guideposts* stopped publishing such incredible tales? To find out, Niemeyer went to the public library to check 1993 issues. In the January issue a man wrote about praying on a ship for guidance about tithing. He felt strangely impelled to send his pastor a check to give to one of his old, bedridden Sunday school teachers. The pastor wrote back that the money was the exact amount needed for a new hearing aid. "She had ordered it C.O.D.," said the pastor, "but now couldn't afford it. Without your gift the post office would have had to return it." The sender of the check told *Guideposts*: "Suddenly I knew what—or rather Who—made me do what I did."

The February issue ran a testimony from a woman whose son Mark had been murdered. After the murderer's trial, she visited the local newspaper office to pick up back issues with editorials about the trial that she wanted to send to relatives. She was astounded to see that one paper contained a crossword puzzle that had been completely solved in Mark's handwriting!

After putting away some groceries, she returned to the paper only to find that the puzzle's solution had vanished. She took this as a sign from God that her son's life, unfinished on earth, had been completed in heaven.

The April issue printed a letter from a man whose car had stalled on a two-lane highway. He got out and tried to start the car by pushing it while his wife sat in the driver's seat. As he stepped behind the car his wife called out "Jake!"

He leaped out of the way just before a car crashed into the back of the stalled Chevy. Both cars were totaled. The husband, who had been knocked unconscious, awoke in a hospital with his slightly injured wife beside him. If she had not called out his name, he would have been killed. The wife was puzzled. "I didn't say anything," she told Jake. "I was so frightened, my lips were clamped shut."

Thousands of such testimonies in *Guideposts* have implied similar paranormal events, usually in response to prayers. Could it be that this mystical, paranormal aspect of the magazine accounts for its circulation of about four million, exceeding that of *Newsweek*?

Readers of *Guideposts* apparently take all such anecdotes seriously. Today millions still take them seriously in the preaching and writing of Peale's most famous protégé, the Reverend Robert Schuller, whose Crystal Cathedral far outglitters Peale's drab Marble Collegiate Church on Fifth Avenue in Manhattan. As far as I can tell, Schuller's theology differs from Peale's in only one respect. What Peale calls "positive thinking" Schuller calls "possibility thinking."

"No book on the life of Norman Vincent Peale could be less than motivating, inspiring, life-changing," reads Schuller's blurb on the jacket of *God's Salesman*. "Dr. Peale is one of the 20th century's most remarkable and influential persons. As an author, motivator, minister, and positive persuader, he changed my life and my ministry."

ADDENDUM

"His Mysterious Ways" is the name of a monthly column in *Guideposts* that publishes miracle tales sent in by readers. Out of curiosity I checked the January 1994 issue. Dorothy Howard, of Amherst, Massachusetts, tells of blacking out after her car skidded on ice and crashed into a guardrail. The impact tossed her into the back seat. When she came to she found her car safely parked on a grassy shoulder. "What happened to your companion?" a policeman asked her. He had seen a man drive her car off the highway. "There had been no man in my car," Ms. Howard writes, "but Someone had been with me."

"His Mysterious Ways" is the most popular feature of *Guideposts*. In 1988 more than a hundred of these melodramatic columns were published by Guideposts Associates in a book titled *His Mysterious Ways*. They are grouped under seven headings: God speaks, God Rescues, God Reassures, God Provides, God Protects, God Heals, and God Uses Human Love.

The anecdotes are out of this world. Thomas Coverdale tells how a grenade nearly killed him in Vietnam. After recovering in the hospital his platoon sergeant asked how he managed to let the medics know he had been hit. Coverdale said he had radioed for help. But the radio he carried was totally demolished by the grenade. "How did the medics get my SOS?" Coverdale asks. "I don't know. But God does."

Chloe Waldrop devotes six pages to how she and her husband had parked their motor-home on a large roadside parking area on the Texas side of the Rio Grande. A young man held them up with a pistol, forced them to walk into the desert, strip to their underwear, crawl under a barbed wire fence, then shot them both in the head.

Mrs. Waldrop prayed to Jesus. A misty white cloud enveloped her, spoke to her audibly, guided her to the fence, and then vanished. The next thing she knew she was on the other side of the fence. "I could not comprehend how I got there." She stumbled her way to the parking area where she found her husband bleeding but still alive. They recovered from head wounds after seventeen days in an El Paso hospital. There was no way she could have made it through—or over—the barbed wire, she writes, without getting scratched, yet there were no scratches on her body. She believes the cloud was none other than "the Holy Spirit of Jesus."

And so on, for more than two hundred pages of sensational letters, carefully edited and rewritten for dramatic effect, with no real effort on the part of editors to verify their accuracy. In his introduction, editor Van Verner speaks of a letter about a man dying of thirst on a broiling hot desert "when suddenly, out from a sunny, cloudless sky fell a deluge of life-giving hail. . . . Who could explain those stories of strange signs appearing unsolicited from nowhere, the screams for help that were heard yet never uttered. . . . Why bother to explain those odd stories? If they happened, if they're true, why not just *believe* them? After all, isn't that the essence of faith?"

Yes, but not the essence of rational faith.

Peale died on Christmas Eve, 1994, at age ninety-five. There used to be a stripper who called herself Norma V. Peel. It occurs to me that she was not a bad symbol of Dr. Peale. He managed to strip Christianity of all its ancient doctrines, but instead of his followers shouting "he has no clothes," they were enchanted by his gyrations in the buff.

CHAPTER NINE
THE CULT OF THE GOLDEN RATIO

> Geometry has two great treasures: one is the Theorem of Pythagoras; the other, the division of a line into extreme and mean ratio. The first we may compare to a measure of gold, the second we may name a precious jewel.
>
> —Johannes Kepler

*W*ebster's Ninth New Collegiate Dictionary* has several definitions of "cult". One is: "great devotion to a person, idea, or thing; *esp*: such devotion regarded as a literary or intellectual fad." For more than a century a cult, in the sense just defined, has flourished with respect to an arithmetic ratio known variously as the "divine proportion," the "extreme and mean ratio," and the "golden ratio."

Place a point on a line so that it cuts the line into two segments, A and B, such that the length of the line is to *A* as *A* is to *B*. *A* and *B* are then in golden ratio to each other.

It is easy to show that this ratio is the positive root of the equation $x^2 - x = 1$. Applying the quadratic formula gives x a value of 1.61803398+, an irrational number that is half the sum of 1 and the square root of 5. In the U.S. this number is customarily designated by ϕ, the Greek symbol for phi.

Phi is almost as ubiquitous in mathematical structures as *pi* or *e*. The reason, of course, is the simplicity of the equation that produces it. As might be expected, it is also the sum of the simplest possible continued fraction:

$$1 + \cfrac{1}{1 + \cfrac{1}{1 + \cfrac{1}{1 + \dots}}}$$

"Notes of a Fringe Watcher," *Skeptical Inquirer* (Spring 1994).

Phi is the only positive number that becomes its own reciprocal by subtracting 1. Because $1/\phi$ is .61803398+, the same infinite sequence of decimal digits, some mathematicians have preferred to call .618 . . . the golden ratio. It doesn't matter because you get the same sequence of decimal digits regardless of whether you divide line segment A by B or vice versa.

Phi is related to a generalized Fibonacci sequence in a startling way. Begin with any two numbers, rational or irrational, add them to get a third number, then add the second and third to get the fourth, and so on, always recursively generating the next number as the sum of the two previous ones. As the sequence goes to infinity, the ratio of two adjacent numbers approaches phi as the limit.

Consider the simplest Fibonacci sequence: 1, 1, 2, 3, 5, 8, 13, 21, 34, 55, 89, . . . Divide 89 by 55 and you get 1.618+, or phi correct to three decimals. Continue five more steps to 987/610 and you produce the golden ratio to five decimal places.

Since the Renaissance, an enormous literature has accumulated, most of it nonsense, about the application of the golden ratio to architecture, painting, sculpture, nature, and even to poetry and music. The first great work defending this inflated worship of phi was a 457-page German treatise, *Der Goldene Schnitt* (The Golden Cut), published in 1884 by Adolf Zeising. Early works in English, following Zeising's lead, were *Nature's Harmonic Unity* by Samuel Coleman (1913), and *The Curves of Life* by Theodore Cook (1914). Similar books have been published since, and others are still being written.

My discussion here of what can be called pseudomathematics is based mainly on George Markowsky's sensible paper, "Misconceptions About the Golden Ratio," in the *College Mathematics Journal* 23 (January 1992): 2–19. Markowsky is a computer scientist at the University of Maine. His paper can be consulted for more details and for its valuable list of fifty-nine references. See also the chapter on phi in my *Second Scientific American Book of Mathematical Puzzles and Diversions*, where I myself fell for some misconceptions.

The most persistent misconception is the belief that the "golden rectangle," a rectangle with sides in golden ratio, is the most aesthetically pleasing of all rectangles. The first effort to prove this was undertaken by Gustav Fechner (1801–1887), an eccentric German physicist and psychologist who held bizarre opinions. He believed, for example, that the sun, the moon, and all the planets are living organisms and that even a pebble has a "soul." In one experiment he exhibited ten rectangles of varying shapes and asked subjects to select the one they considered most attractive. About three-fourths of their choices were rectangles with side ratios of .57, .62, and .67.

As Markowsky writes, far from establishing the golden rectangle as the most beautiful, Fechner showed that people prefer a rectangle within a fairly large range; not too close and not too far from a square. Fechner made other experiments to prove that phi was the most pleasing of all ratios, but they were crude by today's standards.

Recent research has shown that the golden rectangle does not score any better than rectangles similar to it, such as a 3 × 5, the shape of a file card. To demonstrate how vague such preferences are, Markowsky drew the chart shown in figure 1, containing 48 rectangles, and asked students to identify the two golden forms. Most of them could not. He then arranged the same rectangles in linear order (figure 2), their ratios ranging from .4 to 2.5. He found wide variations in choices. Moreover, when asked to pick the most pleasing shape in each chart, subjects rarely chose the same one. The rectangle most often selected was the one in row 3 in column 4 of figure 1—a rectangle with sides in a 1.83 ratio.

The efforts of phi cultists to find golden rectangles in architecture, painting, and sculpture reached absurd heights. It is easy to see how this happened. Measurements of parts of a building, or work of art, have such fuzzy boundaries that it is easy to find phi when ratios close to phi fit just as well. Markowsky demolishes the notion that phi is involved in the proportions of the Great Pyramid of Egypt or in those of the Greek Parthenon. There is not the slightest evidence that the Egyptians, Greeks, or any other ancient people used phi in any of their buildings or art. As Markowsky says: "The dimensions of the Parthenon vary from source to source probably because different authors are measuring between different points. With so many numbers available a golden ratio enthusiast could choose whatever numbers gave the best result."

Because Leonardo da Vinci illustrated one of the earliest books on phi, *De Divina Proportione,* by Luca Pacioli, phi cultists have imagined that the ratio was intentionally used by Leonardo in many of his paintings. In every case the application of golden ratios to a Leonardo painting is extremely arbitrary and obtained only by fudging. Parts of a figure will extend beyond the borders of the imagined rectangle, and other parts will fail to touch the borders. There is no evidence that Leonardo da Vinci, or any other Renaissance artist or sculptor, used phi in his work. This does not apply to the twentieth century. A few modern architects, painters, and even music composers, fascinated by the golden ratio, have made deliberate use of it.

Phi buffs are also fond of asserting that on most men and women the navel divides their height in a golden ratio. Indeed, this was one of Pacioli's claims. Why nature would arrange this is never made clear. In any case, it isn't true. Navel height, in relation to body height, varies consid-

Figure 1. Forty-eight rectangles with ratios from .4 to 2.5 in random order.

Figure 2. The same rectangles in linear order.

erably with race and locale, covering a range that of course includes 1.618. Moreover, as Markowsky points out, such measurements are not precise because navels are not points, but areas of nontrivial diameter.

Four persons at Middlebury College, in Vermont, measured the navel heights of 319 college men and women, reporting their results in "The Golden Midd," *Journal of Recreational Mathematics* 24 (1992): 26–29. They summarize their findings as follows: "For the students who endured a bellyful of statistics, the Golden Midd is no Golden Mean. Admittedly, measurement error in this study was a ticklish problem. But, assuming no systematic bias to these errors, we conclude that a practitioner of navel art who wishes to capture divine proportions would have to place the belly-button of a typical Middlebury College coed about 0.7 inches higher than it really is."

Phi enthusiasts have also found the golden ratio in the forms of birds, insects, fish, and other animals. "Of course, wings, legs and fins can be moved over a wide range of positions," Markowsky writes, "and it is not surprising that the golden rectangle can often be produced." In spite of such arbitrariness, some writers on phi have found the golden ratio in animal forms to a precision of five decimal places!

A fascinating property of the golden rectangle is shown in figure 3. By snipping off squares, it can be divided into an infinite sequence of whirling squares and golden rectangles. The vertices trace a precise logarithmic spiral. It is true that spirals closely resembling logarithmic ones abound in nature—the chambers of a chambered nautilus is the most cited instance—but again the spirals vary within a considerable range even in the case of the nautilus.

It is hard to believe, but phi mania has even invaded literary criticism. George E. Duckworth, in *Structural Patterns and Proportions in Virgil's Aeneid* (University of Michigan Press, 1962), provides the major instance. By measuring the number of lines in various parts of Virgil's epic, Duckworth (who died in 1972) claims that Virgil made frequent and conscious use of the golden ratio. Markowsky summarizes objections to Duckworth's claims, and they can be found at greater length in "How to Find the 'Golden Number' Without Really Trying" by Roger Fischler in the *Fibonacci Quarterly* 19 (1981): 406–10, in "Aeneid I and .618?" by Jane Bews in the *Phoenix* 24 (1970): 130–33, and in "Extreme and Mean Ratio in Virgil?" by William Waterhouse in the *Phoenix* 26 (1972): 369–76. In spite of such vigorous criticism, praise of Duckworth's research turns up in several reputable books of literary criticism.

Although finding phi in nature and art has all the earmarks of pseudomath, no one can deny that the golden ratio is encountered with surprising frequency in geometry and algebra. One of the oldest, most striking

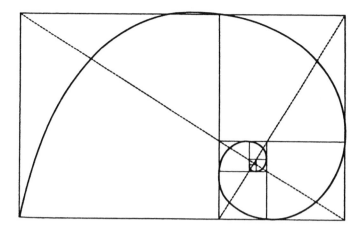

Figure 3. A logarithmic spiral generated by whirling squares and golden rectangles. The spiral "strangles" the intersection point of the two dotted diagonals. The diagonals are in golden ratio.

Figure 4. The pentagram, mystic symbol of the Pythagorean Brotherhood, and the pattern Goethe's Faust used for trapping Mephistopheles. Inverted, it is a satanic symbol.

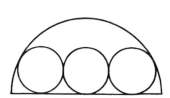
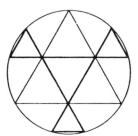

Figure 5. On the left, the radius of a large circle divided by the diameter of one of the small circles is phi. On the right, the side of one of the four larger equilateral triangles divided by the side of one of the three smaller ones is phi. Readers skilled in plane geometry may enjoy proving both assertions.

examples is the pentagram shown in figure 4, the magic symbol of the ancient Pythagorean Brotherhood. Every line segment in the pentagram is in golden ratio to the segment of next smaller length.

Two other delightful constructions in which phi unexpectedly turns up are shown in figure 5.

Of course there is a raft of ratios close to phi that arise from equally simple constructions. The simplest is 3/5 = .6 (or 1.666 . . . , if the fraction is inverted). It would be amusing, if one had the time and inclination, to see how easily 3/5 can be found in the architectural structures of the ancients, in great works of art and literature, and in the forms of animals and humans.

ADDENDUM

The following interesting letter came to the *Skeptical Inquirer* from Dr. Stephen T. Abedon, of Philadelphia:

To the Editor:
    Reading Martin Gardner's "The Cult of the Golden Ratio" I sneaked ahead of the text to look at figure 1 and decide which rectangle

I found most pleasing. Not surprisingly, as I found reading a bit further, I picked the rectangle in row 3 and column 4 (the rectangle apparently most selected). Now why should this particular rectangle be the most selected? To me it just seems to pop out of the page, it is so obvious. Here is my simple hypothesis as to why, all based on position in the figure rather than any factor inherent in this particular rectangle: (1) The rectangle is as close to being at the center of the figure as is possible, being one of the four most central rectangles. (2) Of these four most central rectangles, this particular one is in the upper left hand corner, just where we Americans tend to start our reading. (3) Of all the rectangles shown in figure 1, this is the only one that borders on all four edges rectangles most nearly squarelike. (4) For the life of me I have no clue as to which rectangle this particular rectangle is in figure 2, though I suspect it can be found on the right hand side of row 3. (5) None of the rectangles in figure 2 look nearly as good to me as this particular rectangle in figure 1. It would be interesting to see if this same rectangle would be similarly chosen were the rectangles in figure 1 shuffled differently for each observer, or if a single observer were to look for their favorite rectangle in a series of differently shuffled figures. What all this has to do with the Golden Ratio I don't know, but this may be an example of rectangle "forcing" no doubt holding some insight into human visual processing.

George Markowsky commented:

Stephen Abedon presents some interesting speculations in his letter to the editor about why people chose a particular rectangle as most pleasing when shown in figure 1 as presented in Martin Gardner's "The Cult of the Golden Ratio." I don't really know why people made the selections that they did and I find it plausible that the location of the rectangle affected its selection. My point in carrying out the experiment was exactly to demonstrate that the claim for a particular rectangle to be the "most pleasing" is on very shaky ground. The very limited nature of my experiment suffices only to cast doubt on the claim that the golden rectangle is the "most pleasing rectangle," but is insufficient to explain why people make the choices that they made.

Abedon's letter and Markowsky's comment are published here for the first time.

CHAPTER TEN
EYELESS VISION AND GOD

For four decades Ronald Coyne (pronounced "coin"), a Pentecostal preacher who lives in my hometown of Tulsa, Oklahoma, has been wowing church groups with what magicians call an "eyeless vision" act. But first a little background.

For centuries conjurors have known how difficult it is to blindfold a person so effectively that he or she cannot obtain a peek down the side of the nose. Noses project so far from the cheekbones that an opaque blindfold, covering nose and eyes, invariably leaves two tiny loopholes. This is not the only method of obtaining vision while seemingly securely blindfolded—magic shops sell a variety of blindfold tricks—but it is the simplest, and one still unknown to the public.

Magicians using the nose peek usually add other dodges to strengthen an audience's belief that they cannot possibly see. Powder puffs or silver dollars may be placed over the closed eyes and fastened down with tape. Eyelids may also be taped shut.

Kuda Bux, a magician from India, was famous for his eyeless-vision act. Because he is no longer living, and no performer now uses his method, I will explain here, perhaps for the first time, exactly how he managed to see.

After large globs of soft dough were pushed over Kuda's eyes, a black blindfold was tied over the dough. Assistants then wrapped his entire head with a long strip of cloth of the sort used to make turbans. The cloth swathed his entire face from chin to forehead, giving him the appearance of a mummy.

After his face was swathed, Kuda would raise his hands to adjust the portion of the cloth that crossed his nose. Beneath his fingers, his thumbs, unseen by the audience, would push up through the dough, along the sides of his nose, to form two tunnels that reached to the inside corners of his eyes. In a few more minutes the dough would harden, leaving permanent passages through which both eyes could peek.

"Notes of a Fringe Watcher," *Skeptical Inquirer* (Summer 1994).

Now back to the Reverend Coyne. In 1950 in Sapulpa, a town close to Tulsa, young Ron (then seven) accidentally slashed his right eye with baling wire. His parents rushed him to Tulsa's St. John's Hospital where an ophthalmologist tried to save the eye by surgery. This proved impossible. The eye was removed and a plastic eye substituted. Three months later Ron was "saved" in a rousing conversion experience during the altar call at a local Baptist vacation Bible school.

For ten months Ronald was totally blind in his right eye. Daisy Gillock, wife of an Assembly of God pastor in Odessa, Texas, and sister of the well-known Pentecostal faith healer, L. L. Osborn, came to Sapulpa to conduct a revival. During the faith healing part of the service, young Coyne followed others to the platform. Not knowing Ron's right eye was false, Daisy Gillock prayed that sight in the eye be restored. As Coyne tells us in his literature, he at once began to see with the plastic eye—first the altar steps, then the microphone and his fingers.

This miracle, reported by Tulsa's two newspapers, caused a sensation in the area. Coyne claims that his mother, a devout Christian, accepted the miracle at once; but his father, a professed atheist, refused to believe until one day when Ron asked his dad to blindfold his good eye. After seeing and hearing Ron read print with the other eye, the father was so stunned that he was instantly saved.

Soon young Coyne was appearing in nearby Pentecostal churches to demonstrate how well he could see when his good eye was "securely" covered. From that day to this, more than forty years, Coyne has been presenting his sensational act to believers all over America, and even abroad.

If you send a dollar to Ronald Coyne Revivals, 3702 E. 51st Street, Tulsa, OK 74135 (phone: 918-744-0309), you can obtain Coyne's life story in a 77-page booklet, *When God Smiled on Ronald Coyne.* It was written by his mother in 1952. For four dollars you can buy a long-playing album with the same title. Recorded in the mid sixties by Loyal Records, a Birmingham, Alabama company, its two sides present one of Coyne's entire acts, complete with background organ music and shouts of "Glory to God," "That's Right, Praise the Lord," and "Thank You, Jesus." You can even hear Coyne belt out the lyrics of "Only Believe."

The front cover of this album shows a photograph of a handsome Ronald clutching a Bible. On the back cover are these stirring words by Walter Bailes, president of the recording company:

Can you imagine the shock it must have given a seven-year-old boy to be told that he must have an eye removed from the socket forever because of an injury to that eye and that it would be replaced by a plastic eye. Can you imagine the hurt that a praying, God-fearing, trusting

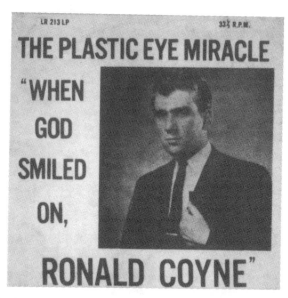

This long-playing album, recorded in the mid-sixties, presents one of Ronald Coyne's entire acts.

mother must have felt at the news. Think of how this must have added even more doubt to an already atheist father. But wait a minute! the story doesn't end here. In fact this is only the beginning. But Ronald tells it so much better himself on this album. I would like to say though that I have personally witnessed this miracle of his seeing through this plastic eye and know that it is a work of the One who created all things.

Now in his fifties and grossly overweight, Coyne is still allegedly flimflamming the faithful. In 1989 the tabloid *Weekly World News* (August 15) featured him on its front page. The inside interview, by Ross Johnson, quoted Coyne as follows:

> The Lord is a mystery. Men cannot understand Him. I often wonder why He gave this miracle to me instead of all the other people who need to be healed.
>
> In fact, the first thing I'm going to ask when I get to heaven is: "Why me, Lord? Why me?"
>
> It's an abnormal thing that goes against everything that is taught by medical science. If a doctor who's a Christian sees me with the glass eye, he'll say, "It's a miracle of God." If a doctor who isn't a Christian sees me read he'll say, "The man really is reading—just don't give me any of that God stuff."

Front page of *Weekly World News,* August 15, 1989.

> Nobody can understand it. Some people try to fight it. But every-body agrees that they've never seen anything like it. I'd say 99 percent of them accept it as the divine miracle that it really is.

Louisiana skeptic Henry Murry attended one of Coyne's performances on April 28, 1989, in a tent on Highway 10 near Jackson, Louisiana. His account of the show appeared in the May–June 1989 issue of *La Raison,* a publication of Baton Rouge skeptics. Murry says at 6:45 P.M., before Coyne arrived, he was subjected to "an hour of electronic noise, accompanied by foot-stomping, hand-clapping, and a wide range of vocal sounds."

Reverend Coyne began his act at eight. Money collections were made before and after the performance while he sat on two chairs because his weight seemed more than four hundred pounds. "As he began to preach," Murry writes, "his thunderous voice hinted that he may have learned to whisper in a sawmill."

Coyne began by recalling sinners who had been saved by Jesus from the eternal flames of hell. His numerous Bible quotes were met with loud amens, hallelujahs, and praise-the-Lords. An elderly woman was called to the platform. After holding her hands and jabbering in the Unknown Tongue, Coyne suddenly yelled "Now!" The poor woman fell backward, "slain by the Lord," into the arms of two women behind her. For five minutes she lay on the floor, arms upraised, lips trembling. A dozen others were similarly "slain."

The show's second half was Coyne's long-practiced act. A borrowed handkerchief was folded and taped over his good eye. "I was seated about twenty feet in front," Murray writes, "and even with my poor eyesight I thought I could see the tape come loose under the eye." With his artificial eye, apparently now made of glass, Coyne read aloud Kipling's "Gunga Din," as well as social security numbers, driver's licenses, and other items handed to him. One woman fell into a trance after he correctly read her driver's license.

Coyne then proceeded to "heal" anyone who came forward with an ailment. A skeptic who had accompanied Murry to the show raised his hands to declare himself an atheist who did not believe Coyne was actually seeing with his glass eye. Unflappable, Coyne calmly said, "The Lord will destroy you, probably on your way home this evening." I should add that Coyne likes to pop out his artificial eye and continue reading with the empty socket.

To make sure Coyne was still performing, I wrote to ask. "Yes," Coyne replied in a handwritten note, "we are still working and traveling for Jesus. I will look to hear from you." Signed "In Him, Ronald Coyne."

When I accuse Coyne of using a nose peek, I am unworried about libel action. Truth is not libelous. Coyne would have to prove in court that he can see through his eyeless socket after an expert covers his good eye so thoroughly that no nose peek is possible. This, of course, Coyne cannot do.

One of the saddest aspects of Protestant fundamentalism is that so many evangelists who are nothing more than greedy con artists are able to take millions from the generous contributions of gullible believers. Steve Martin's marvelous film *Leap of Faith* (1993) is about just such a hustler.

The film is based mainly on the shattered career of faith-healer Peter Popoff. Popoff pretended to have supernatural powers, given to him by the Holy Spirit, to know details about the lives and ills of persons called up to be healed. In reality, as discovered and exposed by James Randi, the Reverend Popoff was receiving this information through a hidden earpiece. His wife and assistants would go through the audience, prior to the show, and converse with spectators. Later, from a trailer outside the auditorium or tent, Elizabeth Popoff, seated in front of a television screen showing the platform, would relay this information to her husband.

Combine the hypocrisies of Popoff and Coyne with the tears and swaggers of Jimmy Swaggart, and you have Steve Martin's phony evangelist. Not until a crippled boy is genuinely made to walk is the healer stricken with remorse—remorse intensified by the desertion of his girlfriend, subtly acted by Debra Winger.

One of his clever "miracles" is secretly painting open eyes on the closed eyelids of a giant wooden Jesus, nailed to a cross behind the tent's platform. This was an invention of the script writers, but such a miracle is not far from those perpetrated by actual faith-healers. Marjoe Gortner, who began his Pentecostal career as a child evangelist at the age of four, made an appalling documentary in 1972 in which he freely confessed his many deceptions. One was to paint a cross on his forehead with a chemical that turned red from perspiration while he preached! "You don't get booked back unless you have a gimmick," Marjoe told *Newsweek* (July 31, 1972). He estimated that he had earned $3 million for his parents, who were part of the scam.

Coyne's gimmick is the nose peek. Now that he is nearing the end of his long and, in my opinion, shabby career, and few congregations today accept him as genuine, he would do well to imitate Marjoe. A documentary explaining his method of seeing, and telling how he has hornswoggled good believers for four decades, ought to bring in much needed loot. My guess is he lacks the guts to make such a film, even though it would be a fine way to atone for his sins.

Coyne's act is an exception among eyeless-vision performers. Most of them are self-styled psychics who pretend they can read print with their fingers or toes, or see through their foreheads. In China in 1980 a group of "psychic" children read printed material after it was shoved into their ears or put under their armpits. For details on the history of eyeless vision by psychic charlatans, see my paper "Dermo-Optical Perception" (*Science*, February 11, 1966). It is reprinted with additions in *Science: Good, Bad and Bogus* (Prometheus Books, 1981).

CHAPTER ELEVEN

THE TRAGEDIES OF FALSE MEMORIES

The greatest scandal of the century in American psychiatry—the topic of chapter 6—is the growing mania among thousands of inept therapists, family counselors, and social workers for arousing false memories of childhood sexual abuse.

No one denies that children are molested, but memories of events that never happened are easily fabricated in the minds of suggestible patients by techniques that include hypnotism, regression therapy, drugs, dream interpretation, and guided imagery. These fake memories become so vivid that patients who acquire them make enormously convincing court witnesses. Jurors tend to believe them rather than the expected denials of those accused. The result: an epidemic of wrong convictions and a mass hysteria that is now far more extensive than the old Salem witch-hunts.

Perhaps the tide is starting to turn. More and more judges, attorneys, police officers, media personnel, and ordinary citizens are becoming aware of the terrible injustices being done. Reputations are ruined, innocent adults are sent to prison for life, and some ten thousand once-happy families are ripped apart by the testimony of patients, mainly children and middle-aged women, who firmly believe their ersatz memories. On the bright side are recent court cases suggesting that innocent victims are finally starting to hit back. Higher courts are beginning to overturn convictions, an increasing number of victims are winning malpractice suits, and many children and adults are recanting their charges.

In Chicago last year, Steven Cook, in hypnotic trances induced by Michele Moul, a Philadelphia therapist, began recalling sexual attacks by Chicago's highly respected Cardinal Joseph Bernardin—memories Cook thought he had repressed for seventeen years. It turned out that Moul's degree in psychology was from a school run by New Age guru John-Roger, who, according to *Time* (March 14, 1994), "claims to be the embodiment of a divine spirit."

On the sole basis of cooked-up memories, Cook sued the cardinal for

"Notes of a Fringe Watcher," *Skeptical Inquirer* (Fall 1994).

$10 million. Fortunately, after a competent clinician convinced Cook his memories were confabulations, he recanted and dropped his civil suit. The vindicated cardinal was too kind to sue Moul for quackery.

All over the United States and Canada Protestant fundamentalists are convinced that Satan is on a final rampage preceding the Second Coming of Christ. Dozens of shabby books have been published about satanic rituals, in spite of a careful study by Kenneth Lanning, of the FBI's Behavioral Science Unit, that found no evidence that such ritual crimes take place. Stimulated by books on Satanism, and by talk shows on the topic, about 30 percent of false memories involved bizarre satanic rituals, and it is claimed that in some of these the babies are killed and cannibalized.

If such cults existed there would be tens of thousands of bodies of mutilated babies buried around the land. Not one has been found. The *Salt Lake Tribune* (September 19, 1993) reported that a Utah task force spent $250,000 trying to find evidence of satanic ritual abuse. It found nothing. How do fundamentalists explain this? Satan is so powerful, they argue, that he obliterates all evidence!

In June 1992, in Martensville, Canada, nine persons associated with a baby-sitting service were charged with ritual abuse on the basis of testimony by thirty young children. The accused included Ronald Sterling and his wife, Linda, their son Travis, an unnamed woman of twenty, and five members of the local police department. The accusations began when a fundamentalist mother decided her two-year-old son had been ritually abused because he had a diaper rash. Constable Claudia Bryden, described by the press as "terribly paranoid" in her fear of Satanism, was chiefly responsible for the arrest of the "Martensville Nine."

The children first denied anything improper had happened, but, after scores of relentless grillings and coaxing by police and counseling by therapists, their "memories" slowly emerged. They spoke of being forced to drink blood and urine and to eat feces. A seven-year-old boy said one of the accused women cut off a child's nipple and swallowed it. Two boys each said that an axe handle had been shoved up his anus, and a vibrator up his penis. No medical evidence for such acts was found.

A child testified he had seen people killed and acid poured on their faces. Another boy claimed he had been put nude in a cage suspended by a rope. He accused Linda Sterling of threatening him with a knife until he sucked her breasts. On another occasion he recalled her saying, "If you don't pee in my mouth I'll kill you." Both Ron Sterling and his son were accused of sodomy.

Seven of the nine were eventually acquitted, their reputations forever scarred. Travis Sterling was sentenced to five years, and the young woman to two years. Some of the acquitted are considering lawsuits of up to $200 million. Mothers of the children remain firmly convinced that the town is infested with secret satanist cults. (Source: "The Martensville Horror," by David Roberts, in Toronto's *Globe and Mail,* February 19, 1994.)

Harold Joseph Levy, 52, a respected attorney and editorial writer on the *Toronto Star,* was arrested in May 1993. A woman undergoing therapy had long-repressed memories aroused of being sexually molested by Levy. A year later, persuaded that her memories were false, she recanted. As the *Toronto Globe and Mail* put it (April 30, 1994), this ended a year of "professional humiliation, social repudiation, and searing gossip." Incredibly, the Crown's attorney, Christine McGoey, said she withdrew her charges "reluctantly." Said Levy's lawyer, "I am completely flabbergasted at the use of the word 'reluctantly.' There was never a shred of evidence. The Crown should be ashamed" (*Toronto Sun,* April 30, 1994).

In 1989, Holly Ramona was suffering from bulimia. Marche Isabella, a family counselor, told her that 80 percent of bulimia cases arise from repressed memories of child abuse—a preposterous claim. There is no such connection. After months of therapy with Isabella, Holly began having flashbacks of repeated rapes by her father, Gary, when she was a small child. After Richard Rose, a psychiatrist, gave her sodium amytal, lurid details of these molestations began to take shape in her mind. Because of her daughter's charges, Gary's wife divorced him and he was fired from his $400,000-a-year job as vice president of a California winery.

Among the signs advanced by Holly's therapists that she had been sexually abused as a child were that she did not like mayonnaise, cream soups, or melted cheese, and that she could not eat a banana until it was sliced. As naive devotees of Freudian symbols, the therapists argued that these foods unconsciously suggested semen and a penis, and were related to Holly's repressed memories of being forced to perform oral sex on her father!

Infuriated by what he called therapeutic quackery, Gary Ramona sued the two therapists for $8 million in damages. In May 1994 a trial jury in Napa County, California, issued a ground-breaking verdict. Ramona was awarded half a million dollars.

Lenore Terr, a San Francisco child psychiatrist, was a chief witness for the defense of the two therapists. A tireless defender of repressed memory therapy, Terr has this year published a book titled *Unchained Memories: True Stories of Traumatic Memories, Lost and Found* (Basic Books). Terr told the jury that Holly's memories were corroborated by her dislike of teeth that resembled her father's and by her aversion to pickles and bananas because they reminded her of oral sex. However, under questioning, Terr admitted that Holly's "memory" of being forced by her father to perform oral sex on the family dog was "dubious." (Sources:

***

Case Study of Implanted Memory

The following dialogue is from Daniel Goleman's article "Studies Reflect Suggestibility of Very Young as Witnesses," in the *New York Times* (June 11, 1993). It is an excerpt from eleven interviews of a four-year-old boy, who each week was told falsely: "You went to the hospital because your finger got caught in a mousetrap. Did this ever happen to you?"

First Interview: "No. I've never been to the hospital."
Second Interview: "Yes. I cried."
Third Interview: "Yes. My mom went to the hospital with me."
Fourth Interview: "Yes. I remember. It felt like a cut."
Fifth Interview: "Yes." [Pointing to index finger.]

.   .   .

Eleventh Interview: "Uh huh. My daddy, mommy, and my brother [took me to the hospital] in our van. . . . The hospital gave me . . . a little bandage, and it was right here." [Pointing to index finger.]

The interviewer then asked: "How did it happen?"

"I was looking and then I didn't see what I was doing and it [finger] got in there somehow. . . . The mousetrap was in our house because there's a mouse in our house. . . . The mousetrap is down in the basement next to the firewood. . . . I was playing a game called 'Operation' and then I went downstairs and said to Dad, 'I want to eat lunch' and then it got stuck in the mousetrap. . . . My daddy was down in the basement collecting firewood. . . . [My brother] pushed me into the mousetrap. . . . It happened yesterday. The mouse was in my house yesterday. I caught my finger in it yesterday. I went to the hospital yesterday."

***

"Dubious Memories," by Jill Smolowe, *Time,* May 23, 1994, and Jane Gross's article in the *New York Times*, April 8, 1994.)

Terr was also an expert witness for the prosecution of George Thomas Franklin, a former California firefighter now in prison for life on the sole testimony of his daughter Eileen. She said she "adored" her father until 1989, when therapy revived a twenty-year-old memory of having seen him murder her best friend, eight-year-old Susan Nason. It had been an unsolved crime, and the details were long familiar to Eileen.

In 1989, Eileen "remembered" her father hitting Susan on the head with a rock after raping her. She also had revived memories of herself being sexually molested by her father, and on one occasion being held down by her father while one of his friends raped her. In 1990 the California Court of Appeals upheld Franklin's life sentence. Terr firmly believes Eileen's long-repressed memories. On CNN's "Sonya Live" (March 13, 1994), I heard Terr say that one-sixth of all women have been sexually abused as children and that the cases of revived memories proving false are only a "drop in the bucket" compared with revived memories that are true.

Dale Anthony Akiki, thirty-five, mentally retarded and physically deformed (he is a hydrocephalic), spent two and a half years in jail after ten children (ages three and four) in San Diego accused him of sexually abusing them in satanic rituals at Faith Chapel, where he taught Sunday school. The children had been pressured to fantasize by parents and therapists. Akiki was accused of hanging them upside down from a chandelier, sodomizing them with a curling iron, dunking them in toilets, forcing them to drink blood and urine and ingest feces, mutilating animals and a human baby, and bringing an elephant and a giraffe to Sunday school class, where he killed them.

Akiki was acquitted in November 1993 by a San Diego jury. Terr testified for the prosecution, insisting that only clinicians, not research psychologists and psychiatrists, are capable of judging the validity of repressed memory theory. In June 1994 the jury lambasted the therapists for their techniques. Akiki's attorneys are bringing a civil suit of $110 million against the San Diego county. (Source: *New York Times*, June 3, 1994.)

In Hendersonville, North Carolina, where I live, a gullible jury convicted Michael Parker in 1993 of ritually abusing his three young children. Their memories had been revived by therapists at the insistence of their mother, who had been impressed by a book about Satanism. As usual, the children's memories were as bizarre as they were unsubstantiated. Not only Parker, but his mother and seven others were accused of satanic cult abuse. The children testified to being surrounded by the accused, who were wearing Ku Klux Klan-type robes with emblems on the sleeves, holding burning candles, and chanting. One little girl recalled her father raping her with a big spoon. It became filled with blood, which he poured into a cup and drank.

Divorced and living alone in a trailer camp in the nearby town of Saluda, Parker was too poor to hire a lawyer. "Sodom and Saluda" was what Mike Edwards, the prosecuting attorney, called the town. (Saludians were of course furious.) He quoted frequently from the Bible while jurors smiled and one man murmured "Amen." It took them only fifty-five minutes to find Parker guilty. He is now in prison, eligible for parole in 160 years. Michael Edney, his court-appointed attorney, plans to appeal.

One of Parker's daughters, who had been in a mental hospital, said Parker had forced her to lie on the ground, her arms and legs pinned down by horseshoes, while he molested her. She told the jury of a time when a poster on her bedroom wall, advertising the "I Love Lucy" show, talked to her and said she deserved all her suffering. None of the children had told anyone about their abuse until undergoing therapy.

In spite of the FBI's report that satanic cults are a myth fabricated by fundamentalists and Pentecostals, the prosecuting attorney says they are widespread in North Carolina. "My experience is when you uncover the evidence of Satanism you get dribs and drabs," he said. "It's a fraternity that has a code of silence like no other. We've got a peek at what it looks like." To escape prison, Parker's mother accepted a plea bargain and pleaded "no contest." Trials of the other seven are coming up soon. (Source: Hendersonville's *Times-News* from February 13, 1993, through February 5, 1994.)

A few earlier cases, out of thousands, deserve mention. The McMartin Preschool case in Manhattan Beach, California, ended in 1990 without convictions of the school's director and her son. They had been accused of hundreds of episodes of rape, oral and anal intercourse, and unspeakable acts involving satanic mutilations of animals—all solely on the basis of memories planted in the minds of suggestible children by honest but quack psychologists. It was the longest (six and a half years) and costliest criminal trial in U.S. history. The accusations had been triggered by a mother who was later hospitalized for acute paranoid schizophrenia. For details see *The Abuse of Innocence: The McMartin Preschool Trial*, by Paul and Shirley Eberle (Prometheus Books, 1993).

In 1993 a New Jersey Court of Appeals overturned the forty-seven-year sentence of Margaret Kelly Michaels for abusing nineteen children at the Wee Care preschool, in Maplewood, New Jersey. An Essex County prosecutor spent almost $3 million of taxpayer money in his zeal to convict Michaels solely on the basis of testimony by children who had been undergoing dubious therapy. They testified that Michaels could toss cars into trees and that she liked to cover her nude body with peanut butter and make them lick it off. They added the charge, so often repeated in books on satanic cults, that they were forced to ingest feces and urine. They said Michaels had pushed Lego toys into their vaginas and rectums. Michaels spent five years in jail before her acquittal. Incredibly, the state is appealing.

Laura Pasley, thirty-nine, a secretary in the Dallas Police Department, sought therapy for her bulimia and was told that all eating disorders spring from repressed memories of child sex abuse. Using hypnosis and dream analysis, her therapist soon persuaded her that she had been abused by her mother, father, and grandfather, and a neighbor, and that her brother once tried to kill her. She "remembered" sex abuse by animals. In 1992 she decided that all these aroused memories were false, and sued both her counselor and therapist. The case was settled out of court.

"These therapists are doing something as evil as evil can be," Pasley told a reporter. She said that when she tried to tell her therapist that certain horrible events had not happened, he shook his head, insisting she was "in denial" and only trying to protect her family. (Source: Pasley's article, "Misplaced Trust," in *True Stories of False Memories*, edited by Eleanor Goldstein and Kevin Farmer.)

The most tragic and still ongoing case of fabricated memories involves the Little Rascals day-care center in Edenton, North Carolina, a town torn apart by the case. On no basis except preposterous claims by children, egged on by angry, mind-closed mothers, and memories evoked by therapists, Robert Kelly, owner of the school, was convicted on ninety-nine counts of first-degree sex offenses. He is currently serving a sentence of twelve consecutive life terms, the longest sentence in North Carolina history. He can apply for parole in 240 years. Early this year his wife, Betsey, pleaded "no contest," which allowed her a reduced sentence on forty-eight counts. She is serving seven years in prison.

Willard Scott Privott, a video-store owner associated with the Little Rascals case, spent almost four years in jail awaiting trial because he could not raise a $1-million bond. At his May 1994 trial, he escaped a possible 363 years in prison by accepting a plea bargain, and was released on a suspended ten-year sentence. He had been accused of sex acts with Betsey in front of the children, as well as sex acts with the children, while photos were taken. No such photos were found. Three other defendants still await trials, and have been offered plea bargains.

"Innocence Lost," a two-part television documentary on the Edenton case, shown in 1993, was a vigorous attack on RMT. It left no doubt that the youngsters confabulated and that those accused were innocent. The town's Christian parents were accurately depicted as hysterical in their blind rage against the day-care workers and their associates. The Associated Press (June 17, 1994) quoted a typical statement by Susan Small, one of the angriest of the mothers:

> One day you [Willard Scott Privott] will stand before Almighty God and be accountable for that which you have done here on earth and no amount of lies and manipulation, no "Frontline" presentation, will be able to hide the truth from Him. He knows every sorted detail and I pity you for that.

There is not the slightest evidence, aside from the wild, garbled testimonies of the disturbed children, that Privott, who ran an audio store and a shoe repair shop in Edenton, ever did anything wrong.

All those charged maintain total innocence. When the children were first interviewed by therapists, they had no memories of sex abuse, but after prolonged therapy, and hundreds of leading questions, memories of abuse began to emerge. Some notion of the accuracy of these "memories" can be gained by one child's recalling that "Mr. Bob" had taken a group of children aboard a ship surrounded by sharks. He threw one of the girls in the ocean. Was she eaten by sharks? No, the boy replied. He had jumped into the water and rescued her!

Children recalled seeing Mr. Bob kill babies with a pistol and take photos of employees engaging in sex. They testified to sodomy by Mr. Bob, and said he routinely shot children into outer space on rocket ships. To this day the children, now young adults, swear their revived memories are genuine. "We know. We were there," they have said many times on TV talk shows. One can only marvel at the intensity with which the prosecuting attorneys continue to pursue the case. Could it be that winning a court victory overrides their consciences?

The cases described only scratch the surface of nightmares that are splintering families all over the United States and Canada and sending innocent adults to prison for life. During the past dozen years, hundreds of preschool teachers have been arrested on the basis of repressed-memory therapy. Leading psychiatrists seem powerless to combat the epidemic. The same techniques used to awaken long-repressed memories of sex abuse are also being used by scores of therapists to revive memories of abductions by aliens in UFOs, as well as memories of traumas experienced in previous incarnations!

John Mack, a Harvard psychiatrist, has just published *Abductions: Human Encounters with Aliens* (Scribner's), a book about his successes in using hypnosis to uncover memories of sex abuse on flying saucers. Mack believes the aliens live in dimensions invisible to us. See his 1994 interviews in the *New York Times Magazine* (March 20), *Time* (April 25), and *Psychology Today* (March/April).

Readers interested in up-to-date information about this mania can contact the False Memory Syndrome Foundation, 3401 Market Street, Philadelphia, PA 19104, which publishes a newsletter. Books on both sides of the bitter controversy are proliferating. Of special interest is Lawrence Wright's *Remembering Satan: A Case of Recovered Memory and the Shattering of an American Family* (Knopf), The book reprints his explosive two-part *New Yorker* article (May 17 and 24, 1993) about the conviction of a pious policeman in Olympia, Washington, on the basis of "recovered" memories of his two daughters. Because I discussed this tragic case, which involved an alleged satanic cult, in my previous chapter on false memories, I won't repeat its crazy details here. It is a book every American should read. Someday you may be called for jury duty on a repressed-memory case that can result in terrible injustice unless you and your fellow jurors are adequately informed.

By far the best, most detailed, most accurate, most compassionate history of this tragic witch-hunt is *Victims of Memory*, by Mark Pendergrast, published in 1996 by Upper Access Inc.

ADDENDUM

The tide against the RMT epidemic is finally starting to turn. Three recent developments are responsible:

1. More and more patients and parents are suing therapists for malpractice and winning large settlements. (A "therapist," by the way, can be a psychiatrist, psychologist, social worker, family counselor, New Age guru, or any untrained person who calls himself or herself a therapist.)

2. The overturning of past convictions by higher courts.

3. The rapid spread of accurate information about RMT to police, attorneys, judges, and ordinary people who serve on juries.

In 1994, Vynnette Hamanne, of White Bear Lake, Minnesota, sued her St. Paul psychiatrist, Dr. Diane Bay Humenansky, fifty-nine, for using hypnosis and sodium amytal to convince her falsely that she had been abused by a satanic cult and was suffering from multiple personalities. She persuaded Hamanne that she had been repeatedly sexually abused by her father, mother, uncle, grandfather, grandmother, and maybe other family members. One of Vynnette's "memories" was of her grandmother stirring a large cauldron containing dead babies! Another aroused memory was of having a child at age eight, then giving the child to a cult to be sacrificed.

On July 31, 1995, a jury ordered Humenansky to pay $2.6 million, the largest such settlement ever imposed on a psychiatrist. Six other recanted patients are also suing Humenansky for arousing false memories of child abuse and convincing them of nonexistent multiple personality disorders. Their attorney is seeking a settlement of $6.9 million. The doctor's beliefs are so weird that the Minnesota Board of Medical Practice has ordered her to undergo a physical and mental examination. In court testimony she said she based her techniques on *The Courage to Heal* and *Sybil*, two "bibles" of RMT believers. She contends that 90 percent of her patients have been sexually abused as children, and that twenty have told her about involvement in cults where babies were killed and eaten. (References: The Minneapolis/St. Paul *Star Tribune*, July 19, 23, 24, and August 1, and an Associated Press release of August 1, all of 1995.)

In Pittsburgh Nicole Althaus recanted after fourteen months of RMT.

She and her parents, Richard and Cheryl, sued therapist Judith Cohen, and were awarded $272,000 by a jury in 1994. Nicole had "remembered" being tortured with a thumbscrew and giving birth to three babies who were brutally murdered. She "recalled" a grandmother who rode on a broom, and a time when she was raped in a crowded restaurant. Her poor father had been taken from his home in handcuffs.

In Mount Holly, New Jersey, Joan and Kenneth Tuman sued a psychiatric group called Genesis Associates, in Exton, for arousing false memories of horrible satanic rituals in the mind of their twenty-year-old daughter Diane. Diane had gone to Genesis to be treated for bulimia. She soon developed memories of being raped by her father, and became convinced that they had murdered a twin brother and other children in satanic cult rituals. Her treatment involved "rage therapy" in which she was urged to beat a pillow with a bat, scream the name of a hated parent, pretending that the pillow was the person she was killing.

Genesis advised Diane to leave her parents and assume a new identity to "hide from the cult." In 1995 a federal judge refused to dismiss the lawsuit as urged by Genesis attorneys. According to a riveting two-part "Frontline" TV documentary, "Divided Memory" (1995), eight other former patients are now suing Genesis for damaging their lives by creating false memories. The documentary showed patients at Genesis sobbing and writhing on the floor. (See the *Legal Intelligencer* 213, no. 17 [1995], for the judge's ruling.)

In Bangor, Maine, after a bitter divorce settlement, Peter Maury's ex-wife Barbara took their two young daughters to therapist Judith Osting. Osting convinced the girls that their behavior problems arose from sexual abuse by their father. In 1995 a federal jury awarded Maury $850,000 in damages for the false accusations. (Source: *Bangor Daily News*, July 10, 11, 12, and 22, 1985.)

In 1985 Donna Sue Hubbard was given a hundred-year prison sentence for alleged child molestations. Her conviction was overturned in 1995 by California's Fifth District Court of Appeals. "There is substantial likelihood that the children's resulting testimony was false," said Appellate Justice Thomas Harris.

These are only a small fraction of hundreds of recent cases in which recanters and/or their parents are suing RM therapists for untold damage to their lives, and cases in which earlier sentences have been overturned by higher courts.

Children sometimes invent stories of sexual abuse without being brainwashed by therapists. Bill Forester, of Greensboro, North Carolina, spent two years of a life sentence in prison before Mindy Coppinger, who had accused him of molesting her when she was six, admitted she made up the story. "I'm very sorry," she said. "I know I shouldn't have told a story because it was wrong." (Source: Associated Press release of December 27, 1993.)

Michael Duane Boykin spent five years of two life terms in prison after his twelve-year-old daughter Tanya accused him in 1989 of rape. He was released in 1994 after Tanya confessed she had concocted the charge because her father had threatened to punish her for skipping school. Boykin had turned down a chance for plea bargaining to get a lessor sentence if he pleaded guilty. (Source: Associated Press release of May 30, 1994.)

The latest, most sensational instances of overturned convictions involve the Franklin case and the Little Rascals case, both covered in chapter 6. In April 1995 a state court in Washington ordered a new trial for George Franklin because of contradictions in his daughter's testimony. Another ground for overturning the verdict was that the jury had not been told that details the daughter "remembered" about the murder of her friend had all been widely published by the print and electronic media before her "memories" were "revived."

In May 1995, a North Carolina court of appeals ordered a new trial for Robert Kelly, Jr., co-owner of the Little Rascals day-care center, and Kathryn Dawn Wilson, the center's cook. Both are serving life sentences and will remain jailed until they are retried. It turned out that three of the jurors never doubted the innocence of Kelly and Wilson, but were under such pressure by the other jurors that they finally went along with a guilty verdict only to avoid a hung jury. Three other former workers at the day-care center still await trial. Attorney General Mike Easley vows to prosecute them as long as the brainwashed children are able and willing to testify.

After six years in prison Kelly was finally released in 1995 on a $200,000 bond after the state supreme court refused to reverse the court of appeals ruling. Incredibly and sadly, he may be retried by a district attorney more concerned about his reputation among hysterical Edenton mothers than in justice to a falsely accused man.

Although Michael Parker is still serving a life sentence, all charges were dropped in July 1995 against seven of his codefendants—innocent bystanders living in Saluda, near Hendersonville where Parker's trial took place. Flagrant contradictions had been found in the testimonies of Parker's disturbed children. Parker's mother had escaped her son's fate by pleading no contest without admitting guilt. Here is how I put it in a letter that our local paper refused to print:

> It is heartening news (July 27) that charges of child abuse have been dropped against Cheyenne Hill and six codefendants living near Saluda. The charges rested mainly on the conflicting testimonies of three men-

tally disturbed children brainwashed by an angry divorced mother and by incompetent therapists.

If the district attorney is genuinely concerned about justice he should drop charges against Michael Parker, now in prison for life, for alleged crimes based on the same confabulations of his three children. Charges also should be rescinded against Parker's distraught mother who pleaded no contest solely to escape her son's fate.

The children testified to repeated abuses while surrounded by satanic cult members holding candles, wearing robes with mysterious emblems on the sleeves, and chanting. The nine-year-old girl said her father had pinned her arms and legs to the ground with horseshoes while he sexually assaulted her. The twelve-year-old daughter claimed her father raped her with a big spoon that became filled with blood which he drank. The twelve-year-old son said his grandmother took off all her clothes and "jumped up and down" on him while his hands were tied to bedposts. (See *Times-News*, January 21 to February 5, 1994.)

These and even wilder scenes related by the children are straight out of books on nonexistent satanic cults written by paranoid fundamentalists. Officers, attorneys, judges, and juries, unaware of how easily false memories can be fabricated, have sent hundreds of innocent parents to prison for abuses that never occurred. Of many recent books about this greatest scandal in modern psychiatry, I recommend Mark Pendergrast's *Victims of Memory: Incest Accusations and Shattered Lives*.

There *are* no satanic cults in Saluda. There never have been. It would be a gracious gesture if the district attorney who spoke of "Sodom and Saluda" in his zeal to sway a jury with biblical citations would apologize for this crude canard.

John Mack has become such an embarrassment to Harvard that its medical school conducted a year-long secret investigation to determine whether Mack should be publicly censored. In August 1995 the investigators announced that no adverse action would be taken. The investigating committee's preliminary report found Mack "in violation of the standards of conduct expected of a member of the faculty," and said he deserved rebuke for "affirming the delusions" of his patients. Arnold Relman, chairman of the committee, was quoted by the *Boston Globe* as saying, "John Mack may win the Nobel Prize and go down in history as the modern Galileo."

*   *   *

It goes without saying that adults do rape and molest children. Where there is solid evidence, such criminals should of course be punished. The point is that equally terrible tragedies occur when judges and juries refuse to believe that children can lie convincingly for a variety of reasons, and can develop totally false memories under treatment by well-meaning but self-deluded therapists. The same techniques can arouse false memories of past sexual abuse in the minds of vulnerable adults. It is sad that so many leading feminists have defended RMT without taking the trouble to learn much about it. It would be to their interests not to support a mania which has the effect of turning women into powerless victims of abuse that never took place.

*　　*　　*

A selected bibliography of articles on RMT in academic journals, popular magazines, and leading newspapers would require dozens of pages. Among the many recent books on RMT, I recommend the following:

Campbell, Terrence. *Beware the Talking Cure.*

Crews, Frederick. *The Memory Wars: Freud's Legacy in Dispute.*

Eberle, Paul, and Shirley Eberle. *The Abuse of Innocence: The McMartin Preschool Trial.*

Goldstein, Eleanor. *Confabulations: Creating False Memories, Destroying Families.*

Goldstein, Eleanor, and Kevin Farmer. *True Stories of False Memories.*

Loftus, Elizabeth, and Katherine Ketcham. *The Myth of Repressed Memory: False Memories and Allegations of Sexual Abuse.*

Nathan, Debbie, and Michael Snedeker. *Satan's Silence: Ritual Abuse and the Making of a Modern American Witch Hunt.*

Ofshe, Richard, and Ethan Watters. *Making Monsters: False Memory, Psychotherapy, and Sexual Hysteria.*

Pendergrast, Mark. *Victims of Memory: Incest Accusations and Shattered Lives.*

Smith, Susan. *Survivor Psychology: The Dark Side of a Mental Health Mission.*

Wakefield, Hollida, and Ralph Underwager. *Return of the Furies: An Investigation of Recovered Memory Therapy.*

Wright, Lawrence. *Remembering Satan: A Case of Recovered Memory and the Shattering of an American Family.*

CHAPTER TWELVE
LITERARY SCIENCE BLUNDERS

Unfortunately, there are people in the arts and humanities—conceivably, even some in the social sciences—who are proud of knowing very little about science and technology, or about mathematics. The opposite phenomenon is very rare. You may occasionally find a scientist who is ignorant of Shakespeare, but you will never find a scientist who is *proud* of being ignorant of Shakespeare.
—Murray Gell-Mann, as quoted in John Brockman,
The Third Culture: Beyond the Scientific Revolution (1995)

C. P. Snow, in his famous little book *The Two Cultures,* maintained that scientists usually know more about the arts than leaders of the humanities know about science. One could fill this page with the names of great scientists and mathematicians—Einstein is a notable example—who loved classical music, many of whom were even skilled in playing it. Other scientists, eminent and not so eminent, have been unusually knowledgeable about poetry, literature, painting, and philosophy.

Contrariwise, it is not easy to find musicians, painters, novelists, poets, and especially actors who have a knowledge of science beyond what they learned in grade school. There are, of course, exceptions. Snow himself was a physicist-turned-novelist who bridged the two cultures. H. G. Wells was an earlier example. Milton and Dante were well acquainted with the science of their time. So was Shelley. The same can be said of such modern writers as Nabokov, Borges, Auden, Pynchon, Vonnegut, and Updike. By and large, however, persons trained in the arts tend to be appallingly ignorant of the most elementary science. I recall a confusing conversation I once had with a graduate student in English literature before I realized he did not know, as Shakespeare did, that what the bard called the moon's "pale fire" was "snatched" from the sun.

Over the decades I have gathered a list of amusing howlers involving science that occur in literary works. Because it is far from exhaustive I would welcome hearing of any blunders I have missed. It goes without

"Notes of a Fringe Watcher," *Skeptical Inquirer* (January/February 1995).

saying that a science mistake in a work of fiction is only a minor blemish that in no way mars the literary value of the work.

Let's start with a little-noticed mistake by F. Scott Fitzgerald in his masterpiece, *The Great Gatsby*. In chapter 2, Fitzgerald describes a huge sign in front of an oculist's shop in Queens, New York: "The eyes of Doctor T. J. Eckleburg are blue and gigantic—their retinas are one yard high. They look out of no face but, instead, from a pair of enormous yellow spectacles which pass over a nonexistent nose." Throughout the novel the giant eyes symbolize the eyes of God. Did you get the mistake? One cannot see retinas. Fitzgerald meant pupils or irises.

The first edition of Willa Cather's best-known novel, *Death Comes for the Archbishop,* had the following incredible passage:

> . . . A chasm in the earth over two hundred feet deep . . . through the sunken fields and pastures, flowed a rushing stream which came from the high mountains. Its original source was so high, indeed, that by merely laying an open wooden trough up the opposite side of the arroyo, the Mexicans conveyed the water to the plateau at the top. This sluice was laid in sections that zigzagged up the face of the cliff.

Water can flow upward only when confined within siphons and other structures, but not in open troughs. The error was corrected in later editions. In the same edition Cather speaks of mesas in the region of Acoma, New Mexico, as "great tables of granite." Actually they are made of sandstone. Another passage refers to a man's right eye as "overgrown by a cataract." Cataracts are not growths on the outside of an eye lens or cornea, as many believe. They are a clouding of the lens itself.

William Golding's novel *Lord of the Flies* contains two outstanding howlers. Here is how Ralph, in the second chapter, starts a fire by using the spectacles of the myopic Piggy:

> There was pushing and pulling and officious cries. Ralph moved the lenses back and forth, this way and that, till a glossy white image of the declining sun lay on a piece of rotten wood. Almost at once a thin trickle of smoke rose up and made him cough. Jack knelt too and blew gently, so that the smoke drifted away, thickening, and a tiny flame appeared. The flame, nearly invisible at first in that bright sunlight, enveloped a small twig, grew, was enriched with color and reached up to a branch which exploded with a sharp crack. The flame flapped higher and the boys broke into a cheer.

Nearsighted (myopic) persons wear lenses that are concave. Only convex lenses can focus sunlight on a small spot.

James Hugh, in "You Can Be Myopic and Still Survive on a Desert Island," in the *Physics Teacher* (December 1991), pointed out that a lens for correcting nearsightedness is actually convex on the outward side, but strongly concave on the side facing the eye. If such a lens is held horizontally, the concavity can be filled with water to make it a convex lens capable of starting a fire.

Golding makes an even worse mistake in chapter 5. The sun has just set, stars have appeared, and a "sliver of moon" is rising above the horizon. Golding, who majored in science at Oxford before he switched to literature, should have known that a moon rising after sunset has to be full, not crescent-shaped.

Mistakes about the moon are common in both fiction and poetry. Evidently most people are not aware that the moon, like the sun and the stars, rises in the east and sets in the west. They seem to think the moon floats about the sky randomly until it is dark enough for it to become visible.

Coleridge makes the same mistake in *The Ancient Mariner.* In part 3 "The Sun's rim dips, the stars rush out: At one stride comes the dark." This is followed by a "horned moon" climbing in the east. Not only is this moon a crescent, but it has "one bright star within its nether tip." The line originally read "almost atween the tips," so Coleridge may have known that a star inside the moon's crescent is impossible, and intended this to be a supernatural omen.

In George Eliot's *Mill on the Floss,* Maggie Tulliver and her brother are drowned on the river Floss when their frail boat is overturned by a mass of debris floating toward them at a faster rate than the boat is drifting. Actually, both boat and debris, unless there were strong eddies or countercurrents, would move through the flowing river at the same rate.

In spite of lurid books and articles to the contrary, by poorly informed journalists of pseudoscience, chemists agree that no human being ever caught fire by spontaneous combustion. Such events occur only in fiction, the most notorious instance being the sudden combustion of a drunken Mr. Krock in Dickens's *Bleak House.* Other instances of such deaths can be found in Charles Brockton Brown's *Wieland,* Nicolai Gogol's *Dead Souls,* Frederick Marryat's *Jacob Faithful,* Herman Melville's *Redburn,* and Emile Zola's *Le Docteur Pascal.*

The first edition (1885) of H. Rider Haggard's best-selling novel *King Solomon's Mines,* in chapter 11, "We Give a Sign," has a total eclipse of the sun taking place during a full moon, and producing total darkness for an hour and a half. A total eclipse of the sun can occur only when the moon is between the earth and the sun and thus invisible, and totality lasts only a few minutes. Not until the edition of 1886 did Haggard change the event to a lunar eclipse.

It is easy to forget that the moon, like stars, can be overhead in the daytime but nearly invisible. If the moon is full or gibbous, it often shines in the dim light of sunrise or sunset. Apparently T. S. Eliot forgot this when he complained about the seeming obscurity of the fifth stanza of Shelley's "To a Skylark":

> Keen as are the arrows
>   Of that silver sphere,
> Whose intense lamp narrows
>   In the white dawn clear
> Until we hardly see—we feel that it is there.

Is not the meaning obvious? Shelley is describing a silvery full moon at daybreak. As the sky gets brighter, the image slowly fades until it reaches a point when you hardly see it but "feel" it is still there. The vanishing is especially rapid in the foggy, air-polluted skies of London. In a similar way, the song of a retreating skylark trails off into silence.

It is hard to believe, but here is what Eliot had to say about this stanza in "A Note on Richard Crashaw" in his book For Lancelot Andrews:

> For the first time perhaps in a verse of such eminence, sound exists without sense. . . . I should be grateful for any explanation of this stanza; until now I am still ignorant to what sphere Shelley refers, or why it should have silver arrows, or what the devil he means by an intense lamp narrowing in the white dawn; though I can understand that we could hardly see the lamp of a silver sphere narrowing in white dawn (why dawn? as he has just referred to the pale purple even). There may be some clue for persons more learned than I; but Shelley should have provided notes.

Someone must have explained the stanza to Eliot because he removed his objection when the essay was reprinted in a later book.

Thomas Cook, in his crime novel *Flesh and Blood* (1989), has on page 44 an autopsy report saying, "At the moment of her death, her heart had weighed four grams, her brain seven." He must have meant kilograms.

Edgar Rice Burroughs, who never set foot in Africa, made so many boo-boos about Africa's flora and fauna in his Tarzan series that I understand residents of the dark continent read the Tarzan books partly for laughs.

Science-fiction writers are, of course, free to indulge in wild fantasy about traveling faster than light, taking shortcuts through space warps, or going back in time in spite of the logical paradoxes that arise, such as how you could exist if you murdered your father when he was a child. The whole range of psi phenomena (ESP, PK, precognition, and so on) pervades much of science fiction, as do aliens in UFOs visiting earth, the transmission of human bodies by dissolving and reconstituting their molecules ("Beam me up, Scotty"), and a thousand other improbable things.

Of course we can forgive science-fiction writers for introducing Martian canals before it was clear they did not exist, or describing the "twilight zone" on Mercury. H. G. Wells correctly anticipated the dropping of "atom bombs" in World War II, in his most prophetic novel *The World Set Free*, but his airplanes were so primitive that the bombs were released by hand through a hole in the bottom of the plane. Although electrical computers appear in early science fiction, almost no author anticipated the computer revolution. There are stories taking place far in the future with scientists still making calculations on slide rules! Arthur Clarke, in his novel *Master of Space*, was the only writer to anticipate the televising on earth of the first moon landing.

Now and then, however, even the best science-fiction writers nod and make unintended blunders. Jules Verne's *From the Earth to the Moon* is a classic instance. Inertial forces produced by the cannon used to shoot a spaceship to the moon would have killed the astronauts. Verne assumes that on the trip earth's gravity would slowly diminish while the moon's gravity would slowly increase until the ship reached a balance point where the two gravity pulls would be equal. Only then would the astronauts float freely about inside their ship. Verne should have known that his ship would be in free-fall all the way to the moon, with weightlessness experienced inside at all times. Another blunder occurs when the travelers fling out a dead dog and the carcass floats alongside the ship instead of speeding off horizontally.

H. G. Wells trounced Verne for such blunders, but in his *First Men in the Moon* he makes a mistake equally absurd. We cannot fault him for his Cavorite, a substance that insulates the ship from gravity, because Einstein had not yet shown that any sort of gravity shield would be impossible.

Wells describes all the unattached objects in his spaceship as clustering toward the sphere's center by the attraction of their masses. Of course their gravitational pulls would be far too minute to have such an effect.

It is well known that inside a spherical shell, no matter how large, gravitational attraction due to the sphere itself is zero at all points. Ross Rocklynne, in his story "At the Center of Gravity," has men trapped by gravity at the center of a hollow sphere the size of the earth.

Just as many mistakes about space travel turn up in science-fiction films. One of the most common errors is showing a ship moving relative to the stars. Stars are much too far away and too far apart to display such motion.

Electronic conversations back and forth over vast distances, with no recognition of time delays, frequently take place in science-fiction stories and movies. Laser beams often glow as they move through space when in fact they would be invisible in the absence of molecules.

Another frequent blunder of early science fiction was assuming that meteor or meteoroid collisions with spaceships would be a constant hazard. Actually, encounters with meteors, even with asteroids while moving through the asteroid belt, would be rare because of the vast distances between them. Hollow earths play a role in fiction by Verne, Burroughs, Poe, and others. Inertial drives for spaceships violate Newton's third law of motion (conservation of momentum) yet they are featured in many science-fiction yarns. Even Arthur Clarke, who knows better, uses an inertial drive in *Rendezvous with Rama.* For several years John Campbell, the editor of *Analog Science Fiction,* who tumbled for a variety of pseudo-sciences (including Scientology), trumpeted a worthless space drive in his magazine.

Charles Eric Maine, in *High Vacuum,* speaks of astronauts in space suits on an airless planet as being unable to hear their own footsteps. He should have realized that footstep sounds would be transmitted by shoes, feet, legs, and air inside the suits. In *The Tomorrow People,* Judith Meril has a helicopter whirling about the moon, where the absence of atmosphere, as even Kant observed, would prevent birds from flying. In *Hothouse,* Brian Aldiss has giant spiders spinning webs that join the earth and the moon, forgetting that the earth's rotation relative to the moon would rip such webs apart.

It is conceivable that humanoids from other planets might find humans sexually attractive, but early science fiction often had bug-eyed monster males making passes at female earthlings, something akin to an earthling being sexually aroused by an octopus.

Lord Byron's Prisoner of Chillon says:

> My hair is grey, but not with years,
> Nor grew it white in a single night
> As men's have grown from sudden fears.

Hair cannot suddenly turn white, although it does so in many nineteenth-century novels.

How often have you encountered in fiction and films persons who disguised their voices on the telephone by stretching a handkerchief over the mouthpiece, or who listen to conversation in another room by putting an ear to the bottom of a drinking glass, its rim pressing against the wall? Cloth has no effect on the quality of a voice. When eavesdropping on sounds in another room, you do even better by flattening an ear to the wall. As a child, I recall being puzzled by one of Harold Lloyd's comedies in which someone chalked "KICK" on a wall. When Harold leaned against the wall the words, unreversed, were imprinted on the back of his jacket.

I myself once wrote a story called "The Island of Five Colors," based on my confusing the famous four-color-map theorem (unproved at the time) with a completely different theorem, easily verified by graph theory, that five regions cannot be drawn on the plane so each borders the other four. The two theorems are often thought to be the same, as I learned to my embarrassment after the story appeared in an anthology.

I find in my files the following charming poem by Mary Winter, clipped from the *New York Times* (December 4, 1957):

THE STRANGER TRUTH

Forming a bivalve, as before,
The shell close-cupped upon my ear
Gives back the waves' diminished roar.

A child's faith once implicitly
Accepted this fine fantasy.
As clear, oh clear, the surge and whirr
Of surf and wind came back to her.

And magic still returns, though sense
Instructs my muted turbulence;
Rhythm of blood's salt tide in me
Murmurs the cadence of the sea.
Wonder revives, though knowing well,
My ear, it is, informs the shell.

The poem's theme is that the roaring you hear in shells is not an echo of ocean waves but something even stranger—the echo of blood coursing through the veins of your head. The truth is less strange. It is merely the echo of sounds in the air around you as their waves resonate inside the shell's chamber.

ADDENDUM

My roundup of literary science blunders produced a large number of letters. Only the following eight were published (May/June 1995):

I very much enjoyed reading Martin Gardner's "Literary Science Blunders." I marveled at how astute Gardner was at detecting "howlers" in literature, errors that I might not always have detected on cursory reading.

One error I did catch appeared in Ernst Jünger's famous novel *Heliopolis*. Jünger's hero travels to the moon and describes in poetic terms how the landscape colors itself in successive shades of yellow, then orange, then red as the sun sets over the moon's horizon. In reality, of course, the moon's mountains, craters, and plains must remain colorless due to the absence of any atmosphere on the moon.

I was about seventeen when one of my uncles, a poet who wanted to educate me in the literary masterpieces of the world, recommended that I read *Heliopolis*. In fact, so impressed was he by this work that he proclaimed "the world is divided into two classes of people: those who have read *Heliopolis,* and those who have not." Well, read the book I did, then pointed out the error to my uncle, who angrily chided me for calling attention to such trivial matters that in no way detract from the beauty of this work of genius. We had quite an argument about this, which I think I lost.

Didier de Fontaine, Professor of Materials Science,
University of California, Berkeley, Calif.

Permit me to add to Martin Gardner's delightful list of "Literary Science Blunders."

Nikos Kazantzakis, in his controversial novel *The Last Temptation of Christ,* constructed a scene where the disciples of Jesus are fearfully discussing the potential ramifications of the recent beheading of John the Baptist by King Herod. Jacob speaks to his compatriots: "Wait a minute, lads," he said, "don't explode like gunpowder." Of course gunpowder would not be known in the Middle East for another 1,300 years . . . !

Robert R. Weilacher, Palestine, Texas

I was delighted with the premise of Martin Gardner's "Literary Science Blunders." However, I became disappointed, as he seemed to defeat his premise by showing ignorance of literary conventions and of the processes by which books and films reach the public.

While I'm sure it is true that artists and authors are as ignorant about science as the general public, it would have been nice if Gardner had chosen more convincing examples of blunders; this would have shown how such "howlers" detract from otherwise noteworthy works, therefore justifying the posit that artists should be better informed than the general public, as I think they should.

Gardner seems not to know a true conceptual error on the part of the author (the eyeglass scene in *Lord of the Flies*) from an editor's omission. Fitzgerald knew damn well what he was describing, and so does anyone who reads the passage, but his editor should have noticed that he used the wrong word to describe the visible part of the eye, and corrected the manuscript.

Authors may describe things counter to nature for a variety of reasons. In *The Mill on the Floss,* the log that overtakes Maggie Tulliver's boat is a metaphor for the way life has overtaken her; it is a literary device. Yes, physically, it should not have happened; that's the whole point. Cather, in turn, describes the appearance of the man's eye, not the scientific reality of his condition. Often a severe cataract is visible through the pupil, and does appear to grow over the eye. Krock is destined to have drink destroy him, so Dickens decides to use high drama to make a point. Krock is an alcohol-soaked raisin (a Victorian dessert, served flaming) lit by the hand of an exasperated God. . . .

I sincerely hope Gardner has more examples of literary blunders— ones that can stand scrutiny, because it is certainly true that art suffers when artists are ignorant. Would a gifted wordsmith with a small scope have been more prolific and insightful if better informed? Probably. Gardner is the first person that I know of to take a "hard science" tack with this subject, but social scientists have been picking at historical and cultural inaccuracies in literature for generations. I hope they all will continue.

Rebekah Hammer, Bloomington, Ind.

In "Literary Science Blunders," no effort appears to have been made to distinguish mistakes that might be worthy of such characterization from misstatements of scientific truths that more properly should be characterized as literary/poetic license. If an author perceives a need for an occurrence that requires some departure from "truth," it would seem to fall within the millennia-old tradition of deus ex machina. If, quite properly, an "exception" is recognized for science fiction, why are "mainstream" authors not to be afforded the same luxury? Indeed, is Gardner also guilty of a "blunder" when he states that on a trip to the moon the ship "would be in free-fall all the way to the moon." What ever happened to the need to achieve and maintain escape velocity from the earth? Is that an oversimplification, a blunder, or to be overlooked? (Or am I wrong in believing that that is a scientific fact that comes into play on any attempt to leave the earth's gravitational pull, before one can achieve free-fall to the moon?)

Kenneth B. Povodator, Fairfield, Conn.

Gardner's "Literary Science Blunders" serves only to ridicule artists, particularly literary artists, for not being scientists. He mocks writers for not knowing what we know. Such derision requires the assumptions that it is better to know what we know than what they know and that we are superior to them for knowing it. The polite term for Gardner's attitude is "arrogant." The precise term is "bigoted."

Ironically, Carl Sagan's "Wonder and Skepticism" in the same issue warns us that "the least effective way for skeptics to get the attention of . . . people is to belittle or condescend, or show arrogance."

Sagan again: "The chief deficiency I see in the skeptical movement is polarization: Us vs. Them—the sense that we have a monopoly on the truth; that those other people . . . are morons; that if you're sensible, you'll listen to us."

Russell King, Madison, Wisc.

Gardner's essay on writers ignorant of scientific fact was amusing; but perhaps he might also collect lists of science writers who make glaring literary blunders. An off-the-cuff example: a recent overview of dinosaur paleontology (*Kings of Creation,* Lessem, 1992) illustrates the geological time-scale by quoting Mark Twain—that human life on this planet is like the paint atop the Empire State Building. Twain died in 1910, long before the Empire State building existed. This is a minor error of fact comparable to F. Scott Fitzgerald's using "retinas" for pupils.

Unlike Gardner, I am skeptical as to whether scientists are any more knowledgeable about the arts and humanities than painters and poets and musicians are knowledgeable about science. In regard to major errors of understanding, for every blockheaded artist ignorant of the orbits of the moon there are also blockheaded scientists ignorant of their own lunatic fringe. An off-the-cuff example: the "great" biologist Haeckel, who in *Riddle of the Universe* and other popular works recorded dangerous distortions of history, philosophy, and religion, as well as bad science. Fortunately, different human beings have different talents that add checks and balances to the hubris of any expertise. Ultimately, we are all amateurs at living; and while Einstein did play classical music, the joke was that he couldn't keep "time."

James Alan Brown, Willoughby, Ohio

If Gardner wants to ferret out literary science blunders, he should get his literature correct first. In no place in Nikolai Gogol's *Dead Souls* does any character physically "spontaneously combust." Gogol does make references, in his last chapter, to the protagonist Chichikov symbolically being consumed by fire in an expensive suit of "smoke and flame." Later, Chichikov "was shaken to the core of his being and melted too. . . . The strongest men also yield in the furnace of misfortune. . . ." (*Dead Souls,* the Reavey translation, part 2, chapter 5). This is, again, only a symbolic reference. Chichikov, in the last mention Gogol makes of him, is still alive, hardly a pile of cinders. Writers certainly make science blunders, but the converse, scientists making "literature blunders," is equally amusing.

Walter W. Reisner, Durham, N.C.

Gardner writes: "Thomas Cook, in his crime novel *Flesh and Blood* (1989), has on page 44 an autopsy report saying: 'At the moment of her death, her heart had weighed 4 grams, her brain seven.' He must have meant kilograms."

The average human brain is about 3 pounds, or 1.3 kilograms. Unless the brain had swelled up and cracked open the skull, it's unlikely the brain was 7 kilograms.

Mark Gilkey, Palo Alto, Calif.

It is perhaps unfortunate that Gardner's notes on literary science blunders was in the same issue with C. Eugene Emery, Jr.'s "Media Watch" column, because this contained a blunder almost as delicious as the ones that Gardner commented on. Specifically, Emery noted that people were not masked against alien viruses or bacteria in the Roswell TV movie. Infectious agents, at least on our planet, tend to be highly species specific. Infection across species boundaries is unusual. Transmission by species with completely different evolutionary histories is almost inconceivable and certainly far less likely than that a forester would contract dutch elm disease. Emery may have also missed the most entertaining biologic error in the Roswell incident, the assumption that an intelligent, tool-using being would have to be patterned after mankind, obviously the highest point on the evolutionary tree. My parrot, Ralph, suggests that this is the height of speciesism and extraordinarily unlikely from an evolutionary standpoint.

Mark Hauswald, M.D., Associate Professor,
Dept. of Emergency Medicine, School of Medicine
University of New Mexico, Albuquerque, N.M.

Now for some comments on unpublished correspondence.

James M. Rowley reminded me that John Livingston Lowes, in his classic *The Road to Xanadu,* devotes many pages to Coleridge's horned moon. There is no question that Coleridge was fully aware that no star could be between the tips of the moon's crescent. He introduced this image to strengthen his ballad's fantasy. Lowes also argues that the seeming error about the rising full moon at sunset is not a mistake because the stanza implies a passage of time between sunset and moonrise. Actually, I covered this at some length in the notes to my *Annotated Ancient Mariner,* but had forgotten about it.

Bernard David defended George Eliot by arguing that a frail craft on a river can drift much more slowly than a mass of debris.

David J. Simmons sent me pages from Isaac Asimov's chapter in *Of Matters Great and Small* where he apologizes for thinking the North Star was fixed in the sky at the time of the Phoenicians when actually it was then almost 17 degrees away from where the north pole pointed. Subsequent precession of the earth's axis brought the star to its present fixed spot. Asimov quotes Shakespeare making the same mistake when his Julius Caesar says just before being stabbed:

> But I am constant as the northern star,
> Of whose true fix'd and resting quality
> There is no fellow in the firmament.
> The skies are painted with unnumber'd sparks;
> They are all fire and every one doth shine;
> But there's but one in all doth hold his place.

David Todd cited a passage in Virginia Woolf's *Orlando* which described children's balloons floating above a pavilion at Henry VIII's court. There were no rubber balloons then, let alone a way of inflating them with hydrogen. Todd also copied the following lines from Thomas Hood's poem "Forsaken":

> Last night unbound my raven locks,
> The morning saw them turn to gray.

Vincent Ambro quoted the following lines from Roald Dahl's novel *Danny, The Champion of the World.* "He turned his head, fixing me with his pale eyes. The eyes were large and ox-like, and they were so near to me that I could see my own face reflected upside down in the center of each." Seeing one's face reflected in another's eyes is possible, but it is right side up. Only on the invisible retina is it inverted.

D. F. Gibbs pointed out numerous scientific impossibilities in H. G. Wells's two stories "The New Accelerator" and "The Invisible Man," and in Wells's novel *The First Men in the Moon.* I found him right on all counts, but have little doubt that Wells was aware of these contradictions, sacrificing them for the sake of his plots.

William Harmon reminded me of Matthew Arnold's poem "Dover Beach," which speaks of Sophocles long ago hearing tides on the Aegean. The Aegean Sea does not have tides. Harmon also referred to Tennyson's "The Lotus Eaters" where it tells of mariners arriving at a spot where "full-faced above the valley stood the moon."

H. W. Lewis recalled an old science-fiction film titled *Rocketship XM* in which a spaceship suddenly ran out of fuel. This caused the ship to come to a crashing stop that threw the astronauts around the cabin. He also wrote about a Jules Verne novel that featured a large helicopter with an open deck on which passengers could sun themselves if the helicopter was flying downwind. They had to retire to the cabin when flying upwind. "That was of course derived from Verne's seagoing experience. . . . To this day some flight instructors tell their students it is important to maintain airspeed when flying downwind. It is for psychological reasons if you can see the ground, but the airplane doesn't know the difference."

In another letter from David Todd I learned for the first time that the poet Muriel Rukeyser had written in her twenties a biography of the scientist Wilfred Gibbs. On page 156 she quotes the line "Beer not recommended" from one of Gibbs's notes on a speech he had heard. Rukeyser took this to mean that drinking beer was not recommended. Actually, Gibbs was referring to a physicist named Beer.

Ralph D. Copeland found a line in William Diehl's mystery novel *Primal Fear* where he refers to steers used for breeding cattle. Steers are castrated males.

Physicist Allen Janis wrote to tell me about physics blunders in three science-fiction yarns: Jerome Bixby's "The Holes Around Mars" (reprinted in Asimov's collection *Where Do We Go From Here?*), Ross Rocklynne's "Center of Gravity," and Larry Niven's "Neutron Star." Gwydion M. Williams sent seventeen errors he had spotted in science-fiction novels, stories, and films.

Dana Richards, L. Sprague de Camp, and John Geohegan wrote about the many science blunders in Conan Doyle's Sherlock Holmes tales. In "The Speckled Band," wrote de Camp, "Doyle has a captive snake fed on milk and trained by the sound of a whistle though snakes don't drink milk and have no ears."

Geohegan and Richards discussed the curious mistake in "The Adventure of the Priory School." Holmes deduces from mud tracks which way a bicycle was going by the fact that the deeper impression made by the rear wheel (owing to greater weight on it) crossed over the shallower track of the front wheel. If you think carefully, you will realize that this would be the case regardless of the direction traveled by the bicycle. When the error was pointed out to Doyle, after the story appeared in *The Strand,* he couldn't believe it until he tried it out by rolling a friend's bicycle through mud.

Asimov, in a chapter on "Sherlock Holmes as Chemist" (in his anthology *The Roving Mind*), cites numerous chemical howlers in the Holmes canon. To list only a few: Holmes refers to an "amalgam" when he means an "alloy." He calls a carbuncle blue, whereas all carbuncles are red. He thinks the carbuncle is crystallized charcoal, confusing it with a diamond. Holmes assures Watson that he can "distinguish at a glance the ash of any known brand either of cigar or of tobacco." Asimov comments: "If he can, he is the only human being of Earth or in history who can or could."

Mario Milosevec sent me pages from the first edition of Larry Niven's science-fiction novel *Ringworld*. In the first chapter his hero, Louis Wu, follows the sun by transporting himself instantly from city to city in an *easterly* direction. The error was corrected, Milosevec thinks, in a later edition.

Milosevec also copied a letter from Scott Jarrett to *Isaac Asimov's Science Fiction Magazine* (April 1987) listing seven instances earlier than the Clarke novel I mentioned, in which television broadcasts were made or planned to be made from the moon. His earliest instance was J. Schlossel's 1928 short story, "To the Moon by Proxy," in which a robot goes to the moon while monitored on earth by television. Asimov wonders if any readers can go further back than 1928.

Incredibly, such an example was reported by Dennis Lien in a letter to Asimov's magazine in November 1988. Homer Eon Flint, in "The Planeteer" (*All-Story Weekly,* March 9, 1918), has people on earth watch the activities of a crew on the moon by a television device that also allows them to talk to the astronauts!

After my column appeared I came across this blunder in Kahlil Gibran's *The Prophet.* Gibran writes: "The owl whose night-bound eyes are blind unto the day." That owls cannot see in daylight is a common myth. Like cats, owls see well at night, but also see equally well by day.

Doyle's bicycle mistake and some others cited above were not, of course, science blunders. I also collect nonscientific blunders in poetry, plays, and fiction. Others include the time Robinson Crusoe stripped himself of clothing, then swam to the wreckage of a ship where he filled his pockets with biscuits. While Don Quixote was being serialized, Cervantes has Sancho Panza sell his donkey. Later in the story he forgot about it and has Sancho riding the donkey again. Shakespeare's historical and geographical errors are abundant. He speaks of cannon during the reign of King John, of striking clocks in the days of Julius Caesar. Hector quotes Aristotle, Coriolanus refers to Cato, Cleopatra's palace has a billiard table, and Bohemia has a seacoast.

It is well known that Keats, in his sonnet "On First Looking into Chapman's Homer," has "stout Cortez" staring at the Pacific when he should have been Balboa. Kipling made a geographical error in the first line of "Mandalay." Moulmein is on the west coast of Burma. Instead of looking eastward to the sea, it looks westward toward the Bay of Bengal. The dawn may come up like thunder out of China, but not across from any water.

Errors such as those have suggested to critics that the great creative writers are far more careless about such things than lesser writers. Their genius just doesn't bother with such trivia. Mistakes of this sort, however, are a topic for another essay.

CHAPTER THIRTEEN

SCIENCE VS. BEAUTY?

M y previous chapter was about the gulf that too often divides the culture of science from the culture of the liberal arts. Nowhere is this
chasm more noticeable than in the lines of certain poets who believe that
a knowledge of science somehow destroys one's awareness of the wonders and beauty of nature.

Over the decades I've collected some examples:

> The moon shines down with borrowed light,
> So savants say—I do not doubt it.
> Suffice its silver trance my sight,
> That's all I want to know about it.
> A fig for science. . . .
>
> —Robert Service

> The goose that laid the golden egg
> Died looking up its crotch
> To find out how its sphincter worked.
> Would you lay well? Don't watch.
>
> —X. J. Kennedy, "Ars Poetica"

> I'd rather learn from one bird how to sing
> Than teach ten thousand stars how not to dance.
>
> —e e cummings

> While you and i have lips and voice which
> are for kissing and to sing with
> who cares if some one-eyed son of a bitch
> invents an instrument to measure Spring with?
>
> —e e cummings

"Notes of a Fringe Watcher," *Skeptical Inquirer* (March/April 1995).

... Do not all charms fly
At the mere touch of cold philosophy?
There was an awful rainbow once in heaven:
We know her woof, her texture; she is given
In the dull catalogue of common things.
Philosophy will clip an Angel's wings,
Conquer all mysteries by rule and line,
Empty the haunted air and gnomed mine—
Unweave a rainbow. . . .

—John Keats, "Lamia"

"Arcturus" is his other name—
I'd rather call him "Star."
It's very mean of Science
To go and interfere!

I pull a flower from the woods—
A monster with a glass
Computes the stamens in a breath
And has her in a "class"!

—Emily Dickinson

A Color stands abroad
On Solitary Fields
That Science cannot overtake
But Human Nature feels.

It waits upon the Lawn,
It shows the furthest Tree
Upon the furthest Slope you know
It almost speaks to you.

Then as Horizons step
Or Noons report away
Without the Formula of sound
It passes and we stay—

A quality of loss
Affecting our Content
As Trade had suddenly encroached
Upon a Sacrament.

—Emily Dickinson

Sweet is the lore which Nature brings;
Our meddling intellect
Mis-shapes the beauteous forms of things:—
We murder to dissect.

Enough of Science and of Art;
Close up those barren leaves;
Come forth, and bring with you a heart
That watches and receives.
                    —Wordsworth, "The Tables Turned"

Today we breathe a commonplace,
Polemic, scientific air;
We strip illusion of her veil;
We vivisect the nightingale
To probe the secret of his note
The Muse in alien ways remote
Goes wandering.
                    —Thomas Bailey Aldrich

Science! true daughter of Old Time thou art!
    Who alterest all things with thy peering eyes.
Why preyest thou thus upon the poet's heart,
    Vulture, whose wings are dull realities?
                    —Edgar Allan Poe

There's machinery in the butterfly,
There's a mainspring to the bee.
There's hydraulics to a daisy
And contraptions to a tree.

If we could see the birdie
That makes the chirping sound
With psycho-analytic eyes,
With X-ray, scientific eyes,
We could see the wheels go round.

And I hope all men
Who think like this
Will soon lie underground.
                    —Vachel Lindsay

Similar sentiments have been expressed in prose. Here are a few:
Coleridge: "The real antithesis of poetry is not prose but science." Billy
Rose: "I wish the engineers would keep their slide rules out of the bits of

fairyland left in this bollixed up world." Nietzsche: "They [scientists] have cold, withered eyes before which all birds are unplumed."

There is something to be said for such sentiment, though not much. It is possible for scientists to become so wrapped up in their work that they lose all sense of nature's beauty and mystery. "When you understand all about the sun and all about the atmosphere and all about the rotation of the earth," wrote Alfred North Whitehead, a philosopher who stood astride the two cultures, "you may still miss the radiance of the sunset."

G. K. Chesterton made the same point in his amusing story "The Unthinkable Theory of Professor Green," in *Tales of the Long Bow*. Green is an astronomer who forgot about the world around him until one day when he fell in love with a farmer's daughter. He announces a lecture on his discovery of a new planet. The auditorium is packed with colleagues while he describes one of the planet's strange creatures. Slowly it dawns on Green's listeners that he is describing a cow.

I suppose that scientists like Professor Green, before he discovered the earth, exist, but if so, I have yet to encounter one. On the contrary, almost all scientists believe that as their knowledge increases, their sense of wonder also grows. The scientist sees a flower, said physicist John Tyndall, "with a wonder superadded."

Professor Green's unthinkable theory reminds me of stanza xcii from the first canto of Byron's *Don Juan*:

> He thought about himself, and the whole earth,
>   Of man the wonderful, and of the stars,
> And how the deuce they ever could have birth;
>   And then he thought of earthquakes, and of wars,
> How many miles the moon might have in girth,
>   Of air-balloons, and of the many bars
> To perfect knowledge of the boundless skies;—
> And then he thought of Donna Julia's eyes.

The Laputans, in Gulliver's Travels, describe a woman's beauty by "rhombs, circles, parallelograms, ellipses, and other geometrical terms." Arthur S. Eddington, writing on "Science and Mysticism" in *The Nature of the Physical World,* quotes from a page on winds and waves in a textbook on hydrodynamics. He then compares this with the aesthetic experience of watching actual sea waves "dancing in the sunshine."

That knowledge of science adds to one's appreciation of the mystery and splendor of the cosmos has nowhere been more vigorously expressed than by the late physicist Richard Feynman in Christopher Syke's *No Ordinary Genius* (W. W. Norton, 1994). He described an artist friend who would hold up a flower and say: "I, as an artist, can see how beautiful a flower is. But you, as a scientist, take it all apart and it becomes dull."

"I think he's kind of nutty," says Feynman, and he adds:

First of all, the beauty he sees is available to other people—and to me too. Although I might not be quite as refined aesthetically as he is, I can appreciate the beauty of a flower.

At the same time, I see much more about the flower than he sees. I could imagine the cells in there, the complicated actions inside, which also have a beauty. I mean, it's not just beauty at this dimension of one centimeter: there is also beauty at a smaller dimension—the inner structure. The fact that the colors in the flower are evolved in order to attract insects to pollinate it is interesting—it means that the insects can see the color. It adds a question: does this aesthetic sense also exist in the lower forms? Why is it aesthetic? All kinds of interesting questions which a science knowledge only adds to the excitement and mystery and the awe of a flower. It only adds. I don't understand how it subtracts.

Does it make any less of a beautiful smell of violets to know that it's molecules? To find out, for example, that the smell of violets is very similar to the chemical that's used by a certain butterfly (I don't know whether it's true, like my father's stories!), a butterfly that lets out this chemical to attract all its mates? It turns out that this chemical is exactly the smell of violets with a small change of a few molecules. The different kinds of smells and the different kinds of chemicals, the great variety of chemicals and colors and dyes and so on in the plants and everywhere else, are all very closely related, with very small changes, and the efficiency of life is not always to make a new thing, but to modify only slightly something that's already there, and make its function entirely different, so that the smell of violets is related to the smell of earth. . . . These are all additional facts, additional discoveries. It doesn't take away that it can't answer questions of what, ultimately, does the smell of violets really feel like when you smell it. That's only if you expected science to give the answers to every possible question. But the idea that science takes away is something I don't understand.

It's true that technology can have an effect on art that might be a kind of subtraction. For example, in the early days painting was to make pictures when pictures were unavailable, that was one reason: it was very useful to give people pictures to look at, to help them think about God, or the Annunciation, or whatever. When photography came as a result of technology, which itself was the result of scientific knowledge, then that made pictures very much more available. The care and effort needed to make something by hand which looked exactly like nature and which was once such a delight to see now became mundane in a way (although of course there's a new art—the art of taking good pictures). So yes, technology can have an effect on art, but the idea that it takes away mystery or awe or wonder in nature is wrong. It's quite the opposite. It's much more wonderful to know what something's really like than to sit there and just simply, in ignorance, say, "Oooh, isn't it wonderful!"

A famous poem by Walt Whitman tells how he listened to a "learn'd astronomer" lecture about the heavens until he (Walt) became "unaccountably tired and sick." He walks out of the lecture room into the "mystical moist night air" so he can look up "in perfect silence at the stars."

Here is how Feynman, in his Lectures on Physics, reacted to the notion that astronomical knowledge dulls one's sense of awe toward the cosmos:

> "The stars are made of the same atoms as the earth." I usually pick one small topic like this to give a lecture on. Poets say science takes away from the beauty of the stars—mere gobs of gas atoms. Nothing is "mere." I too can see the stars on a desert night, and feel them. But do I see less or more? The vastness of the heavens stretches my imagination—stuck on this carousel my little eye can catch one-million-year-old light. A vast pattern—of which I am a part—perhaps my stuff was belched from some forgotten star, as one is belching there. Or see them with the greater eye of Palomar, rushing all apart from some common starting point when they were perhaps all together. What is the pattern, or the meaning, or the *why?* It does not do harm to the mystery to know a little about it. For far more marvelous is the truth than any artists of the past imagined! Why do the poets of the present not speak of it? What men are poets who can speak of Jupiter if he were like a man, but if he is an immense spinning sphere of methane and ammonia must be silent?

Isaac Asimov, writing on "Science and Beauty" in *The Roving Mind,* quotes Whitman's poem. "The trouble is that Whitman is talking through his hat," says Asimov. Of course the night sky is beautiful, but is there not a deeper, added beauty provided by astronomy? Asimov continues with lyrical paragraphs about the "weird and unearthly beauty" of our sister planets, as recently disclosed by space probes, about the awesome wonders of the stars, of the billions of galaxies each containing billions of suns, of clusters of galaxies, and superclusters fleeing from each other as the universe expands from its incredible origin in the explosion of a tiny point some 15 billion years ago.

> And all of this vision—far beyond the scale of human imaginings—was made possible by the works of hundreds of learn'd astronomers. All of it; *all* of it was discovered after the death of Whitman in 1892, and most

of it in the past twenty-five years, so that the poor poet never knew what a stultified and limited beauty he observed when he look'd up in perfect silence at the stars.

Nor can we know or imagine now the limitless beauty yet to be revealed in the future—by science.

ADDENDUM

The following three letters appeared in the *Skeptical Inquirer* (July/ August 1995):

As always, Martin Gardner makes an excellent point in his piece "Science and Beauty." Knowledge of how the universe works certainly can and should deeply increase one's sense of its loveliness and, yes, mysteriousness.

However, perhaps Gardner overlooks an important source of much emotional reaction against the scientific worldview. Increasingly, scientific findings and theories extend the domain of physical causality into humankind itself. The more thoroughly our thoughts, feelings, and actions are shown to be matters of chemistry and structure, the less room is left for traditional free will, not to mention an immortal soul or a God.

It doesn't really do much good to to say that these questions are not subject to empirical test and therefore lie beyond the purview of science. At best, this simply sweeps them under the rug. At worst, it is dishonest. The fact is, most of them are integrally involved with material reality. For example, St. Paul pointed out quite some time ago that Christianity stands or falls by whether or not the resurrection of Christ is a historical fact, i.e., a testable proposition. Moral and ethical standards depend largely on what the nature of the human organism is. And so on. Whether or not they articulate this to themselves, most people are quite able to perceive it, and to many it is a bitter pill to swallow.

Poul Anderson, Orinda, Calif.

In asserting a conflict between "the culture of science" and "the culture of liberal arts," all Martin Gardner accomplishes is to reinforce the fortress mentality I perceive in the pages of *SI*.

The liberal arts are not competitors with science, but rather serve us all as observers of and commentators on the human zoo. Both areas are complementary in creating and maintaining the well-functioning human being, and neither stands independent of the society in which it is found.

Jack Miller, Port Clements, B.C., Canada

Disparaging Emily Dickinson, Wordsworth, Poe, et al. in the name of scientific skepticism? I can't think of a more foolproof way to alienate the romantics among us.

Surely we can allow the poet enchanted by nature to shun the skeptical lens for a few moments of reverie. I'm a nature poet myself, and I shudder to think that some of my lyrical lines could be skewered by the hardened skeptic as antiscientific.

Please, have some room in your scientific universe for the value of nonscientific experiences—unless you really want the world so entirely intellectually oriented that in your most intimate personal moments you hear the "voice of reason" declaring "I'm so chemically receptive to your pheromones" instead of your heart whispering "I love you"!

Gloria J. Leitner, Boulder, Colo.

David Todd sent me Eden Phillpotts's lyric "Miniature," from *The Oxford Book of Short Poems*:

> The grey beards wag, the bald heads nod,
> And gather thick as bees,
> To talk electrons, gases, God,
> Old nebulae, new fleas.
> Each specialist, each dry-as-dust
> And professorial oaf,
> Holds up his little crumb of crust
> And cries, 'Behold the loaf!'

I came across Christopher Morley's "Autumn Colors" in his collection *Hide and Seek*:

> How tedious it seems, and strange,
> That poets should be raving still
> Of autumn tints: it's just the change
> From chlorophyll to xanthophyll.

I was somewhat appalled by angry letters from readers who seemed to think I had a chip on my shoulder against the arts. The point I wanted to make was the same as in the previous chapter. Most artists, poets, musicians, actors, and professors of liberal arts (especially in England) know less about science than scientists know about the arts.

It would not be easy to locate a physicist who didn't know the difference between a sonnet and an ode. How many Hollywood actors know the difference between a proton and a neutron? The percentage of actors who believe in astrology is huge compared to the percent of scientists.

Indeed, among scientists the percentage is very close to zero. Remember, two astrology buffs, actors Ronald and Nancy Reagan, actually occupied the White House!

Obviously science and the arts complement each other, and no persons today should call themselves educated who are ignorant of either the yin or the yang. I fear that America is a long way from the time when education will give the two sides of our culture equal time.

CHAPTER FOURTEEN

DOUG HENNING
AND THE GIGGLING GURU

Because magic is my main hobby I feel a keener regret than most people over the way in which the Hindu cult of Transcendental Meditation (TM) has taken over the life of one of the best of modern magicians. In the 1970s, Doug James Henning's Magic Show ran on Broadway for more than four years. Henning followed with marvelous NBC-television spectaculars, Las Vegas and Lake Tahoe bookings, and numerous talk-show appearances.

Then something happened to Doug on his way to a magic shop. He discovered TM and became a pal of its founder, His Holiness Maharishi Mahesh Yogi. "The moment I saw him," Doug has often said, "I knew that he knew the truth of life." In a few years Henning became TM's most famous convert since Mia Farrow and the Beatles.

First, some words about TM. Based on ancient Vedic teachings that Maharishi learned from a Himalayan holy man, it stresses a form of meditation linked to the repetition of a Sanskrit word called a *mantra*. The technique is said to relieve stress, slow aging, and promote what TMers call "pure bliss." Moreover, TM instructors promise to teach you, after you fork over thousands of dollars for advanced courses, a variety of awesome supernormal powers known as *sidhis*. They include the ability to become invisible, to see hidden things, to walk through walls, and to fly through the air like Peter Pan and Wendy. Doug's conjuring was fake magic. TM teaches *real* magic.

Yogic flying has been the most publicized of the sidhis. Photographs distributed by TM officials show devotees in a lotus position and seemingly floating in midair. The photos are misleading. No TMer has yet demonstrated levitation to an outsider. The best they can show is the ability to flex one's legs while in a lotus position on a springy mattress and hop upward a short distance. The phony photos were snapped when the supposed floater was at the top of a bounce. One cynic said he never believed the woman in a picture was actually levitating, that instead she was being held up by an invisible TMer!

"Notes of a Fringe Watcher," *Skeptical Inquirer* (May/June 1995).

The flying sidhi has four stages. First, a twitching of limbs. Second, the hop. Third, hovering. Fourth, actual flying. Only the first and second stages have been shown to skeptics, although devout TMers firmly believe that there are Yogic flyers in India and that Maharishi can take off whenever he likes even though no one has ever seen or videotaped him in flight.

"When you reach your full potential," Henning told a reporter, "and you think 'I want to levitate,' you can levitate." And in a lecture: "You can disappear at a high state of consciousness because your body just stops reflecting light."

Amazingly, TMers are greatly entranced by lotus hopping. Last October a demonstration was held at the University of Toronto. Three Vedic "flyers" giggled while they bounced on their bums for five minutes, looking (said one observer) like legless frogs. I was told by Charles Reynolds, who for many years designed Doug's stage illusions, that during one of Henning's TV rehearsals he periodically halted all activity so those present could meditate and send him powerful vibes while he tried vainly to float. He actually believed he might be able to demonstrate levitation on his forthcoming show!

Several disenchanted TMers have sued the organization for failing to teach them powers that were promised. In 1987, for instance, Robert Kropinski, a former TM instructor, asked for $9 million because he was never able to fly. He also charged that TM had caused him "headaches, anxiety, impulses toward violence, hallucinations, confusion, loss of memory, screaming fits, lack of focus, paranoia, and social withdrawal." A Philadelphia jury awarded him $138,000.

Giggling seems endemic among TMers—something similar to the "holy laughter" currently popular in Pentecostal churches. The tiny, white-bearded, beflowered Maharishi giggled constantly during two appearances on the Merv Griffin show. Physicists tend to break into unholy laughter when they hear about Vedic flying.

Since he started TM, the giggling guru has raked in an estimated $3 billion from his millions of gullible followers. He now controls a vast empire that includes a conglomeration of Heaven on Earth Hotels around the world, a consulting corporation, numerous trading companies, medical clinics, and a swarm of other firms here and there.

Maharishi Ayur-Veda Products International (MAPI) sells a raft of herbs, teas, oils, and natural food substances said to cure diseases and reverse growing old. Admirers of the best-selling books on "quantum healing" by Boston's Deepak Chopra may be surprised to know that he is a TM booster with close ties to MAPI, president of a Maharishi Vedic University in Cambridge, Massachusetts, and owner of an Ayur-Vedic clinic in Boston. In 1989 His Holiness awarded Chopra the title of "Lord of Immortality of Heaven and Earth."

Maharishi Research universities are all over the globe. There is one in Lake Lucerne, Switzerland, others in Fairfield, Iowa (the movement's U.S. headquarters), in Buckinghamshire, England, in Asbury Park, New Jersey, and in Vlodrop, Netherlands. Vlodrop is the movement's world headquarters, where Maharishi now lives. The colleges seem to spring up and die like mushrooms.

The word "research" in the names of these universities refers to investigations of what is called Vedic science. It is said to combine the subjective approach of the East with the objective approach of Western science and to usher in what the Maharishi calls the "full sunshine of the dawning of the age of Enlightenment." According to His Holiness, the universe is permeated by a "field of consciousness" underlying the laws of quantum mechanics. The Maharishi, who once studied physics, is keen on the latest results in particle theory.

Expensive double-spread ads in the *New York Times,* the *Washington Post,* the *Toronto Globe and Mail, Time, Newsweek,* and who knows where else, periodically promote the Maharishi's unified field theory. Physicist John S. Hagelin is the movement's top quantum-mechanics maven. He has predicted that Maharishi's influence on history "will be far greater than that of Einstein or Gandhi." Hagelin and other scientists at TM universities have written hundreds of technical papers, most of them published by TM university presses, although a few have sneaked into mainstream science and medical journals unaware of the authors' TM affiliation.

In his paper "Is Consciousness the Unified Field?" Hagelin (who has a Harvard doctorate in physics) conjectures that the sidhis operate by upsetting "the balance of statistical averaging" in quantum-mechanical laws.

> Indeed, the phenomenon of levitation, with its implied control over the local curvature of space-time geometry, would appear to require the ability to function coherently at the scale of quantum gravity, which is the assumed scale of super-unification and the proposed domain of pure consciousness. In this way some of the sidhis, if demonstrated under laboratory conditions, would provide striking evidence for the proposed identity between pure consciousness and the unified field.

TMers have no doubts about the "Maharishi effect." This refers to incredible changes produced by mass meditations. The movement claims that their efforts helped bring down the Berlin wall, resolve the Gulf War, cause stock-market rises, collapse the Soviet Union, decrease traffic accidents, and cut the crime rate in Washington, D.C., and other cities. Such wonders are supported, of course, by highly dubious statistics.

In 1992, longing for political influence, His Holiness founded the Natural Law Party (NLP) in countries that include England and Canada. Henning is senior vice president of the Canadian party. In 1992 he was the NLP candidate in England's general election, representing a residential section of Lancashire. He finished last among four candidates. In a 1994 Canadian election he was the party's candidate from Rosedale, where he and Debbie, his second wife, live. Of 55,928 votes cast, he received 839. Physicist Hagelin was a candidate of the NLP for U.S. president in 1992. The party claimed it had forty candidates running for Congress. The Canadian NLP platform maintains that once the party takes over the government, Canada's crime, unemployment, and deficit will disappear like the elephant that Doug vanished so many times on stage.

I found the elephant simile in Don Gillmor's "Like Magic," a lively article in *Toronto Life* (April 1994), to which this column is heavily indebted. Gillmor quotes Henning as saying, in reference to his party's promises: "We never see the stars going into debt and having to borrow light from the sun. We don't see robins having criminal tendencies and stealing from each other."

Although pushing fifty, Henning still looks like a youth, small, slim, with long dark hair, droopy mustache, a mild, soft-spoken manner, and bucktooth grin. Born in Winnipeg, and a graduate of McMaster University, he began his magic career working parties and nightclubs around Canada. Such skilled magicians as Dai Vernon and Tony Slydini gave him lessons. Henning met the Maharishi in 1975, and for the next ten years he studied TM while still performing on stage. By 1986, convinced that his life mission was to promote TM, he gave up show business and sold his illusions to David Copperfield and other top stage performers.

For the past decade Henning's obsession has been to build a mammoth theme park he calls Veda Land. Plans to locate the park in India, then in Orlando, Florida, adjacent to Disney World, went down the tube. In 1987, with funds from Maharishi, Doug now intends to build Veda Land in Niagara Falls, Ontario. Why there? Because, Henning told Gillmor, the falls are "the greatest natural wonder on Earth. . . . Our purpose is to create wonder for nature."

Unusual rides and exhibits will dramatize Veda Land's central theme—the mystery and beauty of nature. There will be a convention center, a university, and a Tower of Peace, where world leaders can meet to settle disputes. A Magic Flying Carpet will carry 120 passengers onto a rose petal, plunge into its molecular and atomic structure, then finally come to rest in the flower's "pure consciousness." A Corridor of Time will display the history of the universe from the Big Bang to the far distant day when Shiva will dance the universe into oblivion. A preventive-medicine center will sell herbal remedies. Hotels will serve vegetarian and health meals, and there will be a Heaven on Earth housing project.

"Heaven on Earth" is Maharishi's favorite phrase for the world utopia that TM will eventually bring about. As he stirringly put it in the *Maharishi International University News* (Winter 1988), there will be "all good everywhere and nongood nowhere."

In keeping with the Hindu belief that all is *maya,* or illusion, Veda Land will abound with magical special effects designed by Roy Field, who once worked on the *Superman* movies. A large building will appear to float fifteen feet above an artificial pond. Doug won't reveal how this great illusion will be accomplished, although presumably not by real magic. On the opening day a helicopter is expected to move a gigantic hoop over the levitated building the way Doug used to pass a hoop over floating ladies.

Asked if Veda Land will resemble Jim Bakker's fallen Christian theme park, Heritage USA, Doug replied: "It's more like, Wow! Isn't enlightenment great!"

TM recruits are given a mantra so secret that they are forbidden to disclose it to anyone, not even a spouse. The mantra is to be repeated silently while they meditate for twenty minutes each morning and late afternoon or evening. In the 1970s they were assured that their mantra was carefully selected from thousands to fit their personality. A skeptical investigator was puzzled when he joined the movement in three cities under three different names and was always given the same mantra. It turned out that there were just sixteen mantras. The one given was determined solely by a person's age. Today's mantras may be different, but in 1977 if you were twenty-six to twenty-nine your mantra was *shivim.* If over sixty it was *shama,* and so on.

Magicians who perform what the trade calls mental acts were quick to take advantage of the secret list of Sanskrit words before their linkage with ages became widely known. They would ask TMers in the audience to state their birthdate, then pretend to divine their secret mantra by ESP!

In 1994 the cost of a basic TM course jumped from $400 to $1,000. Officials insist that for decades the price has been too low to meet expenses. Besides, they argue, the new price will winnow out dabblers.

Does mantra meditation relieve stress more effectively than praying or just sitting quietly with closed eyes? In 1976, a study of this was made at the University of Michigan and reported in *Science News* (June 19). A group of trained TMers were compared with a control group of subjects unfamiliar with TM. The TM group meditated for a half-hour while the

CHAPTER FIFTEEN

KLINGON AND OTHER ARTIFICIAL LANGUAGES

Do you speak Esperanto?
Like a native!

According to Genesis there originally was only one human language, the tongue spoken by Adam and Eve. Why did Adam name the elephant an *elephant*? Because, goes an old joke, it *looked* like an elephant. Then a terrible tragedy occurred. The Hebrews tried to scale the heavens by building the Tower of Babel. God was so offended by this hubris that he said:

> Behold, the people is one, and they have all one language . . . and now nothing shall be restrained from them. . . . Go to, let us go down, and there confound their language, that they may not understand one another's speech. So the Lord scattered them abroad from thence upon the face of all the earth. (Gen. 11:6–8)

In *Paradise Lost* (Book 12) Milton described it this way:

> To sow a jangling noise of words unknown:
> Forthwith a hideous gabble rises loud
> Among the Builders; each to other calls
> Not understood, till hoarse, and all in rage,
> As mockt they storm; great laughter was in Heav'n
> And looking down, to see the hubbub strange
> And hear the din.

Why God and the angels would find this curse amusing is hard to fathom. At any rate, who can doubt that the multiplicity of world languages is an enormous barrier to world peace. Clearly world unity would be greatly augmented if somehow the babble of tongues could be replaced by a single language.

"Notes of a Fringe Watcher," *Skeptical Inquirer* (July/August 1995).

In ancient times Greek, Latin, and Arabic served as universal languages for large clusters of nations. French was once Europe's international diplomatic language, and for centuries Latin was the favored language of scientists and scholars. Around Mediterranean ports *lingua franca,* Italian mixed with other tongues, became a common form of communication. Swahili, a Bantu speech mixed with Arabic, has long been the lingua franca of East Africa. Today, for better or worse, the new international language is English. In a few years there will be more non-native speakers of English than native ones! Only France is trying desperately to keep its fingers in the dike.

In the seventeenth century, among such philosophers as Descartes and Leibniz, and the Scotsman George Delgarno, the notion arose that perhaps a completely artificial language, based on logic, with simplified grammar and spelling, might serve to unify nations. This grandiose dream quickly gripped the minds of hundreds of linguistic cranks, who during the next three centuries proposed more than three hundred artificial or semi-artificial tongues.

The first major effort was the 600-page *Essay Towards a Real Character and Philosophic Language* (London, 1688), by John Wilkins, Bishop of Chester. His book was greatly admired by Leibniz. All of Wilkins's words are self-defining in the sense that they convey their triple classification as to genus, species, and subspecies. For example, his word for salmon is *zana*—*za* for fish, *n* for scaly, and *a* for red. The language was spoken and also written with symbols resembling modern shorthand. The Bishop wrote other eccentric works, including one arguing that the moon was inhabited by intelligent creatures. His philosophic language was caricatured by the French writer Gabriel de Foigny as an Australian tongue in his novel *The Adventures of Jacques Saleur* (1676).

The *Encyclopaedia Britannica* (14th edition) lists the following other totally synthetic languages: Solresol (1817), Lingualumina (1875), Blaia Zimondal (1884), Cabe aban (1887), and Zahlensprache (1901). Ro, invented in 1904 by Edward P. Foster, an American clergyman, had a monthly periodical called *Roia.* Solresol, created by musician Jean Francois Sudre, combined the syllables of the music scale (*do, re, mi, . . .*) to produce some twelve thousand words. The plan was to send messages by playing a tune.

The *Britannica* does not mention Spokil, perpetrated in France by A. Nicolas in 1887, or Alwato, the creation of Stephen Pearl Andrews, a nineteenth-century American attorney and abolitionist. Alwato was part of Andrews's 761-page crank work *The Basic Outline of Universology* (1872), and he elaborated on it in other books. All his nouns ended in *o.* A human is *ho,* the body is *hobo,* the head is *hobado,* and society is *homabo.* A vegetable is *zho,* an animal is *zo,* a dead animal is *zobo,* and a live one is *zovo.*

Because no completely synthetic language has yet obtained much of a following, one might suppose that efforts of this sort have ceased. Not so! The TV series "Star Trek" has spawned a guttural extraterrestrial language spoken by the warriors of Klingon. It was invented in 1984 for the film *Star Trek III: The Search for Spock,* by Marc Okrand. (He has a doctorate in linguistics.) Poetry has been written and weddings performed in Klingon. "Star Trek" fans are rapidly mastering the language, much to Okrand's amazement, because he does not speak it. He designed the language as a joke—its word for "love" is "bang"—but now his peculiar language has developed a life of its own. There are newsletters in Klingon and an audiotape on conversational Klingon spoken by Michael Dorn, who plays Klingon Lieutenant Worf in the current "Star Trek" television series.

The Klingon Language Institute, headed by Lawrence Schoen, a psychologist at Chestnut Hill College, Philadelphia, is said to be working on a translation into Klingon of Shakespeare and the Bible.* The Bible will not be easy, because Klingons have no words for such concepts as God, holy, atonement, forgiveness, compassion, or mercy. Is all this a put-on? The answer (in Klingon) is *HISlaH* (yes).

On a more useful level than totally contrived languages are the semi-artificial ones based on a blend of natural tongues. Of these, by far the most successful has been Esperanto, the brainchild of Lazarus Ludwig Zamenhof, a Warsaw eye doctor. His first book about it, *Lingvo Internacia* (1887), bore the pseudonym of Dr. Esperanto. The word means "one who hopes." It expressed Zamenhof's quixotic desire that Esperanto would become the world's second language.

Based on Europe's major tongues, Esperanto's sixteen simple grammatical rules have no exceptions. Spelling, using twenty-eight letters, is uniform and phonetic. As in Alwato, all nouns end in *o.* Adjectives end in *a,* verbs in *s,* and adverbs in *e.* A *j* at the end of a word indicates a plural. For example, *grandaj hundoj* means "big dogs."

Over thirty thousand books, including Shakespeare, Dante, the Bible, and the Koran have been translated into Esperanto. A recent translation of Lewis Carroll's *Alice* books calls Humpty Dumpty *Hometo Omleto,* meaning Little-Man Egg. Some hundred periodicals around the world have been written in Esperanto. The Vatican broadcasts in Esperanto, and

---

*The Institute publishes a quarterly journal called *HolQeD* (from "Hol," meaning language, and "QeD" meaning science). It recently sponsored a contest for palindromes written in Klingon. For information, send an SASE to KLI, Box 634, Flourtown, PA 19031–0634.

Espero Kajolika (Catholic Hope) is a magazine published by a Catholic Esperanto group independent of the Vatican.

Here is the Lord's Prayer in Esperanto:

> Patro nia kiu estas en la ĉielo, sankta estu via nomo; venu regeco via; estu volo via, kiel en la ĉielo, tiel ankau sur la tero. Panon nian ĉiutagan donu al ni hodiau; kaj pardonu al ni ŝuldojn niajn, kiel ni ankau pardonas al niaj ŝuldantoj; kaj ne konduku nin en tenton, sed liberigu nin de la malbono.

The movement peaked in the 1920s, especially among one-worlders, but even today about two million people read and speak Esperanto. Enthusiasts hold conventions here and there, and when traveling identify themselves to one another by green lapel pins shaped like stars. The movement continues to be popular in Europe, but in the United States it is now at a low ebb. In 1991 the Modern Language Association sponsored a seminar on Esperanto at its annual convention. No one showed up. Perhaps the main reason for its decline here is the inexorable rise of English as an international second language. In *The Shape of Things to Come* (Book 5, section 7), H. G. Wells predicts that Basic English (the 850 words selected by C. K. Ogden) will "spread like wildfire" and that by the year 2020 "hardly anyone" in the world will not speak and understand it.

The philosopher Rudolf Carnap learned to speak Esperanto fluently. In his autobiography (*The Philosophy of Rudolf Carnap*) he says that Esperanto became for him a "living language." He cannot take seriously "the arguments of those who assert that an international auxiliary language might be suitable for business affairs and perhaps for natural science, but could not possibly serve as an adequate means of communication in personal affairs, for discussions in the social sciences and the humanities, let alone for fiction and drama. I have found that most of those who make these assertions have no practical experience with such a language."

To his surprise and dismay Carnap found that Ludwig Wittgenstein was violently opposed to any form of language that had not "grown organically."

The most popular semiartificial language preceding Esperanto was Volapük—the word means "world speech"—invented in 1879 by Johann Martin Schleyer, a German Catholic priest.* It uses twenty-seven letters, accents all words on the last syllable, and adds "ik" to all adjectives. The

---

*Volapük turns up in James Joyce's *Finnegans Wake* as Vollapluck (p. 34, line 5 from bottom), Volapuke (p. 40, line 4), and Volapucky (p. 116, line 6 from bottom).

"iks" give it a strong icky sound. Some notion of its ugliness can be gained from Volapük's wording of the Lord's Prayer:

> O fat obas, kel binol in süls, paisaludomöz nem ola! Kömomöd monargän ola! Jenomöz vil olik, äs in sül, i su tal! Bodo obsik, vädeliki givolös obes adelo! E pardolös obes debis obsik äs id obs aipardobs debeles obas. E no obis nindukolös in tentadi; sod aidalivolös obis de bad. Jenosöd!

In France and Germany the Volapük cult gained a following of more than a million, with some two hundred Volapük societies meeting around the globe. After its third congress, in Paris in 1899, its leaders began quarreling over how to improve the language. This bickering created rival versions with such names as Balta, Spelin, Dil, Veltpail, Dilpok, Ilingua European, and others. The movement finally evaporated to be replaced by Esperanto.

I found the following anonymous doggerel in an old scrapbook:

> Take a teaspoonful of English,
> A modicum of Dutch,
> Of Italian just a trifle,
> And of Gaelic not too much;
>
> Some of Russian and Egyptian
> Add them unto the whole,
> With just enough to flavor,
> Of the lingo of the Pole.
>
> Some Singhalese and Hottentot,
> A soupçon, too, of French,
> Of native Scandinavian
> A pretty thorough drench;
>
> Hungarian and Syrian,
> A pinch of Japanese,
> With just as much Ojibway
> And Turkish as you please.
>
> Now stir it gently, boil it well,
> And if you've decent luck,
> The ultimate residuum
> You'll find is Volapük!

Many short-lived attempts from 1900 to the late fifties were made to improve Esperanto. They have such names as Perio, Ulla, Mondlingvo, Romanizat, Europeo, Nepo, Neo, Ro, Espido, Esperantuisho, Globaqo,

Novial, and a raft of others. The most successful of these reform efforts was Ido—in Esperanto it means "offspring"—invented in 1907 by the French philosopher Louis Couterat. A monthly titled *Progreso* was written in Ido. Couterat regarded all Esperantists as depraved. In the first volume of his autobiography Bertrand Russell recalls Couterat complaining that Ido had no word similar to "Esperantist." "I suggested 'Idiot,'" Russell adds, "but he was not quite pleased."

Tinkerers with Ido, like the Esperanto tinkerers, soon splintered the movement into variant languages. These included Dutalingue, Italico, Adjuvilo, Etem, Unesal, Esperido, Cosman, Novam, Mundial, Sinestal, Intal, Kosmolinguo, and more.

Here are a few other semiartificial languages developed from the 1880s to the early decades of this century: Weltsprache, Spelin, Blue, Anglo-franca, Mundolingue, Lingua komun, Idiom neutral, Reform neutral, Latinesce, Nov-Latin, Monario, Occidental, Europan, Optez, and Romanal.

Interlingua is of special interest because it was the creation of the great Italian mathematician Giuseppe Peano. It, too, gave rise to dozens of rival variants, such as Simplo, Latinulus, Interlatino, Panlingua, and others. In the mid-1920s Wilfred Stevens developed Euphony, a language that combined words from thirty natural languages. For example, *olc* for eye, *zu* for blue, and *fra* for human combine to produce *frazolca,* meaning a blue-eyed woman. Lancelot Hogben explained his semiartificial language in a Penguin book titled *Interglossa* (1943).

Many of these rival tongues are discussed in Marina Yaguello's fascinating *Lunatic Lovers of Language* (1991) translated into English from the original French by Catherine Slater. Yaguello is a teacher of linguistics at the University of Dakar, in Senegal. I have not seen Mary Slaughter's *Universal Languages* (1982).

Yaguello also covers synthetic languages in works of fiction, such as Newspeak in George Orwell's *1984* and the slang language invented by Anthony Burgess for *A Clockwork Orange*. She also discusses the Martian language created by the French medium Hélène Smith, and neologisms in the works of Swift and Rabelais. To the latter we can add the hundreds of coined words in the fantasies of Lord Dunsany, James Branch Cabell, L. Frank Baum, and in books said to be channeled by supermortals, such as *Oahspe* and *The Urantia Book.*

Edward Kelly, a sixteenth-century crystal-gazer, scoundrel, and friend of the British astrologer John Dee, devised a language called Enochian. He claimed it was spoken by angels and by Adam before it degenerated into Hebrew after the Fall.

For completeness I should also mention artificial languages that arise in subcultures, such as Shelta Thari, spoken by tinkers in England, and Carny, spoken by American carnival workers. A peculiar language called Bootling flourishes only in the small town of Boonville, California. We all know pig latin, and there are other, less familiar ways of distorting a natural language. There are the "unknown tongues" spoken by the early Christians, and by Mormons, Pentecostals, and other recent sects when the Holy Spirit seizes them. Nor should we ignore the sign language used by the hearing impaired, the talking drums of Africa, the smoke signals of American Indians, communication by whistling in the Canary Islands, and the languages used by artificial-intelligence researchers for conversing with computers.

In crude science fiction, extraterrestrials inexplicably speak English, but in more sophisticated science fantasy they speak alien tongues often described with detailed linguistic rules and words. Every conceivable way of communicating without speech has also been exploited: telepathy (as in H. G. Wells's *Men Like Gods*), dancing, whistling, smelling, using musical tones, and so on. In James Blish's *VOR* an alien "speaks" by altering the color of a patch on his forehead. For information about science-fiction artificial languages, see the entry "Linguistics" in Peter Nichols's *Encyclopedia of Science Fiction*, and "Language" in the index of Everett Bleiler's monumental *Science-Fiction: The Early Years*.

ADDENDUM

Novial (New International Auxiliary Language) was invented in 1923 by Otto Jesperson, a Danish professor of linguistics. Itala (International Auxiliary Language Association) was headquartered in New York City during the mid-1920s, and in the Hague, but interest in Novial was short lived.

Loglan, an artificial language invented by James Cooke Brown, has a grammar based on formal logic, and words taken from eight natural languages. Designed mainly to simplify computer communication, Brown described his language in *Scientific American* (vol. 202, June 1960, pp. 53–63). A Loglan dictionary was published.

Loglan spawned a similar language called Lojban, constructed by Robert LeChavlier, a systems engineer. Both languages have a small group of devotees. On Lojban, see Don Oldenburg's "Lojban, a Real Conversation Stopper," in the *Washington Post* (November 10, 1989, p. D5).

Mangani is the language spoken by the great apes who raised Tarzan. Several hundred of its words are scattered through Edgar Rice Burroughs's Tarzan novels. I first learned about this from Joel Carlinsky, who wrote that as a boy he and his brother actually learned to speak Mangani, and that a full vocabulary is in one of the biographies of Burroughs. A related language spoken by the tailed men in *Tarzan the Terrible* is given in that book's six-page glossary.

In his brief tongue-in-cheek introduction to the glossary, Burroughs had this to say:

> A point of particular interest hinges upon the fact that the names of all male hairless pithecanthropi begin with a consonant, have an even number of syllables, and end with a consonant, while the names of the females of the same species begin with a vowel, have an odd number of syllables, and end with a vowel. On the contrary, the names of the male hairy black pithecanthropi while having an even number of syllables begin with a vowel and end with a consonant; while the females of this species have an odd number of syllables in their names which begin always with a consonant and end with a vowel.

Anthony Garrett wrote from England to tell me about Elvish, a complex language invented by J. R. R. Tolkien as the tongue spoken in his imaginary Middle Earth.

Peter C. Speers called my attention to Confluence, the language of the planet Myrin. It was created by the prolific British science-fiction author Brian Wilson Aldiss. Speers sent me a four-page dictionary of principal words, from *Ab We tel Min* to *Zo Zo Con,* that appeared in *Punch* in 1967. The first phrase is defined as "The sensation that one neither agrees nor disagrees with what is being said to one, but that one simply wishes to depart from the presence of the speaker." The second phrase means "a woman of another field." The dictionary is reprinted in Aldiss's collection of short stories *Man and His Time* (1988).

Aldiss explains that the meanings are modified by one's posture. There are nearly nine thousand stances, each with its own name. Aldiss recommends that all statesmen study Confluence before any negotiations break out with Myrin.

On Stephen Pearl Andrews and Alwato, see Madeline Bettina Stern's biography of him, *The Pentarch* (University of Texas Press 1968).

CHAPTER SIXTEEN
FUZZY LOGIC

> When the prophet, a complacent fat man,
> Arrived at the mountain-top
> He cried: "Woe to my knowledge!
> I intended to see good white lands
> And bad black lands,
> But the scene is grey."
>
> —Stephen Crane

Why does traditional logic have so little relevance to how we think? One reason is that, aside from terms in pure mathematics, formal logic, and some words in mathematical physics, almost all words have blurry boundaries. In set theory an element is either in or outside a set. In propositional calculus an assertion is either true or false. No in-betweens. Unfortunately, in the real world, as philosopher Charles Peirce observed, "All things swim in continua."

No sharp line divides day from night. Children grow imperceptibly into adults. Beasts evolved gradually into humans. Red fades into orange and into purple. When is a glass full? A banana ripe? A person rich? Is half an apple an apple? Is Japan a capitalist or socialist state? When is a novel obscene? Exactly what *is* a novel? Is a bar stool with a small back a chair? How can we measure the beauty of a poem, painting, melody, or person?

Such vagueness must not be confused with ambiguity. "There is a bat in the attic" and Groucho Marx's "I shot an elephant in my pajamas" are ambiguous statements. Arguments over whether the moon rotates arise from the ambiguity of *rotate*. The moon rotates relative to the fixed stars, but not relative to Earth. By contrast, "Is there life on Mars?" is vague because "life" is vague. Are viruses alive? "Go wash your face" is vague. Does "wash" require soap? Are ears part of the face?

Problems in logic textbooks often involve such statements as, "If Bill is home, Mary is out." Is Mary home if she is in the garage or on a porch?

"Notes of a Fringe Watcher," *Skeptical Inquirer* (September/October 1995).

You might think that letters of the alphabet can be defined precisely. Far from it. Every letter can be gradually altered on a computer screen until it is any other letter, with unclassifiable intermediates. A well-known example:

TAE CAT

Is the middle symbol of each word an "A" or an "H"? Like so many words, the answer depends on the context. What is warm for an Eskimo may be cool to someone in the tropics. A small hippo is larger than a big ant. Jewelry expensive to a poor person is cheap to, say, Elizabeth Taylor or Donald Trump.

The ancient Greeks dramatized vagueness by the paradox of the heap. From a large heap of sand you remove one grain at a time. When does the heap cease to be a heap and become a few grains? How many are a "few"? How many hairs have to missing from a man's head before he is bald?

From Aristotle on, logicians have, of course, been aware of vagueness and have proposed ways to overcome it. One way is to be more specific. Instead of vaguely declaring, "As someone once said, history is bunk," we specify it by saying, "As Henry Ford said in 1919 . . ." This helps, but still leaves "history" and "bunk" hopelessly vague.

Another way to avoid vagueness is to quantify. Vague words like *fast* and *slow* can be sharpened by saying that a car is going "too fast" on a thruway if its speed is over 65 miles per hour, and going "too slow" if under 40. Hot and cold can be made as crisp as you like by invoking degrees of temperature. Tall and short can be quantified with centimeters.

In recent decades logicians have tried to handle reasoning with vague terms by what are called "multivalued logics." Instead of true and false, a three-value logic may introduce a third term such as *indeterminate.* Proposals have been made to apply three-value logics to quantum mechanics where certain properties are unknowable. Modal logics distinguish between true, false, and possible. Hans Reichenbach and others have proposed multivalued logics based on probabilities. True has a probability of 1, false a probability of 0. In between can be any number of truth values. Instead of saying vaguely that he or she thinks the big bang theory is true, a cosmologist would more accurately give the conjecture a subjective probability of, say, .9 of being true.

The latest, most ambitious, most radical effort to formalize reasoning with vague terms was named *fuzzy logic* by its inventor Lotfi Asker

Zadeh, now a professor emeritus at the University of California, Berkeley. His new logic dates from 1965, when he published a little-noticed paper on *fuzzy sets*. (Zadeh was born Lotfi Aliaskerzadeh in Baku, Azerbaijan, in 1921, of a Russian mother and a Turkish-Iranian father. After graduating from the University of Teheran, he came to America and earned a doctorate in electrical engineering at Columbia University.)

Zadeh passionately believes that Aristotelian black-and-white logic is useless for reasoning about the real world. This view is shared by Alfred Korzybski, founder of *general semantics,* although this earlier movement by Korzybski had no influence on Zadeh. Just as firmly, Zadeh is convinced that fuzzy logic, with its tolerance of imprecision, will soon replace Aristotelian logic in a massive paradigm shift. "Nature," Zadeh is often quoted as saying, "writes with a spray can, not a ballpoint pen."

There is remarkable anticipation of fuzzy logic in H. G. Wells's philosophical work *First and Last Things* (1908). After describing a variety of objects called "chairs," he wrote: "In cooperation with an intelligent joiner I would undertake to defeat any definition of chair or chairishness that you gave me."

> Every species is vague, every term goes cloudy at its edges, and so in my way of thinking, relentless logic is only another name for stupidity—for a sort of intellectual pigheadedness. If you push a philosophical or metaphysical enquiry through a series of valid syllogisms—never committing any generally recognized fallacy—you nevertheless leave behind you at each step a certain rubbing and marginal loss of objective truth and you get deflections that are difficult to trace, at each phase in the process. Every species waggles about in its definition, every tool is a little loose in its handle, every scale has its individual.

Interest in fuzzy logic and fuzzy mathematics is now worldwide, but especially intense in China, Korea, and Japan. Fuzzy conferences are held regularly in the United States, China, and Japan, where hundreds of fuzzy experts are publishing technical papers. Zadeh has become famous in Japan. More than a half-dozen introductory books on fuzzy logic are in Japanese. Technical books in English are finally being published, and several journals are devoted to this mushrooming field, the oldest being *Fuzzy Sets and Systems,* published in Amsterdam. The word *fuzzy* is on its cover in fuzzy red letters.

Every branch of applied mathematics has been fuzzified. Fuzzy arithmetic handles such fuzzy numbers as "almost 10" and "more than 50." Fuzzy geometry deals with almost straight lines, not quite round circles, and even vaguer concepts, such as ovals. Fuzzy graph theory draws graphs based on fuzzy points. There are fuzzy algebras, fuzzy topology, and fuzzy calculus. Work is being done on fuzzy artificial intelligence (AI), pattern recognition, and neural networks.

Fuzzy computer chips for handling fuzzy algorithms are rapidly being used in hundreds of control systems. In Japan, fuzzy silicon chips provide smooth stops and starts on Hitachi's subway in Sendai, Japan. The Japanese are fuzzifying elevators, cranes, washing machines, carburetors, showers, hair dryers, camcorders, electric razors, air conditioners, TV sets, ovens, vacuum cleaners, even entire chemical plants. "Expert systems," such as those used for medical diagnosis, mineral prospecting, and stock market analysis, are being fuzzified.

In 1989, the Japanese government funded the Laboratory for International Fuzzy Engineering Research with an advance of some $35 million and more than forty member firms. Japanese cars are starting to use fuzzy transmissions. In 1989 Honda awarded its prestigious Honda prize to Zadeh for his contributions to Japanese technology. U.S. companies have been extremely reluctant to jump on the fuzzy bandwagon. Exceptions are Rockwell, which markets several fuzzy devices; Otis Elevator; and General Motors, which uses fuzzy logic in the transmission of its Saturn car.

Details of Zadeh's logic are technical, but let me convey some general features. A fuzzy set is one with fuzzy boundaries. Members are graded by a finite number of degrees, with incremental transitions between them. For example, heights of persons can be broken down into such fuzzy adjectives as very tall, tall, medium, short, and very short, each category defined by numerical intervals. A room's temperature is graded by numbers between hot and cold. True and false are replaced by degrees of truth and falseness. Although reasoning with fuzzy is precise, all its conclusions are fuzzy.

Many theorems in traditional logic carry over into fuzzy in modified ways. For example, on a scale of 0 to 1, assume that "Joe is short" has a fuzzy truth value of .2. Its complement, "Joe is not short," has a fuzzy value of $1 - .2 = .8$. An "and" conjunction of "Joe is short" (value .2) with "Joe is handsome" (value .5), has a value of .5. "Joe is either short" or (in the exclusive sense) "Joe is handsome" has a value of .2. Implication: "If Joe is short then Joe is handsome" has a value equal to $1 - (.2 + .8)$, which is zero. Being short does not imply that one is handsome.

Instead of precise fuzzy values one might use what is called a "fuzzy fuzzy" value of, say, "almost .2." Zadeh calls such values a "second order of fuzziness."

"Fuzziness" is distinguished from "vagueness" in terms of (what else?) degree. "Jesus will return in a few years" is fuzzy. "Jesus will return eventually" is so extremely fuzzy that Zadeh calls it vague. He also distinguishes fuzzy from "probability" statements. "The chance it will rain tomorrow is .5" is a probability forecast. The fuzzy equivalent is, "The degree of truth that it will rain tomorrow is .5." The distinctions are subtle. Thus even the term *fuzzy* is "fuzzy."

Fuzzy logic, especially among artificial intelligence specialists in the United States, has persistent detractors. They claim that fuzzy logic is overhyped, seeing it as a momentary fad similar to the "catastrophe theory" craze that befuddled mathematicians in the late 1970s. It has been called a "cult" with Zadeh as its founder and guru. Some have even called it "content free" and "the cocaine of science." Douglas Hofstadter thinks the idea of reasoning precisely about blurry concepts is "rather comical." Michael Arbib suggests that the cult would never have arisen if Zadeh had named his logic "set theory with degrees of membership."

Arguments between promoters and opponents of fuzzy have become acrimonious. In a 1994 conference on fuzzy in San Diego sponsored by *Computer Design* magazine, the main event was supposed to be a debate between fuzzian Earl Cox and antifuzzian Bob Pease. An announcement said the debate would be carefully monitored by the magazine's editor "to keep the contenders from doing each other actual harm." I am told the debate did not take place.

Opponents maintain that algorithms and chips based on probability theory and familiar multivalued logics can do just as well as fuzzy in controlling machinery. After all, probability controls put astronauts on the moon, and guide intercontinental missiles and solar-system probes. The line between fuzzy logic and probability logics is blurry. To assign "very tall" a fuzzy value of *n* is the same as saying that, in a given culture, a person over six feet will be called tall with a probability of *n*. Is fuzzy, detractors ask, merely probability theory in disguise?

To a large extent disagreements may be verbal. A computer program based on an analog algorithm with digital components would be called fuzzy by fuzzians, but not by others. Fuzzy chips, using sieves instead of on-off switches, would be called an analog program by the antifuzzians. Zadeh likes to point out that chess players have fuzzy intermediate goals, and when you park a car you maneuver it into fuzzy positions. Detractors would say that chess players and car parkers are simply making probability estimates.

In many cases, say the probabilists, a simple feedback mechanism such as a flywheel or a thermostat can serve adequately as a control mechanism. Fuzzy experts are proud of the fact that the Japanese have a fuzzy stability program that balances a pole on one end. Detractors say the same thing can be done with nonfuzzy programs. Fuzzians insist that fuzzy chips balance the pole, as well as handle other control systems, more efficiently, with simpler rules and lower costs.

In 1993 two popular books on fuzzy logic were published in the United States: *Fuzzy Logic* (Simon and Schuster) by Daniel McNeil and Paul Freiberger, and *Fuzzy Thinking* (Hyperion) by Bart Kosko. Both books are breathless paeans to fuzzy, hailing it as a revolution of monumental proportions in computer technology—a revolution destined to transform the world.

Fuzzy Logic is the more restrained of the two. The authors give space to detractors, but argue that their opposition springs from a failure to understand fuzzy logic and from the slowness of a stubborn establishment to recognize a new paradigm shift. They agree with Zadeh that it will be many years until the United States catches up with Japanese technology in fuzzifying control systems. Although they are convinced that fuzziness will soon invade world technology, they grant the possibility that this prediction may "harden into garish embarrassments like the predictions of AI (artificial intelligence) and neural networks."

Bart Kosko, author of *Fuzzy Thinking,* is the movement's most controversial and combative promoter. He is the hero of the McNeil/Freiberger book, which devotes an entire chapter to him. Born in 1960 in Kansas City, Kansas, Kosko obtained his Ph.D. in 1987 from the University of California, San Diego, with a thesis on fuzzy systems. He now teaches electrical engineering at the University of Southern California, Los Angeles.

Kosko is also a karate expert, body builder, music composer, and fiction writer. Politically he is a libertarian. A believer in the future of cryonics—freezing human bodies to resuscitate them later when medical science is more advanced—he made this the basis of his science-fiction novella *Wake Me When I Die.* He was an ardent logical positivist, steeped in the binary thinking of Carnap and Quine, before Zadeh's work overwhelmed him and Kosko moved from black and white to gray. Since then his contributions to fuzzy have been immense, notably his recent work on "fuzzy entropy" and "fuzzy systems."

Kosko is also into Zen meditation. He believes U.S. logicians and manufacturers are still mired in the binary either/or thinking of Western philosophy. By contrast, Southeast Asia, with its Buddhist background, is more tolerant of continuity and vagueness. True, the yin/yang symbol is binary, but each half contains a spot of the other suggesting the fuzziness of both sides. Perhaps Japanese fuzzians will fuzzify the symbol by fading the white and black sides through a continuum of grays.

Kosko is good at inventing fuzzy phrases, such as "fuzz-up" and "fits" (fuzzy units to replace fuzzy bits, or binary units). Rubik's cube suggested to him a clever way to model fuzzy values as fuzzy points within cubes and hypercubes. He likes to speak of the day he learned that "science is not true"—that is, all its laws are fuzzy.

Fuzzy Thinking is an entertaining tour de force that ranges widely and smoothly over such topics as relativity theory, quantum mechanics, psychology, ethics, philosophy, and even theology. Everything is, of course, fuzzified. "God," Kosko writes in his last chapter, "is He who wrote the math. Or She who wrote the math. Or It that wrote the math. Or the Nothingness that wrote the math.The Mathmaker."

Is fuzzy logic as revolutionary as Kosko and his mentor Zadeh believe? Maybe.

ADDENDUM

Two letters about my column on fuzzy logic ran in the *Skeptical Inquirer* (January/February 1996). The following letter was written by William Dress, of Knoxville, Tennessee:

> As usual, Martin Gardner has an unerring instinct—or a highly trained mind—to identify amphigory even in the hallowed halls of science.
>
> I have used Bart Kosko's technical book *Neural Networks and Fuzzy Systems* as the text for a graduate course on "advanced methods" for signal processing and found it clear, concise, and quite useful, as it contains a valuable summary of the various "neural network" models and a good exposition of fuzzy sets, including Kosko's own contributions to the field.
>
> However, as I was careful to warn my students, there are places in the book where Kosko leaves the realm of science and reason to conduct a personal vendetta against benighted practitioners of "Western logic" and, in particular, the Aristotelian principles of reason. Kosko forgets that fuzzy logic was created to allow a consistent mathematical treatment of fuzzy and ambiguous *linguistic* terms, not objective behaviors of physical reality. Indeed, quantum electrodynamics has shown us that the physical reality is crisp at least to a part in 10^{16}—not even remotely fuzzy on a human scale. So much for the fuzziness (impreciseness) of quantum phenomena.
>
> Chapter 7 (Fuzziness versus Probability) is the key chapter in Kosko's book as it serves both as a misguided polemic against reason and logic in science and provides a reasonably clear discussion of Kosko's two main contributions mentioned by Martin Gardner (the geometry of fuzzy sets and the fuzzy entropy theorem). A careful reading of this chapter, keeping in mind that fuzzy logic is a description of linguistic behavior, quickly reveals numerous inconsistencies and non-

sensical statements. The latter are easy to rectify by applying a little common sense. For example, his Figure 7.1 shows a crude sketch of what might be an oval or an ellipse. Kosko wants us to accept that either "It is probably an ellipse" or "It is a fuzzy ellipse." This false dichotomy, directed against probability theory, which he rightly contrasts to fuzzy logic, is easily resolved by allowing more linguistically diverse statements, such as, "It is a poor representation of a circle," or "it is my shaky sketch of an egg," or any of a number of other statements that attempt to convey, in linguistic terms, the possible interpretations of a picture to a human mind. His wavering circle does not compel us to adopt the fuzzy metaphor.

The telling point against Kosko's anti-Western and antirational polemic against "crisp" logic is very simple and quite devastating: Each theorem proven in his book, including the fuzzy set theorems, makes a fundamental appeal to the Aristotelian laws of logic—those of identity, noncontradiction, and the excluded middle that he so despises! In essence, in denying that $A = A$, he no longer has the right to use the word "is"; and the famous "Q.E.D." following his proofs of theorems can have no meaning. Likewise, the very structure of a mathematical proof is grounded in the law of noncontradiction, and the essence of mathematical consistency is tightly bound with the law of the excluded middle. Thus Kosko has himself denied the validity of his own work.

Concisely stated, *fuzzy logic does not and cannot violate the laws of ordinary logic!* It merely allows a consistent way to express linguistic concepts in a "machine" or computer environment. As such, it is a wonderfully useful tool that can enlighten our understanding of linguistics and make computers much more useful to humans, but it has nothing to say about objective reality apart from the human mind and its cultural concepts.

Anytime someone starts talking about "Western science" in contrast to "Eastern science" or some other putative science, the alarm bells start to ring. There is only science. There may be personal approaches, or flavors, to doing, thinking about, expressing, and reporting science, but there can be only science. It is not Western, not Eastern, not African, not northern European, neither male nor female, not socialist, nor communist, nor bourgeois, nor proletarian; science transcends all ethnic, racial, religious, economic, and philosophical strife that so divides our modern world. As such, science becomes an archetype that has the potential to heal our painful rifts of diversity. Fuzzy logic and fuzzy sets do us poor service when used to widen these rifts.

Bruce I. Kodish, of Baltimore, a great admirer of Alfred Korzybski, wrote as follows:

In his column "Fuzzy Logic," Martin Gardner demonstrates his finely honed talent for overgeneralizing when he states: "Zadeh passionately believes that Aristotelian black-and-white logic is useless for reasoning about the real world. This view is shared by Alfred Korzybski, founder of *general semantics,* although this earlier movement by Korzybski had no influence on Zadeh."

Throughout his career Gardner has misrepresented Korzybski's work. Korzybski *did not* consider Aristotelian black-and-white logic useless, only limited. Discussing an either-or orientation, Korzybski wrote, "In living, many issues are not so sharp, and therefore a *system which posits the general sharpness of 'either-or,' and so objectifies 'kind,'* is unduly limited; it must be revised and made more flexible in terms of 'degree'" (*Science and Sanity,* fifth edition). Zadeh, I believe, shares this viewpoint.

Gardner does accurately note that Korzybski's work had no direct influence on Zadeh when he started his work. However, I happily report that connections between general semantics and fuzzy logic have begun to be made. Zadeh presented the 1994 Alfred Korzybski Memorial Lecture and participated in the colloquium on "Exploring Life Applications of Fuzzy Logic." Some material from these events were to be published in late 1995 in the Institute's *General Semantics Bulletin,* Number 62.

I conclude by noting Gardner's careless disregard for the difference between label and actuality. He first writes that "it [fuzzy logic] has been called a 'cult,' with Zadeh as founder and guru." Later in that paragraph Gardner writes that "Michael Arbib suggests that *the cult* [my emphasis] would never have arisen. . . ." From being called a cult, fuzzy logic becomes a "cult." I find this curiously irresponsible formulating from someone touted as a premier "skeptic."

BOOK
REVIEWS

CHAPTER SEVENTEEN
FROM HERE TO INFINITY

Outside a church in Rome is a large stone face with a gaping mouth. Legend has it that if you put your hand in the mouth and make a false statement, you'll never get it out. "May God forgive me," writes Rudy Rucker. "But I have been there, and I stuck my hand in the mouth and said, 'I will not be able to pull my hand back out.' "

The anecdote conveys the flavor of *Infinity and the Mind* (Birkhauser, 1981), an informal, witty, brilliant, and profound book. For the first time a mathematician has surveyed, from a modern point of view, every aspect of infinity—that blinding spot at which the mystery of transcendence shatters the clarity of logic, mathematics, and science. You will learn about Georg Cantor's paradise of transfinite numbers, and (in the opposite direction) the infinitesimal numbers of nonstandard calculus. You will be introduced to the paradoxes of logic and set theory, with their infinite regresses and infinite levels of metalanguages. You will learn about Kurt Gödel's staggering discovery that there are mathematical truths that can never be proved true by mind or computer.

Is there an infinity of universes? An infinity of spacetime dimensions? Will our own cozy little cosmos expand forever or "bounce" forever? Do you know about Gödel's rotating universe in which travel into the past is theoretically possible? Or the "many worlds" interpretation of quantum mechanics in which every microsecond the universe splits into billions of parallel worlds? You will also learn of Rucker's own cyclical model, made half in jest, that starts with universes, then continues down a ladder of suns, planets, rocks, molecules, atoms, particles, quarks, . . . until it becomes an infinite set of the same universes it started with!

A great-great-great-grandson of Hegel, with a doctorate in set theory, Rucker now teaches mathematics at Randolph-Macon, and writes science fiction on the side. His first fantasy, *White Light* (Ace, 1980) is based on the work of Cantor and Gödel. (Ace will soon publish two more: *Spacetime Donuts* and *Software.*) Rucker got to know Gödel, and his book on

This review first appeared in *Isaac Asimov's Science Fiction Magazine* (February 1982).

infinity records several delightful conversations with this great man. Like Gödel, Rucker is a Platonic realist, for whom infinite sets are no less "real" than the number 8 (infinity rotated). All mathematical concepts "exist" in what Rucker calls the Mindscape. Beyond the Mindscape, beyond all the transfinite sets, lies the transcendent infinity that Hegel and Cantor called the Absolute. It is the Unknowable of Herbert Spencer, and it goes by many other names such as Brahmin, the Tao, and God.

Last March *Analog* published a story called "Schrödinger's Cat," based on the most notorious paradox of quantum mechanics. Who could have written it except Rucker? Read his marvelous book and your mind will flood with strange waters—waters that you can be sure will seep more and more into serious science fiction, written for those who are bored with Hollywood's crude mix of sex, violence, galactic wars, and paranormal powers.

CHAPTER EIGHTEEN
HOW SCIENCE WORKS AND FAILS

Why do scientists treat with respect such wild concepts as quarks and black holes but dismiss as nonsense extraterrestrial UFOs and the cosmology of Velikovsky? This is one of the central questions raised by Richard Morris, a physicist turned science writer, in *Dismantling the Universe: The Nature of Scientific Discovery* (Simon and Schuster, 1983). It is an admirable popular account of how science operates by dismantling faulty theories and replacing them with better ones. The process may never end, and final truth may be unreachable, yet who can deny the fantastic success of the enterprise?

Morris begins with an excellent nontechnical summary of how relativity theory, in spite of its wrench to common sense, improved on Newton's physics. Compared with the slow swing in earlier centuries, from Earth-centered cosmologies to heliocentric models, the relativity revolution was amazingly rapid and painless. Quantum mechanics, the next great revolution, was even swifter.

Morris has little enthusiasm for Fritjof Capra and other physicists who contend that quantum mechanics supports Eastern mysticism. He knows that Erwin Schrödinger, one of quantum mechanics' architects, was profoundly interested in Eastern philosophy and that Niels Bohr saw the yin-yang design as a symbol for complementarity—the view that seemingly contradictory aspects of quanta are opposite sides of an incomprehensible truth. But it takes a lot of distortion, Morris believes, to find quantum mechanics closer to Eastern than to Western thinking. Eastern sages have no monopoly on interconnectedness. Western mystics had similar visions of a supernal Oneness, not to mention the long lines of European pantheists from Plotinus to Alfred North Whitehead. It was not a Taoist but nineteenth-century English poet Francis Thompson who wrote: "Thou canst not stir a flower/Without troubling of a star."

A chapter on the pitfalls of intuition tells how Copernicus, having no way to know that planetary orbits are elliptical, was forced to use epicy-

---

This review first appeared in *Science 84* (March 1984).

cles as ugly and complicated as those of the Ptolemaic models. So entrenched was the belief that orbits must be circular that even Galileo refused to accept Kepler's ellipses. Kepler's intuition led him far astray when, in a burst of bogus illumination, he related the orbits of the known planets to the five Platonic solids. Einstein's remarkable intuition failed him utterly when he introduced a "cosmological constant"—a repulsive force between particles—to prevent gravity from collapsing his elegant steady-state model of the universe.

Of course none of these mistakes detracts from the monumental achievements of the three men. For Morris, they highlight the fumbling way that guesses in science are made. When it became apparent that the universe is expanding, Einstein lost no time in calling his constant "the chief blunder of my life." Morris is surely right in seeing this corrective process as operating with increasing efficiency as science more and more becomes a vast cooperative enterprise with rapid exchanges of information between its various research centers.

A hard-hitting chapter on crackpottery should be read by anyone who thinks the term useless. Velikovsky in *Worlds in Collision*, for example— in which he theorized that Venus was originally a comet expelled from the planet Jupiter that eventually collided with Mars and Earth—did not really challenge anything. "On the contrary," Morris says, "he behaved as though modern science did not exist." In Morris's opinion, now shared by everybody except a few tiresome diehards, Velikovsky's fantasies were so far outside the bounds that he became the very model of a crackpot.

The term should not, however, Morris cautions, be indiscriminately applied to research programs merely because they prove to be mistaken. Consider polywater, a strange jellylike water that excited chemists in the mid-1960s; Vulcan, a tiny planet once thought to be inside Mercury's orbit; and the fictitious N-rays that some French physicists at Nancy believed they had observed. Were the defenders of these notions crackpots? Morris thinks not. The science community became skeptical, he points out, "when these theories became so convoluted that they began to take on crackpot proportions." Unnecessary insults may have been tossed back and forth, but the speed with which these three controversies vanished is a striking tribute, Morris contends, to science's constantly improving skill in self-correction.

Is it possible for a theory to be reputable, yet so bizarre that no one can believe it? Morris introduces two recent instances: the many-worlds interpretation of quantum mechanics, in which the cosmos fractures every microsecond into billions of parallel worlds, and a speculation of physicists Robert Dicke and P. J. E. Peebles that there are countless universes within universes, each of them expanding from an exploding black hole.

That establishment journals regularly publish such outlandish but possibly useful ideas surely belies the view that mainstream science is a rigid orthodoxy, contemptuous of off-trail thinking.

Morris ends his book by wondering just what is meant by *real*. The question is unusually troublesome on the subatomic level where particles seem not to exist until they are measured. Are the particles no more than figments of human imagination? In an obvious sense they are mental constructs, yet in another sense, Morris wisely insists, they model something out there, independent of human life, that is sufficiently structured to impose severe restraints on the modeling.

What roles do simplicity and beauty play in the invention of a good hypothesis? Here I think Morris is right in general, but in spite of Keats's famous line about truth and beauty, I must question the book's final sentence: "Science seeks to create pictures of the order in nature which are so logically elegant that we cannot doubt that they are true." No one knows how to measure a theory's elegance—that mysterious mix of simplicity and beauty. It is a theory's success in passing new empirical tests that must always be the final arbiter. Particle physicists now like to say that the recent theory of supersymmetry is much too beautiful to be false. Alas, this has been said many times before about theories that bit the dust because, though very beautiful, they were also very wrong.

CHAPTER NINETEEN

THE FAITH OF THREE SCIENTISTS

The Southern Baptist faith of science journalist Robert Wright did not survive his youthful discovery of evolution, but it left an aching void. Does the universe have a purpose? Mr. Wright's search for the meaning of life brought him into contact with three controversial, out-of-the-mainstream scientists. *Three Scientists and Their Gods* (Times Books, 1988) is his valiant effort to extract from their thinking as much light as he can to illuminate his central question.

Alas, the light on Wright is mainly not so bright. Although he sees the computer concept of "information" as a common thread in the speculations of his three sages, only Edward Fredkin makes much of it, and as for the "gods" in his book's title, only Kenneth Boulding seems to have one. Indeed, just about the only thing these three wise men have in common is Robert Wright, now an editor at the *New Republic,* who decided to write about them.

Edward Fredkin is a computer scientist, formerly with MIT, who sees the universe as a gigantic digital computer. In his wild vision, called "digital physics," space and time are not continuous, but made of discrete bits of pure information. There are no energy transfers or particle movements, only shifting patterns as these bits of information alter their states, like the illusory motions on a computer screen produced by the changing states of pixels.

He isn't kidding. "I feel like I'm the only person with eyes in a world that's blind," he told Mr. Wright when he was interviewed at his enormous villa on Moskito Island, in the Caribbean. (Fredkin bought the island with the millions earned from his computer hardware company.) Few physicists buy his vision. "If Fredkin were a cheese merchant," physicist Philip Morrison says, "he'd be telling you that everything in the universe is made of cheese."

Was our universe programmed by a "great hacker in the skies"? Mr. Fredkin does not believe there is a God, but he does suspect that something

---

This review first appeared in the Raleigh, N.C., *News and Observer,* October 30, 1988.

akin to our intelligence is using the universe "to reach some final state, the solution to some problem, but we can't know what the problem is."

As for the future, although totally determined, the program is so complex that the only way to know what will happen is to let the show go on. Even God, says Mr. Fredkin, if there is one, can't know the outcome "any faster than doing it."

Edward O. Wilson, Mr. Wright's second scientist, is the well-known promoter of sociobiology. Like Mr. Wright, Edward Wilson abandoned his born-again beliefs when he encountered science. His career began with research on the social insects (bees, ants, wasps, termites) whose behavior is totally determined by genes. Although Mr. Wilson recognizes that human behavior is a mix of genetic programming and environmental influences, he has become the world's most passionate champion of the view that genes play a far greater role in human culture than social scientists want to admit.

As Mr. Wilson, now a Harvard biologist, has grown older and written more books, he has become increasingly persuaded that aesthetics, altruism, and even religious beliefs are strongly conditioned by genes, which are in turn products of random mutation and natural selection. Many of his colleagues think he has carried genetic determinism too far. Some have even called him a racist.

He is not a racist, but as an honest atheist, what is he doing in a book about scientists and their gods? Mr. Wright tells of an occasion when Edward Wilson found himself at a memorial service listening to an old gospel hymn. He began to cry. "It was tribal," he explained. "It was the feeling that I had been a long way from the tribe."

Kenneth Boulding, Mr. Wright's third expert, grew up in Liverpool as a Methodist, later becoming a Quaker and a follower of Teilhard de Chardin, the heretical Roman Catholic paleontologist. Mr. Boulding's first book, *Economic Analysis,* was once a popular college text. His later books (there are dozens) tend to be rambling with endless quips and asides. They focus on Spaceship Earth (he coined the phrase) as a "total system" that is evolving into a unified superstate of love, peace, and justice.

Now in his late seventies, with unkempt snow-white hair, Kenneth Boulding impresses Mr. Wright as a gentle, lovable Wizard of Oz, so agreeable that "he uses the word yes the way children use ketchup." Is he a charlatan—"a mush-minded do-gooder who finessed his way into the academic limelight with his wit and British charm"?

Mr. Wright isn't sure, and I cannot say; but as for Teilhard de Chardin, I agree with the late Sir Peter Medawar, whom Mr. Wright quotes—that Teilhard's speculations are "nonsense tricked out with a variety of tedious metaphysical conceits." Apparently, Mr. Boulding believes in a Christian God, but his musings tend to be so vague and plat-itudinous that it is hard to know. I keep expecting him to reveal that the past is behind us and the future lies ahead.

Mr. Wright finishes this fascinating book without having learned whether the universe has a purpose or not. "Personally," he writes, "I don't know what to think. But I do think about it often." I enjoyed his skillfully etched portraits and his commentary, and learned a lot from them, but the book's Casey-strikes-out finish reminded me of another man who went searching for the meaning of life. After many years of searching the world he came upon an aged Tibetan monk who was said to know the answer.

"The universe," the monk told him, "is like a flower."

"Do you mean," the irate man responded, "that after my twenty years of pilgrimage, and weeks of climbing this miserable mountain, all you can tell me is that the universe is like a flower?"

The old monk shrugged and spread his hands, "Perhaps it's not like a flower."

CHAPTER TWENTY

SPECULATIONS OF FREEMAN DYSON

Physicists divide today over an awesome question. Are all the fundamental laws of nature about to be discovered? Stephen Hawking, for one, answers yes. Freeman Dyson's new book is an impassioned defense of the contrary—that the universe is infinitely mysterious in all directions. "If it should turn out," he writes, "that the whole of physical reality can be described by a finite set of equations, I would be disappointed. I would feel that the Creator had been uncharacteristically lacking in imagination."

British-born, trained in mathematics at Cambridge University, in physics at Cornell, Dyson is the most esteemed resident of Princeton's famed Institute for Advanced Study. His contributions to physics, technology, and cosmology have been enormous. But there is another side to this remarkable man, a side that relishes fiction and poetry, that likes to dream. His technical papers bristle with equations, but few scientists can write for laymen with more elegance, clarity, humor, and enthusiasm.

Dyson's earlier book, *Disturbing the Universe,* was mostly about his opinions and speculations, although it was disguised as autobiography. *Infinite in All Directions* (Harper and Row, 1988) ranges even more widely. When asked to give the prestigious Gifford Lectures in Aberdeen, Scotland (on which the book is based) he decided not to focus on a single topic, but simply to talk about all the things that interested him. These are some:

• Superstrings—inconceivably tiny pulsating loops that may explain all the weird properties of matter.

• The Oort Cloud of millions of comets, orbiting the sun in spaces beyond Pluto.

• Nemesis, a star not yet identified but which may be a companion to our sun.

• The Monarch butterfly—"The world of biology is full of miracles, but nothing I have seen is as miraculous as this metamorphosis of the Monarch caterpillar."

This review first appeared in the Raleigh, N.C., *News and Observer*, April 10, 1988.

- The benefits and perils of nuclear energy, genetic engineering, and Star Wars.
- The need for world government, and the hope for increasing democratization of the USSR and the real possibility of nuclear disarmament. And with these, doubts about Carl Sagan's nuclear winter.
- The possibility that life on Earth had not a single biochemical source but a double origin. A molecule of nucleic acid, capable of crude replication, latched onto a molecule of protein, he suggests, to become "the oldest and most incurable of our parasitic diseases"—life.

Dyson remarks that while a hundred years ago the intelligent layman had no difficulty understanding the language of Darwin, today science moves ever further beyond the ken of all the but the specialists:

> The chemistry of living cells is the essence of life. The beauty of their variegated architecture is inescapably tied to the ugliness of chemical terminology. The further we penetrate into the mysteries of their behavior, the longer and the uglier our words become.

Dyson likes to entertain science-fiction schemes, one of the wildest being his "astro-chicken." By combining future techniques of genetic manipulation and artificial intelligence, Dyson thinks we may be able to grow an organic robot capable of walking around the moons of Uranus, sending back information from its sensors, and supplying its own energy by eating the ice and carbon of Uranus's rings. "If one ring tastes bad it will try another. . . ."

For me the most fascinating portions of Dyson's book are its theological musings. Dyson's God is the finite, pantheistic god elaborated by the Australian philosopher Samuel Alexander, a world-soul "inherent in the universe and growing in power and knowledge as the universe unfolds."

Dyson first learned he was not alone in this "process theology" from the philosopher Charles Hartshorne, whose "panpsychic" views he shares. Mind permeates the universe, and "is to some extent inherent in every electron." Although Dyson doesn't mention it, his mentor H. G. Wells actually wrote an entire book about this theology, *God the Invisible King,* before he decided he was an atheist.

In Dyson's dream scenario the universe will not vanish in a Big Crunch, but will expand forever. As it approaches death from the cold, he thinks, intelligence will by then have invented ways to continue existing in forms now utterly beyond our comprehension.

What is the purpose of it all? Dyson disagrees with physicist Steven Weinberg that the universe is pointless. The point is to maximize diversity. Leibniz thought ours was the best of possible worlds. Hawking thinks it the most probable of possible worlds, while other cosmologists think it the most improbable. For Dyson it is merely "the most interesting of all possible universes, and our fate as human beings is to make it so."

Aptly, Dyson closes by returning to the mystery of metamorphosis. He recalls the passage from "Purgatorio" where Dante likens the soul to a worm born to become an angelic butterfly. For Dante the metamorphosis refers to you and me. For Dyson the wings belong not to individuals who are destined to perish, but to a "million intelligent species exploring diverse ways of living in a million different places across the galaxy."

I thought of the lines he quoted, in *Disturbing the Universe,* from Wells: "Beings who are now latent in our thoughts and hidden in our loins, shall stand upon this earth as one stands upon a footstool, and shall laugh and reach out their hands amid the stars."

CHAPTER TWENTY-ONE
SHELDON GLASHOW ON SCIENCE AND SUPERSTRINGS

Sheldon Glashow, the Harvard physicist who shared a Nobel Prize in 1979 with his old high school buddy Steven Weinberg and the Pakistani physicist Abdus Salam, is the latest in a line of distinguished scientists to favor us with their memoirs. Written with Ben Bova, former editor of *Omni* and *Analog Science Fiction Magazine, Interactions* (Warner books, 1988) is a marvelous, witty double introduction: to the basic ideas of relativity, quantum mechanics, and particle theory, and to the life and mind of one of the world's most creative explorers of the universe's wild and wonderful underworld.

Shelly, as his friends call him, grew up in Manhattan, the son of Lev Glukhovsky, a Russian Jewish immigrant. Neither his "father the plumber" nor his mother went to college, but somehow they managed to rear three children (Shelly has two sisters) who became Ph.D.s. Shelly's first words almost were "What's that?" As with all great physicists, his childhood curiosity was insatiable. He recalls wondering what a rainbow is, and why an uncooked egg won't spin. He collected comic books. He tinkered with chemistry in his basement lab, and won a ribbon at the Bronx High School of Science for building a stroboscope. He and classmate Weinberg put out a science-fiction "fanzine" called *ETAOIN SHRDLU*, in which appeared his first published article, "On the Nature of Nothing."

"Our trajectories through the world of physics," Glashow writes of himself and Weinberg, "are hopelessly intertwined." They both went to Cornell, where Weinberg's roommate was Daniel Kleitman, now an MIT mathematician who became Glashow's brother-in-law. Their wives are sisters. A third sister was married for a time to Carl Sagan, who persuaded her to become a biologist. In Glashow's barbed opinion, she was "Carl's greatest contribution to science."

Friends and collaborators, Glashow and Weinberg taught at the University of California at Berkeley during the 1960s, and moved to Harvard in 1967.

This review first appeared in the Raleigh, N.C., *News and Observer*, June 19, 1988.

Then, in 1968, there occurred one of the saddest, most spectacular ruptures of friendship in modern science. Glashow, curiously, provides scant details, but says that for an entire year he and Weinberg did not speak to each other even though both were at Harvard and had been friends for thirty years. A partial reconciliation took place when they won the Nobel Prize (for unifying electromagnetism and the "weak force," which plays a part in radioactive decay). Weinberg would later leave Harvard for a post in Texas.

Glashow's title has two meanings: the interaction of particles, and the author's interactions with friends and colleagues. He tells how at Harvard he "painfully" shed two girl friends. One ran off with a student, the other married a mathematician. "I tried to convince her to wed me," he says, "but she told me it was too late; they had already bought the furniture." Weinberg advised Glashow to get married so he could concentrate on physics.

Like many physicists, Glashow enjoys combinatorial play with words and letters. After referring to the "tedium of Ithaca (New York)," he wonders if it isn't better called the "tedia of Ithacans." His father's "sole perversion" was his love of a certain fish. A theory of Jogesh Pati and Abdus Salam is called "pate and salami." Sam Ting makes an observation, and later another physicist sees the Sam Ting. His friend Murray Gell-Mann, who discovered and named the quarks, is dubbed Murray the *OM*niscient to introduce into the adjective the Hindu prayer word "Om" that signifies the unity of everything. CCNY—City College of New York—stands for the "circumcised citizens of New York." Writing about the physicist Eugene Wigner brings to Glashow's mind a riddle: "What is the question whose answer is 9W?" The answer: "Professor Wigner, do you spell your name with a V?"

In his final chapter Glashow introduces a riddle of his own. "Name two grand designs that are incredibly complex, require decades of research to develop, and may never work. . . . Star Wars and string theory." String theory is the latest craze among particle physicists. Gell-Mann and Weinberg are gung ho for it, but Glashow is skeptical. He calls it a "new toy" that is perverting "impressionable students" who are likely to become unemployable after the "string snaps." String theory replaces the pointlike elements (leptons and quarks) of particle physics with inconceivable tiny loops whose vibrations generate the properties of all the particles. Glashow likens it to medieval theology. Because no great breakthroughs in particle physics have taken place in the last ten years, he thinks, physicists are playing "Let's Pretend" so they will have something to talk about.

Physicists have always spent vast amounts of mental energy on crazy ideas, most of which turn out to be wrong. "I do it all the time," Glashow writes. "Having a lot of crazy ideas is the secret to my success. Some of them turned out to be right!"

String theorists hope and believe that strings will tie up all the loose ends of physics, leaving no basic laws to be discovered, but Glashow is betting against it. "Can anyone really believe," he asks on his last page, "that nature's bag of tricks has run out? Have we finally reached the point where there is no longer a new particle, a 'fifth' force, or a bewildering new phenomenon to observe? Of course not. Let the show go on!"

ADDENDUM

Because of space limitations, I did not discuss in my short review where Glashow stands on the conflict between mathematical realists and those who see all of mathematics as a human construction. I am happy to say that Glashow, like almost all mathematicians and physicists, is a realist in the sense that both the laws of nature and the theorems of mathematics are discovered, not invented.

"Are the Simple Lie groups merely an invention of human thought, like the Polish language?" Glashow asks on page 156. They are so essential to physics, he writes elsewhere, that to talk about physics to an audience not knowing group theory is like trying to eat spaghetti with a spoon.

> Surely, intelligent aliens in other galaxies could hardly be expected to speak Polish, but I bet my boots they know about Lie groups. Mathematical entities, like integers, complex numbers, calculus, and Lie groups, are real things, even if we cannot touch or smell them or build rabbit hutches out of them. But it seems to be a reality quite apart from physical reality. Electrons exist in a very different sense than Lie groups.

Eugene Wigner titled a famous paper "The Unreasonable Effectiveness of Mathematics." Glashow shares Wigner's puzzlement. "It is a mystery to me that the concepts of mathematics . . . which are purely inventions of the human imagination, turn out to be essential for the description of the real world of natural phenomena. But so it is."

Purely inventions? If the objects of mathematics are in some sense "out there," waiting to be discovered by human minds, permanently embedded in the structure of the cosmos in the way the "form" of a vase is essential to the material vase, then what is surprising about the fact that having extracted mathematics from the universe, of which our brains are a part, we are able to put it back in?

CHAPTER TWENTY-TWO

HEINZ PAGELS ON
MINDS AND COMPUTERS

M any a beautiful theorem has been discovered in the past by mathematicians playing with numbers and diagrams, but the computer has raised the level of such experimenting to new highs. Because most natural laws are modeled on what mathematicians call the nonlinear differential equations of the calculus, much too complex to be explored on paper, the computer has become a research instrument comparable in power to the telescope and microscope. Where all this will lead, nobody knows, but that it will alter our lives in radical ways is the theme of this admirable third book by Heinz Rudolph Pagels, *The Dreams of Reason* (Simon and Schuster, 1988).

Pagels, a physicist at Rockefeller University and executive director of the New York Academy of Sciences, is one of those rare scientists able to communicate with nonscientists in clear, delightful prose. His first book, *The Cosmic Code,* was about the weird world of quantum mechanics. His second, *Perfect Symmetry,* explored cosmology and the struggle to unify all of nature's laws. His wife, Elaine Pagels, is a distinguished historian of religion, best known for her book *The Gnostic Gospels.*

The two areas in which computers are making the most dramatic breakthroughs are "complexity theory" and "chaos." Complexity theory is concerned with the time it takes a computer to solve a problem. Some tasks that, in earlier centuries, would have required a mathematician years to complete are now finished in seconds. Other problems take hours or weeks, and still others are so complex that no computer could solve them in "reasonable" time. There are problems no computer can solve even if it runs forever, and there are problems that we don't know could be ever solved, no matter the time.

Chaos theory (recently popularized by James Gleick's best-selling book *Chaos*) studies dynamic structures that change in strictly deterministic ways—ways precisely defined by equations—but which quickly plunge into unpredictable behavior indistinguishable from pure random-

---

This review first appeared in the Raleigh, N.C., *News and Observer*, July 11, 1988.

ness. Although mathematicians are having a field day exploring complexity and chaos, the work has endless practical applications in areas as diverse as weather control and economics, all of which Pagels skillfully surveys.

Pagels shares the scorn of most physicists for the philosophers of science, though he has read their books and his pages are peppered, or perhaps I should say "poppered," with their names. Karl Popper gets the most attention. "I am convinced," Pagels writes, "from reading Popper's recent books on quantum theory that he does not understand the theory." Thinkers who stress the influence of social forces on the history of science—Thomas Kuhn, for example, and Paul Feyerabend, who carries the cultural approach to such extremes that Pagels calls him a "punk philosopher"—come in for special drubbing.

Like almost all physicists, Pagels is a thoroughgoing realist who sees our minds as part of a material world "out there," independent of the existence of you and me, though of course what we observe is conditioned by our culture. Scientists do not manufacture laws the way firms manufacture clothes. Scientific revolutions, from Pagels's perspective, are not like changes in fashion. They are linked to a real world, and although science meanders, in the long run it gets closer and closer to the secrets of what Pagels calls the Demiurge. It is his term for a pantheistic deity—not a personal God, but a Mind behind cosmic order. His model of the history of science is evolution, a selective process moving haphazardly into an uncertain future, but always shaped and constrained by a structure that is more than simply a projection of our feeble little brains:

> The "revolutionary" metaphor has been given such currency that many people, who ought to know better, develop and popularize the view that science is simply another social enterprise. This misconception, like occultism, deserves rebuke. I insist that scientific ideas, because of their special vulnerability to failure imposed by the actual order of nature, are subject to a unique, self-imposed selective pressure, a criterion for survival that is transcendent to the particular culture in which these scientific ideas originate.

From antiquity to our own century, philosophers have distinguished between "mind" and "body." Pagels is convinced that the computer revolution, with its spinoffs of artificial intelligence and the cognitive science of mind, its "dreams of reason," is rapidly blurring this ancient duality. "The dualism of mind and nature," he writes, "will not so much be solved as it will disappear."

And as it vanishes, so also will vanish the mystery of how it is that mathematics, a construction of human minds, is so unreasonably effective in explaining and predicting how nature operates. Behind the universe is the Demiurge, a cosmic code of pure mathematics. Is it so surprising that our minds, a part of the universe, can write equations that fit the mathematical structure from which they emerged?

ADDENDUM

Heinz Pagels, less than two weeks after my review was published, died tragically in Colorado of a fall while mountain climbing. He was forty-nine. "I have never known anyone quite like Heinz," his good friend Jeremy Bernstein concluded his moving tribute to Pagels in the *Sciences* (September/October 1988), "and I shall think of him every day for the rest of my life."

CHAPTER TWENTY-THREE

SYMMETRY FROM A TO ZEE

There seems no end these days to books intended to give laymen insight into what particle physicists are up to, and this is one of the best.

Anthony Zee, a Chinese-born physicist at the University of California in Santa Barbara, is the author of *The Unity of Forces in the Universe,* a two-volume, densely technical work. *Fearful Symmetry* (Macmillan, 1989) was written for nonscientists, and is happily available now in both hardback and paperback.

The book's title is taken from William Blake's famous poem about the burning tiger in which "symmetry" is a synonym for awesome beauty, not just the bilateral symmetry of the tiger's body. Mathematicians define symmetry by operations on an object that leave something unchanged, such as rotating it, reflecting it in a mirror, or shuffling parts about like permuting a string of symbols. A circle has strong symmetry because you can rotate it to any degree and reflect it without altering its shape. But a circle is as boring as a one-note melody or an all-pink painting. Zee writes:

> For the Ultimate Designer, herein lies the rub. Symmetry is beauty, and beauty is desirable. But if the design is perfectly symmetrical, then there would be only one interaction. The fundamental particles would all be identical and hence indistinguishable from one another. Such a world is possible, but it would be very dull: there would be no atom, no star, no planet, no flower, and no physicist.

How could the Ultimate Designer, Zee's euphemism for God, start the universe off with "icy perfection," the mother field that preceded the big bang, then manage to frame the strangely beautiful world that permits the existence of forests, tigers, and you and me? The answer lies in broken symmetry. As the expanding fireball cooled, its former supersymmetry, with its single quantized particle, broke into fields and particles of lower symmetry. Water has high symmetry because it looks the same no matter how you turn it. Cool it sufficiently and you get the lower but more

---

This review first appeared in the Raleigh, N.C., *News and Observer*, February 26, 1989.

interesting symmetry of snow crystals. Beauty is a mysterious mix of unity and diversity, or order and disorder.

The book's title page lists the author simply as A. Zee, and his book does indeed cover symmetry from A to Z. There are splendidly clear chapters on the symmetries of relativity theory, of quantum mechanics, of the GUTs (Grand Unification Theories), and the TOEs (Theories of Everything). Modern physicists, in Zee's vision, "have entered the forest of the night in search of the fundamental design of Nature and, in their limitless hubris, have claimed to have glimpsed it."

I know of no book of this sort written more informally and with such humor. There are quotes from Lewis Carroll, clever cartoons, and amusing anecdotes about great scientists. Opponents of GUTs are gutless. Expressions such as Whew! What in blazes? Look, wait a minute; Yeah, sure; Poof! Whoosh! and blah, blah pepper its pages. Physicists who suspect there is no top quark are topless. What would the strong force be like were it weak? It is like asking what your mother would be like if she were your father. A deep unanswered question known as the "triplication problem" is likened to Goldilocks finding bowls and beds of three different sizes. "Quark" is a word taken from James Joyce's *Finnegans Wake*. Zee actually locates a passage in Joyce's *Ulysses* where Bloom speaks to a prostitute about "gauge symmetry."

When God said "Let there be light," Zee thinks He really meant:

Let there be an SU(5) Yang-Mills Theory with all its gauge bosons, let the symmetry be broken down spontaneously, and let all but open of the remaining massless gauge bosons be sold into infrared slavery. That one last gauge boson is my favorite. Let him rush forth to illuminate all of my creations!

It doesn't sound as dramatic, Zee writes, "but it is probably closer to the truth."

The rules of the universe, he says, are more like the simple rules of go than the complicated rules of football. God is playing the great game of Guess the Rules with us. And what is the best guessing strategy? It is to pick the right groups. (Groups, it will help to know, are abstract algebras that define symmetries.)

Oops, I chose the wrong group and ended up without any massless gauge boson. Well, my universe would not have any light in it. No good. Try again. I choose another group, but now I end up with two massless gauge bosons. This universe would have two different kinds of photons. Well, another possible universe hits the wastebasket. Want to play?

CHAPTER TWENTY-FOUR

MATHEMATICAL BREAKTHROUGHS

The front cover of Keith Devlin's Penguin paperback, *Mathematics: The New Golden Age* (1989), is a dazzling computer image reproduced from a Springer Verlag book, *The Beauty of Fractals*. If it looks familiar it's because you've seen it on the front cover of James Gleick's recent best-seller, *Chaos*, published by Viking. Two books with identical covers are rare enough, but to make things worse, Viking is now owned by Penguin. I take this blunder to reflect the chaos that develops when big publishing houses merge.

A research mathematician at the University of Lancaster, Devlin is best known in England for his column on mathematics in the *Guardian,* and for his television appearances. This new book (his ninth) is an effort to introduce general readers to some of the more exciting recent breakthroughs in what he calls "mankind's most impenetrable subject." Devlin's choice of material is excellent, and he is to be praised for the clarity and accuracy with which he presents it.

The book's first topic is prime numbers: integers greater than 1 that have no divisors except themselves and 1. The largest known prime—it has 65,050 digits—is obtained by raising 2 to the power of 216,091, then subtracting 1. Primes of this form are called Mersenne primes. Only thirty-one are known, and no one has yet proved whether there are infinitely many, or only a finite number, maybe no more at all.

For the past decade there has been an intensive search for faster ways to factor composites—numbers that are not prime. One reason, Devlin tells us, is that improved computer methods of factoring could destroy a widely used cipher known as the RNA system after the initials of its three MIT inventors. It is called a public-key cryptosystem because the method of encoding secret messages can be published and used by anyone. Decoding is something else. It is possible only if one knows the two factors of a gigantic composite, obtained by multiplying two primes, which serves as the cipher's secret key. When the RNA system was first proposed in 1977

This review first appeared in the *New York Review of Books*, March 16, 1989. Reprinted with permission from the *New York Review of Books*. Copyright © 1989 Nyrev, Inc.

prime numbers of eighty digits were recommended because there were then no known ways to factor the product of two such primes in "reasonable" computer time—say, ten years. The RNA system is still secure, but because of recent improvements in factoring speed, primes of one hundred digits are now used to make two-hundred-digit keys.

Here are quick rundowns on Devlin's other topics. A chapter on infinite sets includes Kurt Gödel's famous proof that even in systems as simple as arithmetic there are statements impossible to prove true or false. A discussion of different kinds of numbers centers around an amazing property of 163. A chapter on fractals—structures that always look the same, either exactly or in a statistical sense, as you endlessly enlarge portions of them—introduces the famous Mandelbrot set. It is named after IBM's Benoit Mandelbrot, who invented the term *fractal* and pioneered the study of these marvelous patterns.

In his book on chaos theory Gleick calls the Mandelbrot set the most mysterious object in geometry. When a computer zooms in on its infinite structure, progressively magnifying regions, there is an endless sequence of surprises. A periodical devoted entirely to investigations of the M-set, as it is called, even runs occasional science fiction based on the set's unfathomable depths. How mathematicians who pretend that mathematical structure is not "out there," independent of human minds, can view successive enlargements of the M-Set and preserve their cultural solipsism is hard to comprehend.

A chapter on simple groups (abstract algebraic structures based on such symmetry operations as ways of rotating a cube so that it returns to its original state) introduces the concept of symmetry. The concept is fundamental in modern physics, especially in particle theory and the new TOEs (Theories of Everything). Not until 1980 were all the finite simple groups (finite here means that a group has a finite number of symmetry operations) identified. Proof that they are now all classified followed the discovery of the Monster, a group whose number of symmetry operations is 8 followed by fifty-three digits. The proof runs to about 15,000 pages in some five hundred papers by more than one hundred mathematicians. Devlin calls it the longest proof in mathematical history.

A discussion of a famous algebraic problem posed by David Hilbert in 1900, and solved in 1970, leads into Diophantine analysis—finding integral solutions to equations. Devlin gives an up-to-date account of efforts to crack the greatest of all unsolved Diophantine problems—proving Fermat's conjecture that $a^n + b^n = c^n$ has no solutions when n is higher than 2. (If n is 2 there is an infinity of solutions starting with $3^2 + 4^2 = 5^2$.) Lest you be tempted to search for a counterexample, know that if one exists n must be greater than 125,000. The media gave widespread coverage early in 1988 to a supposed proof by a Japanese mathematician, but like hundreds of earlier claims it turned out to be flawed. The most recent development on Fermat's conjecture is a proof that for every n greater than 2 there are at most a finite number of solutions.

"Hard Problems About Complex Numbers," the book's toughest chapter, discusses three more conjectures: the Riemann hypothesis (unsolved), the Mertens conjecture (proved false in 1983), and the Bieberbach conjecture (proved true in 1984). The solving in 1976 of the notorious four-color theorem—the conjecture that all maps can be colored with four colors—is the topic of another chapter. The proof hides in a computer printout so massive that only computers can check it, and to this day some mathematicians are not convinced it is flawless.

The latest proof of this sort was announced last December by Clement Lam and his associates at Concordia University, Montreal. Does a finite projective plane of order-10 exist? This longstanding combinatorial question would take too much space to explain, but the point is that a Cray supercomputer, after running for several thousand hours, answered no. Can we be sure this answer is correct? Some philosophers contend that proofs so lengthy and complex that no human mind can "see" their validity are turning mathematics more and more into an empirical science where results are only probable to varying degrees.

Knot theory, a whimsical branch of topology (the study of properties that are unchanged when an object is continuously deformed), is currently enjoying a revival. It even has applications in organic chemistry, where protein molecules can take knotted forms. Devlin's chapter on knot theory is the most entertaining in his book.

A final chapter on computer algorithms (procedures) discusses a class of closely related problems known as NP-complete, for which no reasonable-time algorithms have been found, or probably exist. The best-known example is the task of finding the shortest route for a salesman who must visit each of n cities just once and return to where he started. Karmaker's algorithm, a recent breakthrough in speeding computer solving of such problems, is explained. Because the algorithm is based on the structures of solids in higher dimensions, Devlin sees it as "an exemplary blend of the pure and abstract with the world we live in and an excellent place to bring to an end a survey of mathematics' New Golden Age." Modern computers have given mathematicians a tool of incredible power. It is the book's recurrent theme that these mindless machines are not only solving old problems that could never be solved without them; they are also opening up vast new regions, of great beauty and utility, that mathematicians are just starting to explore.

William Poundstone's first book, *Big Secrets*, annoyed professional magicians because it exposed the workings of some of their most cherished stage illusions. He followed it with *Bigger Secrets* and *The Recursive Universe*, a book centered on the philosophical implications of a computer game called Life. *Labyrinths of Reason* (Doubleday/Anchor, 1989), his fourth and best book, is a lively, freewheeling discussion of the most bewildering and most profound of many paradoxes still hotly debated in philosophical journals.

"Paradox" has a broader meaning than "fallacy." You can seemingly prove, as Poundstone does, that $1 = 2$, but not without making a subtle mathematical error. A paradox is any line of reasoning that strongly contradicts common sense. Fallacies are trivial. Paradoxes can be far from trivial.

Poundstone's first example is a paradox put forth by Carl Hempel, a distinguished philosopher of science, to show how little we understand what is meant by "confirming evidence." Everyone agrees that each time we observe a black crow it confirms the conjecture "All crows are black." A logically equivalent way to say the same thing is "No nonblack object is a crow." We see a red apple. Surely it confirms "No nonblack object is a crow." If so, it must also confirm the equivalent "All crows are black." Something clearly is wrong, but just what? Poundstone skillfully capsules the various positions philosophers have taken in recent years on this mystifying question.

Sometimes what seems to be a confirming instance turns out to be the opposite. Poundstone cites Paul Berent's amusing paradox of the 99-foot man. Consider the hypothesis "All men are less than 100 feet tall." Each observation of a man less than 100 feet surely confirms the conjecture. Suppose you encounter a man 99 feet tall. Strictly speaking, he confirms the conjecture, but in a stronger way he disconfirms it because you now have good reason to believe that men can grow close to 100 feet. To get around the paradox one must consider Rudolf Carnap's important proviso. Degrees of confirmation must rest on all the evidence that bears on a conjecture, not on the conjecture alone.

Other chapters in Poundstone's racy volume cover such mindbenders as Nelson Goodman's "grue-bleen" paradox of induction; Henri Poincaré's claim that if everything instantly doubled in size overnight we would be unable to detect the change (or would we?); infinity machines, such as a lamp that turns on and off in time intervals expressed by the halving series of one minute, one half minute, one quarter minute, and so on—at the end of two minutes, the sum of the series, is the lamp on or off?; John Searle's much discussed "Chinese Room," designed to attack the notion that computers "understand" their instructions; and Hilary Putnam's "Twin Earth," intended to show that the meanings of words are linked to the external world. "Cut the pie any way you like," Putnam is quoted as saying, " 'meanings' just *ain't* in the head!" If not, Poundstone asks, where are they?

The paradox of the unexpected hanging, the topic of another chapter, continues to generate bizarre debates. A judge tells a prisoner, "You will be hanged at noon on a day next week, but there is no way you can know in advance what day it will be." The prisoner reasons: "They can't hang me Saturday, the last day of the week, because on Friday afternoon I'll be able to deduce that my hanging will be Saturday. So Saturday cannot be the day. Nor can Friday. On Thursday afternoon, knowing that Saturday has been eliminated, I will know Friday is my day of doom. This again contradicts what the judge told me, so Friday has to be eliminated also."

Of course such reasoning will extend backward through the week to Sunday. Does this prove that, assuming the judge spoke truly, the prisoner cannot be hanged? No, because on, say, Tuesday morning the judge orders the hanging at noon. This comes as a total surprise to the prisoner. What was wrong with his logic?

Newcomb's paradox, the topic of the book's last chapter, has produced more confusing argument among philosophers than any other paradox since physicist William Newcomb thought of it in 1960. Ten years later Harvard's philosopher Robert Nozick introduced it to his colleagues in a book of essays honoring Hempel. When I gave it still wider currency in my *Scientific American* column it brought more than a thousand letters. I passed them over to Nozick, who, after summarizing them in a guest column, regretfully concluded that the paradox remains inscrutable. (Both columns are reprinted in my *Knotted Doughnuts and Other Mathematical Entertainments.*)

Imagine, said Newcomb, that in front of you are two closed boxes, *A* and *B*. *A* is transparent. Inside you see a thousand-dollar bill. *B* is opaque. Either it is empty or it holds a million dollars. You must make an irrevocable choice between taking both boxes or taking only *B*. In both cases you keep what is inside.

On the day before the test, a Superbeing from another planet (God if you like) has scanned your brain to determine how you will decide. If he thinks you will take only *B* he puts a million in the box. If he thinks you will greedily take both boxes, he puts nothing in *B*. He then leaves the scene. You know exactly what the conditions are. Moreover, you have seen this test performed a hundred times before with others, and in every case the Superbeing predicted accurately. The greedy who took both boxes got only the visible thousand dollars. Those who took just the opaque box got a million.

What is your best decision? From a pragmatic point of view you are impressed by the Superbeing's past accuracy. (Incidentally, the paradox holds even if the accuracy is only slightly better than 50 percent.) Because all of science, as well as your daily behavior, rests on induction from past experience, should you not take just *B* and be almost certain of joining the millionaire's club? About half the philosophers who have written about the paradox see this as "obviously" the best way to maximize your take.

Unfortunately, an equal number find it just as obvious that you should make a "logical" decision and take both boxes. Assume *B* is empty. If you take only *B* you get nothing, but if you take both boxes you get at least a thousand. Assume *B* is not empty. If you take it alone you get a million, but if you take both boxes you get a million plus a thousand. In each case, taking both boxes will increase your gain by a thousand. Because nothing can change the fixed state of the boxes, why not take everything there?

The paradox leads into deep questions about decision theory—questions that bear on decisions in economics and politics, perhaps even on metaphysical questions about free will and determinism. As Nozick insists, the paradox is not resolved by giving a vigorous defense of either strategy. You must show why the other strategy is inferior.

Scattered throughout Poundstone's book are many lesser paradoxes and puzzles. Here is the most amusing:

> A man gets an unsigned letter telling him to go to the local graveyard at midnight. He does not generally pay attention to such things, but complies out of curiosity. It is a deathly still night, lighted by a thin crescent moon. The man stations himself in front of his family's ancestral crypt. The man is about to leave when he hears scraping footsteps. He yells out, but no one answers. The next morning, the caretaker finds the man dead in front of the crypt, a hideous grin on his face.
>
> "Did the man vote for Teddy Roosevelt in the 1904 U.S. presidential election?"

Answer: A crescent moon is visible at midnight only in regions near the poles. The man, therefore, must have lived in northern Alaska. Because Alaska was not part of the United States in 1904, he could not have voted for Teddy Roosevelt.

ADDENDUM

Since I wrote the foregoing review, three more Mersenne primes have been found: The thirty-second such prime is 2 raised to the power of

756839, minus 1. A thirty-third Mersenne prime, found in 1994, is 2 to the power of 858433, minus 1. I say "a" thirty-third Mersenne prime rather than "the" thirty-third because a Mersenne prime between the last two has not yet been ruled out. Still another Mersenne prime was discovered in 1996: 2 raised to the power of 1257787, minus 1. It has 378,632 digits and is the largest prime now known.

Fermat's last theorem has almost certainly been proved by Andrew Wiles, though at the time I write (August 1995) a final verdict is not yet in.

Logicians disagree on how best to resolve the unexpected hanging paradox. I side with W. V. Quine and others who find the prisoner's first step of reasoning invalid. The prisoner is saying: "If the judge spoke truly, and I am not hanged by Friday noon, I will know that I will be hanged Saturday. But I will also know that I will not be hanged Saturday." Because the two conclusions are contradictory, nothing can be deduced on Friday or any other day. It follows that the judge can select any day he wishes, including Saturday, and the day will be unexpected.

For a discussion of the paradox, and a lengthy bibliography, see the first chapter of my *Unexpected Hanging and Other Mathematical Diversions*. Quine's analysis, "On a So-called Paradox," appeared in *Mind* 62 (January 1953): 65–67.

CHAPTER TWENTY-FIVE
TECHNOLOGY'S AWESOME MARCH

No one can dispute the central theme of this handsomely produced book by Thomas Hughes, a University of Pennsylvania historian and sociologist. For more than a century the United States led the world in inventing technologies and developing massive systems of production that altered the face of the earth and the course of history.

But I put down *American Genesis: A Century of Invention and Technological Enthusiasm, 1870–1970* (Viking, 1989) with mixed feelings of admiration and puzzlement—admiration for the rich details, colorful writing, and striking photographs; puzzlement over what was left out.

Hughes is at his best covering the lives and personalities of the great independent inventors responsible for America's electrification: Thomas Edison, Nikola Tesla, Reginald Fessenden, Lee de Forest, Edwin Armstrong, William Stanley, Elihu Thomson, and many others. There are vivid accounts of other solo inventors such as Alexander Bell, Hiram Maxim (the machine gun), Elmer Sperry (the gyrocompass), and the Wright brothers. Among the system builders the emphasis is on Henry Ford and Frederick Taylor, the efficiency expert whose "Taylorism" was copied so enthusiastically by Lenin and the German industrialists.

Hughes traces the rise of giant corporations, builders of huge research laboratories where the lonely inventor has been replaced by teams of experts. He is quite good in describing mammoth government-funded projects: TVA, the Manhattan Project, the NASA space program, and the military-industrial complex now hard at work on Star Wars.

Nor does he fail to look beyond the obvious. In one chapter he deals with the influence of modern technology on architecture and painting. Others cover recent rebellions against unbridled technology—the "small is beautiful" trend, the antinukers, the whole earthers, the third wavers. Hughes reminds us that this revolt has been intensified by such disasters as Three Mile Island, the *Challenger* explosion, and Chernobyl. (Exxon spilled its oil too late for the book.)

This review first appeared in the Raleigh, N.C., *News and Observer,* April 16, 1989.

Now for some puzzles. Rarely does Hughes refer to the creative mathematicians and physicists, most of them unknown to the public, whose work lies behind technological change. Industrial inventors, engineers, and scientists are, of course, also creative: but they build on what they have learned from obscure theoreticians. And those who found and run corporations are usually mathematical and scientific illiterates. (This was true even of Edison, who puttered around trying this and that while a large staff of assistants did most of the work.) Mathematicians and physicists scribble equations in their university labs or private studies, then years or even decades later up go the factories. Splitting the atom was implicit in relativity theory, yet Einstein is mentioned only as a signer of a famous letter urging research on the atom bomb.

There are other blanks. The latest technological sea change, comparable to the introductions of steam, electrical, and gasoline power, is the computer revolution. Although it began well before 1970—the last year mentioned in the book's subtitle—computers are glossed over in one sentence: "Recently, the general all-purpose digital electronic computer and the laser have been added to the list [of inventions]." The book skillfully portrays the rise of AT&T, DuPont, RCA, General Electric, and General Motors. Nothing is said about Big Blue (IBM).

There is similar silence about America's greatest contribution to the arts, the motion picture. After learning how to talk it moved into everybody's home to become an incredibly potent force in shaping political and social behavior.

Xerography gets just one word in a list of inventions, yet surely dry photocopying sparked a revolution in communication.

At the book's close, Mr. Hughes wonders if our lead in technology will continue. But he says nothing of the decay in our teaching of science and mathematics. There is nothing about Japan's pioneering in robotics; nothing about our decline in research and development while the technological lead shifts to nations where long-term gains take precedence over short-term greed.

In sum, the book does a splendid job encompassing most of the high spots in U.S. technology from 1870 to World War II. A thorough history to 1970 it is not. Perhaps it was a Viking editor and not the author who wrote the book's subtitle.

CHAPTER TWENTY-SIX

TO PLUTO AND BEYOND

Thirty years ago, introducing an essay on the moon in my anthology *Great Essays in Science,* I cautiously wrote: "Our children may well live to see a rocketship circle or land on the moon." I never dreamed I would live to see it.

The rapidity with which space technology has developed in the last three decades is awesome. More has been learned about the sun and her offspring during this period than in all earlier centuries together, and no one has surveyed this fantastic history more skillfully and entertainingly than Bruce Murray. The prospect of studying extraterrestrial geology hooked the interest of this MIT geologist when he was young, and for thirty years he has been at the center of the nation's space programs. For six years he was director of the Jet Propulsion Laboratory in Pasadena, where he now teaches at Cal Tech. *Journey into Space: The First Thirty Years of Space Exploration* (Norton, 1989) is his fifth book about exploring space.

And what a story it tells! I still find it hard to believe, when I look up at a full moon, that two earthlings actually walked upon it. Remember how closely the televised pictures resembled science fiction about trips to the moon?

Space probes of more distant heavenly bodies have produced and are still producing endless surprises. Mercury's surface, like the moon's, is pockmarked by the same bombardment of meteors or comets, some 4 billion years ago, that blasted craters on the moon and Mars. For more than a century astronomers believed that Mercury always kept its same face to the sun, creating a circular "twilight zone" that divided a hemisphere of intense heat from a hemisphere of intense cold. Not so. Mercury rotates slowly with respect to the sun. Unlike Venus and Mars, and to the astonishment of astronomers, Mercury has a weak magnetic field. No one knows why.

Mercury's craters bear curious names: Shakespeare, Cervantes,

---

This review first appeared in the Raleigh, N.C., *News and Observer*, July 23, 1989.

Chopin, Homer, even Mark Twain. After bitter wrangling over what to name them, the humanities won out.

Probes below the thick carbon-dioxide atmosphere of Venus have disclosed a rocky, cratered surface much too hot to support life. Jupiter turned out to have a ring around it, and close-up photos of the giant planet's four largest moons (each bigger than our own) showed that no two are alike. Europa, the strangest, resembles a spherical white egg splattered with black paint by Jackson Pollock. Its icy crust may cover an ocean that Murray calls the largest body of water outside the earth.

Saturn's lovely rings proved to consist of hundreds of thin bands of light separated by dark gaps. Its largest moon, Titan, has a methane atmosphere that could support unearthly forms of life. Uranus has rings like Saturn, and more moons than anyone had guessed, though only Miranda has been seen close up. Neptune has three moons and probably a ring, though not much is yet known about it. Even less is known about Pluto, the smallest, most distant planet.

The old sci-fi dream of life on Mars, as well as public enthusiasm for space travel, took a nosedive when photographs of Mars disclosed a desolate surface devoid of any hint of life. As Murray puts it: "no Martians, no canals, no water, no plants." This absence of life was soon underscored by the analysis of Martian sand scooped up by a robot. Murray and Carl Sagan are friends—together they founded the Planetary Society to promote interest in space exploration—but over results of the Mars probes they sharply disagree. Murray estimates the odds against any form of life on Mars as overwhelming. But Sagan still thinks microorganisms may lurk beneath the sand. There are features on Mars looking exactly like dry river beds. Did water flow on the red planet billions of years ago? If so, microorganisms could have evolved, and later adapted to the arid surface and to the deadly ultraviolet radiation from the sun.

Most of Murray's history is devoted to the anonymous and brilliant technicians behind our space programs, and to their triumphs and failures. Although a harsh critic of NASA, he believes that its programs are slowly recovering from the *Challenger* disaster and will soon be on track again. Former President Ronald Reagan is praised for accepting the vision of exploring and eventually colonizing alien worlds, but Murray faults him for total ignorance of science—an ignorance shared by every one of his close associates. In contrast, former President Carter understood the technology, but subordinated space funding to what he believed were more pressing human needs.

At the close of *The Great Gatsby* its narrator reflects on the emotions of the first sailors to land on the American continent, coming "face to face for the last time in history with something commensurate to [humanity's] capacity for wonder." F. Scott Fitzgerald couldn't have been more wrong. Our new frontier of wonder is the solar system, and the next giant step for mankind will be a walk on Mars. Perhaps, as Carl Sagan and Bruce Murray passionately hope, it will be a cooperative effort of the United States and the Soviet Union. "To Mars—together!" is the rallying cry that runs through Murray's final pages.

We now know there have been no Martians in the past, but, as Ray Bradbury likes to remind us, there are sure to be Martians in the future. They are us. And even colonizing Mars will not be the last frontier. Beyond little Pluto are the stars.

CHAPTER TWENTY-SEVEN
ASTRONOMERS AND GOD

NASA's careless failure to test the Hubble telescope's mirrors may seem a minor disaster to many, but to astronomers it was a crushing blow. Revolutionary observations in the past fifteen years have thrown cosmologists onto a battlefield where rival theories clash as vigorously as when proponents of the big-bang and steady-state models of the universe were ridiculing one another. The Hubble telescope could have settled many of the new controversies. Astronomers will now have to wait years before the Hubble can be repaired or a new one launched.

Starting in 1987, MIT physicist Alan Lightman interviewed twenty-seven of the world's top cosmologists about their family background, their early history, their work, and their beliefs. Stephen Hawking, Roger Penrose, Fred Hoyle, Steven Weinberg, Dennis Sciama, and Robert Dicke are perhaps the best known, but all twenty-seven have made enormous contributions to astronomy. There is no better way to understand their current confusions than by reading this timely and admirable anthology, edited by Lightman and Roberta Brawer, a graduate student in cosmology at MIT. Titled *Origins: The Lives and Worlds of Modern Cosmologists*, the book was published by Harvard University Press in 1990.

At the heart of the debates are the "horizon problem" and the "flatness problem." The horizon question is: Why is the universe so homogenized? The microwave background, left over from the big bang, implies a universe with the same overall structure in all directions. The best explanation is an inflationary model which has the universe popping into existence from almost nothing, expanding at an exponential rate before the bang, then settling down to a slow linear growth.

But is the universe really homogeneous? A few years ago Margaret Geller and others, studying red-shift maps, found that the universe is lumpier than anyone suspected. Galaxies lie on the surfaces of monstrous "bubbles" that surround huge voids. Other galaxies form long filaments and flat "walls." To make things worse, some galaxies are streaming the

This review first appeared in *Book World* (September 2, 1990). © 1996, Washington Post Book World Service/Washington Post Writers Group. Reprinted with permission.

wrong way, against what is called the "Hubble flow"—the universe's steady expansion. Most of the interviewed cosmologists hope that on vaster scales the universe will be smoothed out. All agree that if peculiar structures and motions persist on still larger scales, the big bang model will be in deep trouble.

The flatness question is: Why is the curvature of space so close to zero? This is the same as asking why the Hubble flow is so nearly balanced by the pull of gravity that only a tiny increase in the amount of mass in the universe would eventually halt the expansion. Lightman likens it to tossing a rock in the air with a velocity exactly enough to let the rock escape earth's gravity. Inflation models solve this problem also, but unfortunately require far more matter in the cosmos than can be observed. Indeed, to make space so nearly flat, there must be ten times as much matter as can be seen.

There are solid grounds for thinking that the universe contains the required amount of dark (unseen) matter. Vera Rubin and others have shown that galactic motions cannot be explained without assuming this dark matter, but there is no agreement on how much, or what and where it is.

Most cosmologists accept the flatness, and believe that the dark matter will soon be found. A few, notably John Wheeler and Robert Dicke, lean toward enough matter to "close" spacetime, halt the expansion, and send the universe the other way toward a Big Crunch. The notion that after the crunch it will bounce back again—the so-called oscillating universe—is almost ruled out by the lack of known laws to explain it.

Lightman's interviews follow a fairly fixed set of questions about the above problems, and end metaphysically by asking for a reaction to a famous statement by Steven Weinberg in his popular book *The First Three Minutes*. The more the universe is understood, he wrote, the more pointless it seems.

To me, this is asking whether there is a transcendent Mind behind the universe that gives it a purpose we cannot fathom. I was struck by the fact that a majority of those interviewed were unwilling to make such a leap of faith, and in that sense agreed with Weinberg. Indeed, only four believe the universe has a purpose: Charles Misner, a Catholic; Don Page, an evangelical Protestant; Andrei Linde, a devotee of Hindu theology; and Allan Sandage, who became some sort of Christian convert about 1980. (For a full account of Sandage's distinguished career and evolving beliefs, see Dennis Overbye's *Lonely Hearts of the Cosmos*, HarperCollins, 1991).

Fred Hoyle may also belong to this group even though he did not say so. He is alone in the book in clinging to a steady-state model, rejecting the big bang mainly because he thinks it does not allow enough time for life to evolve. I found it surprising that so many astronomers spoke with regret of having been forced by the microwave radiation to accept a beginning for the universe. Like Aristotle's earth-centered cosmology and Einstein's static first model, a steady state avoids the messy task of explaining how a universe can explode from a quantum vacuum. Several of those interviewed stressed how emotionally satisfying it once was to believe that the universe has always been and always will be just what it is.

Sandage, more than anyone else, spoke of being overwhelmed by the dark riddle of why a universe exists at all, and why it is so beautifully and intricately structured. Let him have the final word:

> The greatest mystery is why there is something instead of nothing, and the greatest something is this thing we call life. I am entirely baffled by you and me. We were both there near the beginning. The atoms in our bodies were made then, yet their sum now, in a living thing, is greater than the whole . . . perhaps the universe is the only way it can be for us to exist.

CHAPTER TWENTY-EIGHT

READING THE MIND OF NOBODY

James Trefil, a physicist at George Mason University, has risen to the highest ranks of science popularizers with a series of excellent books of which *Reading the Mind of God: In Search of the Principles of Universality* (Scribner's, 1989) is the latest. It is a nontechnical account of post-Newtonian science woven around a central theme: the gradual recognition that laws of nature are everywhere and at all times the same. True, speculations are occasionally made about the slow altering of certain constants, such as gravity, but these do not violate what Mr. Trefil calls the "principle of universality." They just "push the parameters," as he phrases it, to deeper levels.

There is no logical foundation for the principle. It rests solely, Mr. Trefil makes clear, on empirical evidence, but evidence so overwhelming that physicists now take it for granted. Many have even forgotten how astonishing the principle seemed in past centuries while it was becoming firmly entrenched.

Greek, Roman, and medieval thinkers had no inkling of the principle. They knew, of course, about natural laws on earth, but it did not seem possible that those laws would also govern the heavenly bodies. It took the genius of Newton to demonstrate that the moon, planets, and comets move under the influence of the very same laws of gravity and inertia that make apples fall.

From Newton on, science slowly, inexorably extended the domain of natural laws outward in space and backward in time. William Herschel mapped the universe—in Mr. Trefil's words, enlarging Newton's orchard to include the stars. In the nineteenth century Auguste Comte so underestimated the growing powers of science that he insisted humanity would never understand the chemical composition of stars. Mr. Trefil skillfully traces the work of scientists who developed techniques for doing precisely what Comte thought impossible.

Relativity theory and quantum mechanics apply everywhere in space,

---

This review first appeared in the Raleigh, N.C., *News and Observer*, September 3, 1989.

and at all times past and future. If Alan Guth's inflationary model is right, the universe began with a quantum fluctuation in a "false vacuum." In a microsecond it jumped from a size smaller than an atom to that of a grapefruit, then the big bang occurred and the universe began a slow expansion to its present size. "The universe," Mr. Trefil quotes a physicist, "is simply one of those things that happen from time to time." Michelangelo's Jehovah, whose grim visage glares from the book's jacket, seems to have played no role in the event. So much for science reading the mind of God.

Not everyone accepts the principle of universality. There are those who argue that science does not discover laws that are independent of human cultures. Instead of getting closer to the mind of God, it is more like the shifting fashions of art. If there are intelligent creatures in other galaxies, presumably their technology rests on an entirely different periodic table of elements, perhaps even on a mathematics in which 17 is not a prime. No one denies that culture influences the motivation of scientists, what they study, how they are funded, how their results are received and used, and so on. But it does not follow, Mr. Trefil argues, that "everything is English Lit":

> In other words, do Newton's ideas express a truth about the external world that is independent of the Age of Reason, or are they nothing more than an expression of that age, equivalent in some sense to a symphony or poem? Obviously, if the latter statement is true, then a scientific theory cannot be objectively true, any more than a symphony can be.
>
> You may think that I am overstating things here, setting up a straw man. It may seem incredible that anyone could seriously propose such an argument, but I have been involved in enough faculty club arguments to know that many academics—particularly philosophers and sociologists of science—do indeed hold these sorts of views. I have yet to meet a serious natural scientist who does, but as one progresses away from the hard sciences into the social sciences and the humanities, this sort of scientific relativism becomes more common, although I am happy to say that its proponents are far from being a majority.

Mr. Trefil closes with some of Mr. Guth's recent wild speculations. If we could compress a mere twenty-two pounds of matter to the size of a proton, it might explode into another universe that would pinch off from our spacetime and balloon into a parallel world. Could our universe be the outcome of such an experiment by a physics student in some alien spacetime? Aside from these forays into fantasy, Mr. Trefil's book is a sober, easy reading, entertaining tribute to the glorious efforts of scientists to read the mind of nobody.

CHAPTER TWENTY-NINE

IS WESTERN CULTURE VANISHING?

It has been a long time since I have had so much fun reading a book while also disagreeing so strongly with its central theme. Advancing along the path of his previous book, *Ending the Maze*, O. B. Hardison, Jr., an English professor at Georgetown University, has constructed his new book on one overriding point: Science and technology have so radically altered our culture that all sorts of old values and ideas are rapidly vanishing through the skylight of modernity.

Disappearing Through the Skylight (Viking, 1989), a series of essays about disappearances, opens with a sequence of pictures by Picasso showing the gradual vanishing of the human form. You will not find human faces in the works of abstract expressionists, either, or in the swirling patterns of computer art. An entire chapter is devoted to "Mandelbrot's Monstrosities," those startling forms generated on computer screens by simple algebraic formulas.

Buildings once mirrored human history. Now they are huge glass boxes or cylinders "as free of history as a Mondrian abstraction." Old-fashioned symphonies and popular melodies are giving way to mediocre computer music, and the experimental compositions of John Cage and others. Musical structure has all but vanished from poetry. One chapter deals with "concrete verse" (poems printed in representational shapes), other chapters with computer doggerel, and the puzzle poems of the Oulipo, a bizarre French group of writers who apply combinatorial mathematics to verse and fiction. Mr. Hardison sees these trends as the disappearance of art and language.

Although books will continue to be printed, he assures us, they will no longer hold center stage. "We are coming," he says, "to the end of the culture of the book." What is displacing them? Television, for one thing, but also computer novels. One punches keys to explore portions of a hypertext in which characters and plots "disappear like water in a sponge."

This review first appeared in the Raleigh, N.C., *News and Observer*, December 2, 1989.

Science likewise is making things vanish. Evolution erased the line between humans and beasts. Run the big-bang scenario backward and the entire universe fades into nothing. Matter long ago dissolved into mathematics. Even the external world, quantum mechanics seems to say, has become a projection of our minds onto whatever mysterious fog is "out there."

The book closes with the wild speculation that humanity itself may be on the way out as silicon robots acquire intelligence superior to ours. They will be immortal, flourishing in outer space, as unable to talk to us as we are to the ants. "Man," he writes, "is in the process of disappearing into the machines he has created." The book's last page is a photograph of the fading earth as seen from the moon. It is captioned, "Earth disappearing into space."

This is nonsense. Science and technology have altered human life in obvious ways, but human nature—a different matter—has not fundamentally changed since the time of the Greeks. Indeed, I suspect only our science and technology would be incomprehensible to Aristotle. Everywhere I look I am struck, not by the vanishing of old ideas, but by their renewal.

A few decades ago God was supposed to have died in mainline churches. Today we are in the midst of a religious revival, albeit taking such strange forms (none mentioned by Mr. Hardison) as fundamentalism and the New Age obsession with reincarnation. Even Norman Mailer, writing in the December 1989 *Esquire,* has rediscovered process theology, seemingly unaware of his distinguished predecessors.

In the art world, realism is all over the lot. Nobody pays much attention these days to abstract expressionism or minimalist sculpture outside a tiny subculture of artists, *New York Times* critics, museum and studio directors, and other aesthetic flimflammers. Who sits at home listening to computer music or the noises of Cage? Computer buffs play with hypertext fiction the way children play with new toys, but this has had little effect on the novel or motion pictures. Only the poets are still allergic to formal structure, churning out unmusical prose broken into vapid lines that look like poetry.

Not many physicists think quantum mechanics allows the moon to disappear when no one looks at it. If you run the Genesis account of creation backward, the universe vanishes as completely as it does in the backward scenarios of modern cosmology.

The most incredible example of the revival of old ideals is the discovery in Marxist nations of democracy and human rights. History vanishing? On the contrary, what George Will has aptly called a great Reformation without Luther is taking place even as you read these lines.

As for humanity giving way to silicon intelligence, this is a whimsical hoax perpetrated by workers in artificial intelligence who devoured too much science fiction in their youth. A healthy antidote is Roger Penrose's just-published *The Emperor's New Mind*. Supercomputers, let's face it, no more know they are playing chess than dishwashing machines know they are washing dishes.

The earth is not vanishing. It is being rediscovered for what it is, the miraculous spherical home for a family of creatures ruled by a sentient species struggling painfully to become worldwide siblings.

CHAPTER THIRTY

PENCILS

I was afraid Dr. Henry Petroski was going to tell me more about pencils than I cared to know. To my happy surprise I found *The Pencil* (Knopf, 1990) so engrossing that I read it through at one sitting. Petroski, a professor of engineering at Duke University and the author of several books on engineering, has written an utterly absorbing history of the most commonplace instrument around—the simple lead pencil. Moreover, he has woven around this history a rich commentary on the role of research and development, industrial design, free-market competition, and everything else related to it.

There is a famous section in Adam Smith's *The Wealth of Nations,* Petroski reminds us, in which a pin factory is featured as a paradigm of modern industry. His latter-day disciple Milton Friedman, in *Free to Choose*, does the same thing with pencils. The cover of its paperback edition shows him conspicuously holding a classic yellow pencil. Now Petroski has expanded the paradigm into a book, lavishly illustrated, and almost impossible to put down.

The word *pencil,* from the Latin, means "little tail," referring to the tiny brushes used by Renaissance artists. The first known picture of what is now called a pencil is in a book about fossils published in Zurich in 1565. The nature of "lead" in this wooden pencil is not known, but it probably was graphite, which had just been discovered in a British mine in Cumberland. The world's first pencils were made in England, with square rods of graphite, although the substance was then called black lead, English antimony, plumbago, and many other strange names. In Paris, Nicolas-Jacques Conte invented the modern process of pulverizing graphite and mixing it with clay, the proportions determining the hardness of the so-called lead. Worldwide competition quickly grew fierce, with the rise of the Faber pencil company in Germany, Dixon pencils in the United States, and the first Russian pencil factory, founded in Moscow by the American industrialist Armand Hammer.

This review first appeared in the Raleigh, N.C., *News and Observer*, January 7, 1990.

How on earth does the graphite get into the pencil? Simple. The wood "infrastructure," as Petroski calls it, is two identical halves, each with a groove down the middle. The graphite-clay mixture is pressed into one groove, the halves glued together, and the outside painted. (Look at a pencil's point and you will see the line between the two halves.) The book will tell you how dyes are added to clay to make colored leads, about the amusing controversy in schools over the addition of erasers, the rise of mechanical pencils and ballpoint pens, the making of mechanical sharpeners, and even the best technique for sharpening a pencil with a knife. You will learn the pros and cons of pencil shapes: round, hexagonal, triangular, or square. The triangular form won't roll off a desk, and is the most comfortable to fingers, but then you can't twirl it easily to keep the point sharp.

I was amused to learn of the facility Henry David Thoreau had in counting pencils quickly. Before he became a writer, he called himself a "civil engineer" and worked in his father's pencil factory, where he was responsible for research and development. Like the hundreds of women who worked for his father, young Thoreau developed a curious skill for picking up exactly the right number of pencils to be packaged in sets of twelve. Here is how his friend Emerson described it: "From a box containing a bushel or more of loose pencils, he could take up with his hand fast enough just a dozen pencils in every grasp." A dozen—no more, no less.

Then there was Harold Ross, the driven and eccentric editor of the *New Yorker*, who seemingly chewed on his pencils to the point where he had all but eaten them. Truman Capote, Jane Austen, Conan Doyle, Elbert Hubbard, John Steinbeck, Carl Sandburg, Ernest Hemingway, John Updike, Douglas Hofstadter—all figure in entertaining and informative stories about the leaded subject. Petroski does not miss cartoonist Saul Steinberg's infatuation with pencils, Johnny Carson's habit of tossing them away, or "Aristotle's illusion" in which a single pencil, touched by two crossed fingers, feels like two.

Given its long history, it's surprising that antique dealers have habitually thrown away early pencils that turn up in boxes of carpentry tools. That's apparently changing. In spite of their increasing rarity, old pencils are now collectibles. There is an American Collectors Society of several hundred pencil lovers that issues a monthly newsletter. Petroski's own collection includes such novelties as the pencil with a loop of string that can be fastened to a buttonhole in such a puzzling way that it is difficult to remove, joke pencils with rubber points or with erasers at both ends, pencils a yard long, and pencils that produce lines of swirling colors.

The only kinds that Petroski misses—understandable since conjuring is a semisecret art—are those sold in magic shops, such as pencils that rise mysteriously on one's palm. Magicians also know ways to break a pencil in half with a dollar bill, push a pencil through a handkerchief, produce spirit raps when pressed against a wall, and guess a pencil's color when it is handed to you behind your back.

For Petroski, the history of the pencil has been dominated by its "invisibility." It is so common, so taken for granted, that until now its history has been virtually overlooked—one reason it was never of much interest to antique dealers. If in a few years an old Dixon Ticonderoga or Eberhard Faber No. 2 is worth many times more than the few cents it cost, perhaps Petroski's charming book will have added to its value. But the pencil's value in larger respects—as the means by which we recorded (and sometimes erased) our innermost thoughts and tallied up bills and designed buildings—will be harder to calculate.

Even Thoreau, that close observer of the quotidian, did not always notice the pencil. When he listed every item he took to Walden Pond, the one thing he failed to record was the instrument that may have been in his very hand.

CHAPTER THIRTY-ONE

ALLAN SANDAGE'S COSMOLOGY

Modern cosmology is seething with controversy. New observations keep demolishing old theories, while fantastic new theories sprout like mushrooms. Books, too, are proliferating to meet public curiosity about what is going on. To Dennis Overbye, a science writer who calls himself a "cosmological camp follower," astronomers are a lonely breed. They are lost in the immensity of the universe, battered by the the unexpected data pouring out of giant telescopes, and in perpetual conflict with one another.

Lonely Hearts of the Cosmos: The Scientific Quest for the Secret of the Universe (HarperCollins, 1991) differs from similar popular books by going into more technical details, and by stressing the appearances and personalities of the leading combatants now struggling to read, as Stephen Hawking has put it, the Mind of God. Swarming with anecdotes, Overbye's book—it is his first—is written with such wit and verve that it is hard not to zip through it at one sitting.

Although most of today's cosmologists are covered, the book's central figure is Iowa-born Allan Sandage, who began his legendary career as a disciple of the great Edwin Hubble. It was Hubble who first confirmed Kant's bold conjecture that nebulae are vast islands of stars, and who found that these billions of galaxies are rushing away from one another. Einstein's first model of the cosmos was a static one, prevented from collapsing by what he imagined to be a repulsive force. After the "Hubble flow" became obvious, Einstein called his conjecture the greatest blunder of his life. His model remained closed, like a sphere's surface, but enlarging like an inflating balloon. This expansion clearly implied a moment of creation, or what Fred Hoyle derisively called the big bang.

Hoyle's rival theory, the steady state, had hydrogen atoms constantly entering space from somewhere to preserve an expanding universe that has always been and always will be overall the same. His theory exploded with a bang after the microwave radiation from the primeval fireball was detected.

This review first appeared in *Book World* (January 21, 1991). © 1996, Washington Post Book World Service/Washington Post Writers Group. Reprinted with permission.

In Overbye's racy account of this, and of the battles that followed, we are told that Sandage "haunts" the narrative "simply because he has been doing cosmology, trying to solve the universe, so much longer and more intensely than anyone else." I do not know how accurate Overbye's picture of Sandage is, but no one emerges from the book in more incisive detail—a person Overbye sums up as "a cosmic quipster, edgy as a razor, scat quick, and humorously dry as a lemon."

Sandage's great contributions are set forth in detail for the first time, alongside his many bitter conflicts with colleagues. "You weren't anybody in astronomy," Overbye writes, "if Sandage hadn't stopped speaking to you at one time or another." For years he and Halton ("Chip") Arp were irreconcilable enemies. Arp continues to be a pebble in the shoes of cosmologists because he keeps finding evidence that quasars may not be far distant objects of enormous energy, but nearby objects of low energy. If he is right, the red shift is an unreliable measure of distance and all modern cosmology is wrong.

Hawking, John Wheeler, Roger Penrose, Dennis Sciama, Robert Dicke, Allan Guth, Margaret Geller—these are just a few of the top cosmologists who weave in and out of Overbye's colorful history. Most of them believe in black holes, but are these invisible monsters really crouching out there, or are they just dubious extrapolations from relativity theory as Philip Morrison suspects? "Black holes are out of sight," reads a sign on Hawking's door. You will learn why Hawking thinks they are not totally black, but radiating energy, and why he thinks the universe may be peppered with tiny black holes that eventually will explode.

You will learn about Vera Rubin's shrewd deduction from the way galaxies rotate that the universe must be saturated with invisible "dark matter." The nature of this matter, and whether it is massive enough to halt the universe's growth and start it shrinking, are unsolved mysteries. If there is a Big Crunch, will the universe bounce back or will it "drag itself into oblivion" to become, in another Overbye metaphor, eaten by God?

You will learn about recent evidence that the galaxies are not randomly distributed, but form a soapsudsy structure. Cosmologists are working hard on far-out theories to explain this lumpiness, and why so many local galaxies are streaming the wrong way, against the Hubble flow.

The most bizarre of recent speculations is that the universe spontaneously emerged from nothing. But of course it isn't really nothing because there must have been laws of physics to give the almost nothing what Overbye calls the "twitch" that exploded some 15 billion years ago into our time and space, and a universe capable of producing such peculiar life forms as you and me.

Only a few cosmologists, Sandage among them, have the courage to go against the scientific community's zeitgeist by entertaining the wild notion that basic laws are in God's Mind. Although impressed by the awesome mystery of existence, most cosmologists seem to agree with such atheists as Bertrand Russell that nothing is gained by positing an eternal Creator when eternal laws will do the job just as well.

"Astronomy is an impossible science," Sandage said to Overbye. "It's a wonder we know anything at all."

CHAPTER THIRTY-TWO

THE MYSTERY OF CONSCIOUSNESS

Time's arrow points only one way. Events leave traces of an unalterable past, not just in the outside world, but also stamped like moon craters on the gray terrain inside our skulls. Without memories we would be more like pebbles than potatoes. How does the brain do it? By what magic does it store memories that can be called up at will? This is the dark question that George Johnson bravely tackles in *In the Palaces of Memory: How We Build the Worlds Inside Our Heads* (Knopf, 1990).

An editor of the *New York Times*'s "Week in Review," Johnson rightly sees this as the most profound of all science questions. His previous book, *Machinery of the Mind*, surveyed the efforts of artificial intelligence (AI) workers to imitate thinking with digital computers. His new book cuts a wider swath. It concerns not just AI, but decades of research on actual brains.

Although many neuroscientists play colorful roles in Johnson's opening section, it centers on the controversial conjectures of Gary Lynch, now at the University of California, Irvine. There are many conflicting theories, but most of Lynch's colleagues agree with him that memory is stored by chemical changes in neurons. Neurons are the little gray cells of the brain. Billions of them, each containing thousands of different proteins and enzymes, are linked together by their nerve fibers called *axons* (that transmit signals) and *dendrites* (that receive) in an inconceivably complex network. A given neuron may be connected to a thousand others. Electrical pulses from sensory organs constantly invade this network, zipping silently through its fibers to be ferried by neurotransmitters across tiny gaps called *synapses.*

Neuroscientists divide into two rival schools. The *presynaptics* think memories are stored mainly in those neurons that send signals across the synapses. *Postsynaptics* think they are stored mainly in the neurons that receive signals. We see the face of a friend. Electrical pulses from our retinas travel to the brain, where they reactivate circuits in a cluster of neurons that may spread throughout the entire brain. The cluster lights up, so to

This review first appeared in *Book World* (February 17, 1991). © 1996, Washington Post Book World Service/Washington Post Writers Group. Reprinted with permission.

speak, and we recognize the face. Ideas are similarly stored. A universal such as cowness is simply a circuit that holds thousands of overlapping memories of cows, a kind of average picture of all the cows we have known.

About thirty-five years ago there was a flurry of interest in trying to simulate thinking with intricate networks of neuronlike wires and switches called *neural nets*. By a massive use of parallel processing, these nets could learn from experience. Marvin Minsky, MIT's famous AI pioneer, collaborated with an associate on a notorious book, *Perceptrons*, that almost killed neural-net research by contending it was a blind alley. Thanks to improved technology, neural nets are now the most fashionable AI field of study. This is the topic of Johnson's second section, which focuses on the work of physicist Leon Cooper, at Brown University.

Neural nets have learned how to recognize signatures and objects on assembly lines, and even how to balance a broom on its handle. Minsky now regards his attack on them as "overkill," and is pleading for a merger of neural-net theory with his own approach, which relies on conventional computers that twiddle symbols.

Johnson's third section stars the Canadian philosopher Patricia Smith Churchland, now at the University of California, La Jolla, and author of *Neurophilosophy*, a recent MIT textbook. For decades she has been trying to make sense of both AI and neurobiology. Essentially a pragmatist, she sees the universe as a vast mindless tinkerer which, by the bumbling process of evolution, has created brains that resemble Rube Goldberg contraptions. She has the curious notion, common to most pragmatists, that truth is less a correspondence of ideas with structures "out there" independent of minds, than the brain's efforts to order its experience in useful ways. Sentient beings on other planets, she believes, may have minds so different from ours, with such exotic physics and mathematics, that we would find their science unintelligible. If an alien in another galaxy counted stars, could it find that two stars plus two stars did not make four stars? Could an alien particle physicist conclude that a hydrogen atom has more than one electron—maybe none at all? Are atoms really out there, or are they just figments of our minds?

Johnson's philosophical musings have little to say about any of the deepest problems. In particular he never comes to grips with self-awareness and free will, actually two names for the same mystery. Try to imagine being aware of your existence without free will, or to imagine yourself with free will but no consciousness. You'll find both impossible. How is it that an infinitesimal portion of the universe, a tiny pattern of molecules, is capable of wondering why the universe exists, and of planning ways to alter its future? A year spent in AI research, so goes an old aphorism, is enough to make one believe in God.

John Searle, a shrewd opponent of AI metaphysics, is dismissed in two lines. Unfortunately, Johnson wrote before the appearance of Roger Penrose's *The Emperor's New Mind*, which argues that we will never understand the brain until we know more about physics, and especially know more about laws below quantum theory.

Aside from six poetic pages of memories about two of Johnson's trips to New Mexico, his book closes with an admission by Churchland that her subjective view of truth—that rain in Spain falls mainly in the brain—is one that "usually sends people absolutely crawling up the walls. But I really don't see why. If the only alternative is that there are truths in Plato's heaven, then it seems to me that the basic story has to be told in terms of the brain."

I am among those Platonists who are indeed driven up a wall by this view. Some readers will close Johnson's book by marveling at how much about the brain has been discovered in recent years. I close the book overwhelmed by how little has been learned. It will be centuries, I am persuaded, before science fully understands the mind of a mouse.

ADDENDUM

George Johnson, understandably, did not care for my review. His letter to *Book World* and my reply ran in the April 14, 1991, issue.

> As a long-time admirer of *Book World*, I was delighted that the editors decided to feature my new book, *In the Palaces of Memory*, so prominently on the cover. I'd like to suggest, however, that assigning a book about the frontiers of brain research to Martin Gardner is a little like assigning a book on genetic engineering to someone who still believes in the ancient doctrine of vitalism. It seems ironic that Gardner, who has spent so much of his life debunking pseudoscience, has come to embrace the mystical notions of mind and consciousness that neuroscientists are trying so hard to expel.
>
> George Johnson, New York, N.Y.

Martin Gardner Replies

> My view of the brain is no more mystical than Richard Feynman's view of quantum mechanics, which he repeatedly called "crazy" and said that no one knows why it works. I believe with Aristotle and almost all modern psychologists and philosophers of science that the mind is a function of a material brain that evolved slowly from lifeless matter. I have no interest in Bergson or any other vitalist.

The trouble is, no one fully understands matter. The particles and their fields are crazy. I agree with Roger Penrose (see my foreword to his book *The Emperor's New Mind*) that free will and consciousness cannot be explained by known laws of physics or simulated by any known type of computer. Johnson is oversensitive. It is not denigrating of neuroscience to call it a science in its infancy.

CHAPTER THIRTY-THREE

IS THERE A GOD?

If *God* is the name for everything there is, then, of course, everyone is a theist. Between this meaningless pantheism and the traditional creator-gods of the major religions stretches a continuum of shades. Here we will assume, with Michael Martin, that God is an invisible transcendent super-being somehow analogous to the human mind, who created our universe and provides a purpose for its history.

Thousands of philosophers—from the ancient Greeks to modern thinkers—have defended atheism, but none more comprehensively than Martin, a professor of philosophy at Boston University. His lengthy arguments, detailed and incisive, are sharpened by modern developments in logic and inductive reasoning and by special attention to contemporary thinkers whose subtle writings are unknown to the general public. In the first half of *Atheism: A Philosophical Justification* (Temple University Press, 1990), Martin argues for "negative atheism"—the view that there are no reliable reasons for believing in God. In the second half, he defends "positive atheism"—the view that there are strong grounds for believing that God does not exist.

The book's first half contains vigorous critiques of the great traditional "proofs" of God. Anselm's ontological argument—especially as revived by Charles Hartshorne, Norman Malcolm, Alvin Plantinga, and Carl Kordig—is so flawed that Martin is amazed it still fascinates certain types of minds. He agrees with Schopenhauer that it is no more than a "charming joke." The cosmological argument and its close cousin, the proof from design, are ripped to shreds. Martin's objections are essentially the same as Kant's but have the added interest of examining closely the sophisticated views of such modern philosophers as William Craig, Bruce Reichenbach, Richard Swinburne, George Schlesinger, and Richard Taylor.

Although I agree with Martin's criticisms, it seems to me he underplays the enormous emotional appeal of the design argument. In the light

This review first appeared in the *Humanist* (March/April 1991).

of today's cosmology, we must assume that you and I were embedded in the quantum laws that generated and controlled the big bang. Particles produced in the first few minutes had the incredible potential of forming, billions of years later, organisms capable of reflecting on the meaning of their lives. Wondering why we exist, or why anything at all exists, can arouse in some persons such an overwhelming sense of awe that William James once called it a "metaphysical sickness." Although logically flawed, the design argument can have a powerful emotional impact that Martin seems never to have experienced.

Pragmatic arguments for God based upon feelings and experience come next under Martin's sharp hatchet. Kant's moral argument, especially as given by W. R. Sorely, John Henry Newman, and A. E. Taylor— that belief in God follows from the assumption that the universe is just— is found seriously defective. After all, Martin reminds us, the law of Karma allows for the righting of wrongs in future lives without requiring a deity to enforce it.

William James defended the right to make a leap of faith under certain circumstances, which Martin expertly summarizes. He rightly perceives that James's fideism is a broad form of "Pascal's wager," in which the benefits of faith are said to outweigh its disadvantages. Kierkegaard's version of the leap, tied as it is to Christian orthodoxy, can only lead to fanaticism, in Martin's view; indeed, Kierkegaard wrote an entire book justifying Abraham's willingness to murder his son because his faith assured him that God had commanded it. I was disappointed that Martin had nothing to say about the greatest of all recent fideists, Miguel de Unamuno. Kierkegaard thought the leap justified even though unsupported by evidence. Unamuno went further: he maintained that the leap is justified in spite of *better* evidence against it!

Wittgensteinian fideism, which treats religions as "language games" that are neither true nor false, is demolished next, along with the even more bizarre view of Louis Pojman—that atheists are justified in *hoping* God exists and living "as if" he or she does.

The second half of Martin's book banishes agnostic fence-sitting by reasoning intended to show that God's existence is extremely improbable. Here the most persuasive arguments spring from the ancient recognition that irrational evil is difficult to square with the existence of an all-powerful, all-good deity. Augustine reasoned that evil behavior is an inevitable consequence of free will—of our not being automatons. Natural evils (diseases, earthquakes, and the like) have been rationalized on the similar ground that we could not exist except in a universe of unalterable laws; given such laws, natural disasters are as inevitable as human sin. Individuals advance by overcoming sin, and humanity advances by the steady conquest of natural evils. No one in recent times has defended these views more skillfully than John Hick, and for this reason it is on Hick that Martin concentrates his fire. He grants that such arguments have some merit but insists that the evils are far too excessive to permit harmonizing them with a beneficent deity.

Only a few pages are devoted to the "finite god" of the process theologians. I was sorry to see Martin limit his attention to a recent bestseller, Rabbi Harold Kushner's *Why Bad Things Happen to Good People.* John Stuart Mill and Edgar Brightman, both finite theists, are cited in a footnote, but it would have been appropriate to recognize also the similar views of Alfred North Whitehead, Hartshorne, Samuel Alexander, and Charles Peirce. There is no reference in the book to Peirce, although he was one of our nation's most interesting theists.

The final chapter speculates tentatively on what Martin thinks would be the long-run social benefits if atheism became the dominant belief. He foresees no falling off of "moral" behavior. There would be a decline in church attendance. Theistic folkways such as the phrase "In God We Trust" on our currency, holidays like Easter and Christmas, prayers in public schools and at inaugurals, and blue laws would all fade. Televangelism, religious bookstores, and Gideon Bibles would disappear. People would stop saying "God bless you." There would be more liberal laws concerning birth control, abortion, divorce, and homosexuality. Birth rates would decline. There would be fewer wars.

Because Martin supports a clear separation of church and state and tolerance for all religious opinions, he has no sympathy for the police-state atheism that prevailed in the Soviet Union. Writing before glasnost, he buys the surely low estimate that only 10 percent of Soviet citizens believe in God. We now know that the Soviet people all along had little use for communism but were afraid to say so. I suspect they kept their religious convictions concealed for similar reasons.

Martin's book contains a few factual mistakes. On page 3, he includes Voltaire, a deist, and Upton Sinclair, a spiritualist, among nonbelievers in God. On page 178, where he describes Hinduism as a pantheism, he misses the belief that Brahman is as "wholly other" as the God of Karl Barth. But these are trivial blemishes on an admirable work. Atheists should read it to bolster their creed, and theists should read it to test their faith against the deadly force of Martin's attack.

CHAPTER THIRTY-FOUR
THE WORLD OF
STEPHEN JAY GOULD

Stephen Jay Gould may be a paleontologist by trade, on Harvard's faculty since 1967, but his knowledge of the liberal arts, especially literature and music, not to mention his familiarity with that elegantly choreographed dance called baseball, far exceeds the knowledge of science on the part of most experts in the humanities. No living scientist who writes for the public has a better claim to the mantle of Thomas Huxley in range of interests and felicity of style.

Bully for Brontosaurus (Norton, 1991) is the fifth and finest selection from the columns that Gould has contributed to *Natural History* magazine since 1973. There is not a lame essay in the lot. Obviously no short review can do justice to all thirty-five.

The title essay is about the unsuccessful efforts of paleontologists to change the name of Brontosaurus (which means thunder lizard) to Apatosaurus (deceptive lizard). Gould sides with the Brontosaurians. In other chapters you will learn about a frog whose tadpoles grow in the mother's belly to be disgorged later through her mouth; the gigantic kiwi egg; the beheading of the great French chemist Antoine Lavoisier; racism in the textbook from which John Scopes, of Tennessee's famous "Monkey Trial," taught evolution; little-known facts behind Huxley's debate with Bishop Samuel Wilberforce; and Freud's crazy effort to persuade women to shift from clitoral to vaginal orgasms.

Other essays concern the typewriter's inefficient QUERTY-keyboard, with an aside on pangrams, short sentences containing all twenty-six letters; the probability that Joe DiMaggio would make a hit in fifty-six consecutive games; Huxley's bitter clash with Gladstone over how to interpret Genesis; the anatomy and behavior of that most bizarre of all mammals, the duck-billed platypus; Prince Kropotkin as a pioneer stressing the survival value of animal altruism; why the family tree of the horse is a bush, not a ladder; and how lazy textbook authors keep copying from one another in describing eohippus, the earliest horse ancestor, as the size of a fox terrier.

This review first appeared in *Book World* (May 19, 1991). © 1996, Washington Post Book World Service/Washington Post Writers Group. Reprinted with permission.

Gould does not consider *debunking* a pejorative term for a scientist's obligation to enlighten the public about extreme pseudoscience. An entertaining chapter on Mesmer tells how Lavoisier devised foxy "sting" operations, conducted in Benjamin Franklin's French home, that thoroughly debunked Mesmer's claim that a magnetic fluid went from a mesmerist's fingers into the bodies of persons mesmerized.

A chapter on the Baseball Museum at Cooperstown debunks the absurd myth that baseball was invented there by Abner Doubleday who, as someone said, didn't know a baseball from a kumquat. The game actually evolved from British ball-and-stick games. In a barn behind Cooperstown's Farmer's Museum you can see P. T. Barnum's great fossil hoax, the Cardiff Giant. Gould gives an amusing account of its history.

A fascinating essay opens with Gould visiting Mount Rushmore and wondering why Teddy Roosevelt is up there with the others. Gould changed his mind when he discovered that Teddy had written a witty book to debunk the views of Abbot Thayer, an artist-naturalist who tirelessly promoted his theory that all animal coloring is an adaptation to render animals less visible to predators. Thayer actually painted pictures (some are reproduced in the book, alas only in black and white) to prove that flamingos are red because it makes them almost invisible against pink sunsets! Another painting shows how hard it is to see a peacock against a backdrop of flowers!

A chapter that should be read by all creationists deals with one of their perennial arguments against evolution. How can a structure such as a wing, which supposedly evolved by small increments, have survival value until it is fully formed and flapping? Gould focuses on the evolution of insect wings, describing ingenious experiments that suggest the wings started out as tiny temperature regulators, then slowly enlarged until they became useful for gliding and flying.

The "incipient stages" argument was first advanced, Gould informs us, by George Mivart, a student of Huxley who was excommunicated by the Roman Catholic church for trying to convince it that if it failed to accept evolution it would be repeating the mistake it made with Galileo. A devout theist, Mivart contended that new species, especially homo sapiens with immortal souls, could not arise unless evolution was somehow orchestrated from above.

Although most theists today, who see evolution as God's method of creation, no longer invoke the incipient stages argument, they like to dwell on the improbabilities that seem to dog the history of life, and to see those improbabilities as evidence for divine direction. Gould strongly rejects this view. He quotes a long-forgotten letter of William James to a geologist in which James crisply rebuts such reasoning even though

James was himself a theist. In another chapter, Gould tells of a surprise phone call from President Jimmy Carter to express sympathy when he learned of Gould's abdominal cancer. Gould prints a portion of a letter in which Carter contends that the improbabilities of evolution are too immense to be accounted for apart from a divine plan.

Gould devotes one chapter to his cancer, the statistics surrounding it, and its happy remission. He is amused when his death is announced at a meeting in Scotland, not so amused when two European periodicals do the same thing. Lacking Mark Twain's willingness to shrug off such mistakes, Gould admits that he "squawked very loudly."

One of Gould's persistent themes is that we can learn from nature absolutely nothing about morals, that we are but a "tiny and accidental evolutionary twig," a mere "mammalian afterthought," in a universe that gives not a damn about the fate of individuals or even the human race. "When my skein runs out," he writes, "I hope to face the end calmly. . . . For most situations, however, I prefer the more martial view that death is the ultimate enemy—and I find nothing reproachable in those who rage against the dying of the light."

CHAPTER THIRTY-FIVE

INCREDIBLE RAMANUJAN

On the eve of World War I, Srinivas Ramanujan appeared like a sorcerer who had stepped out of a mist. In 1913, G. H. Hardy, the renowned Cambridge University mathematician, received a humble ten-page letter that began, "I beg to introduce myself." It was from a twenty-three-year-old clerk in India who said he was poor and uneducated, but nonetheless had made some amazing discoveries in number theory. He enclosed a small sample of his work.

Ramanujan's theorems were unlike any Hardy had seen before. At first he dismissed the writer as a crank. Later when he and his colleague J. E. Littlewood examined the bizarre equations more carefully, he realized they could have been found only by a mathematician of the highest rank. An exchange of letters began and more theorems followed. Working alone, with no knowledge of recent mathematics, Ramanujan had rediscovered some old but deep theorems, had made a few mistakes in others, but for the most part had presented something that was profoundly original and strange. Ramanujan tossed them off by the thousands, jotting them down in notebooks without ever troubling to prove them because somehow he knew they were true. It was decades before Western mathematicians realized how sound his intuitions were.

Hardy brought Ramanujan to Cambridge in 1914. Ramanujan's teenage wife, Srimathi Janaki—the marriage had been family arranged when she was nine—stayed behind in India. For five years Hardy and Ramanujan enthusiastically collaborated in proving and elaborating the theorems that kept floating into Ramanujan's head by some magic process no one yet fully understands. For mathematically literate readers Robert Kanigel, in *The Man Who Knew Infinity* (Scribner's, 1991), gives a lucid account of the most famous of these equations, a formula that expresses the precise number of partitions of a given integer. It has turned out to have many practical applications, including a surprising one in the currently fashionable particle theory called superstrings. Another beauti-

---

This review first appeared in the Raleigh, N.C., *News and Observer*, June 2, 1991.

ful formula is now the basis for the fastest known computer algorithm for calculating the number pi.

Mr. Kanigel, a science writer who teaches journalism at Johns Hopkins University, has written one of the finest, best-documented biographies ever published about a modern mathematician. Even if you hate mathematics you will find yourself captivated by this brilliant study of one of the most remarkable and enigmatic minds of the century.

Ramanujan was brought up in an orthodox Hindu family of Brahmin caste, and Mr. Kanigel argues that Hardy failed to appreciate his friend's religious beliefs. Ramanujan never abandoned his strict vegetarianism or his devout faith in the gods. Throughout his life he prayed to Namagiri, his family's favorite goddess, and believed that it was she who inspired his work. Namagiri, Mr. Kanigel tells us, is the consort of the lion-god Narasimha. Ramanujan never forgot that his grandmother, who conversed with Namagiri during trances, told him that the goddess said she would someday speak through him to the world. Ramanujan practiced astrology, believed in palmistry, and was intrigued by the spiritualist views of the British physicist Oliver Lodge.

Robert Kanigel is convinced that Ramanujan, out of deference to the atheism of his benefactor, played down his mystical side, misleading Hardy into supposing he practiced his religion only mechanically. Indeed, Hardy once called him "as sound an infidel as Bertrand Russell or Littlewood."

So fervent was Hardy's atheism that once on a whimsical list of New Year's resolutions he included, "Find an argument for the nonexistence of God which shall convince the general public." Mr. Kanigel makes clear that in spite of this gulf between Eastern faith and Western nonfaith, the two friends shared a profound Platonism—a belief in a transcendent realm of mathematical truth independent of human minds.

For many modern Platonists, mathematics is the "only" reality. Newton's hard little pebbles of matter long ago dissolved into fields and particles that are pure mathematical constructs, not made of anything. "I believe that mathematical reality lies outside us," was how Hardy put it. "Our function is to discover or observe it." Mr. Kanigel quotes Ramanujan: "An equation has no meaning unless it expresses a thought of God."

Every positive integer, said Littlewood, was "one of Ramanujan's personal friends." Hardy told a now famous story of visiting Ramanujan in the hospital. He happened to take a cab whose number was 1729, and he remarked to Ramanujan that it seemed to him a dull number. The ailing Ramanujan shot to life. "No!" he said, "It is a very interesting number. It is the smallest number expressible as a sum of two cubes in two different ways" ($1,729 = 1^3 + 12^3 = 9^3 + 10^3$).

The portrait Mr. Kanigel draws is of two quite different but very close friends. Ramanujan was of medium height, plump, with a pock-marked face and dark luminous eyes. Hardy was small, wiry, handsome, athletic, and passionately devoted to cricket. Among many eccentricities, Hardy never shook hands, and was so averse to seeing his face in mirrors that he covered them with cloth even while shaving. I did not know until I read this book that Hardy was gay. "A nonpracticing homosexual" was how Littlewood described him.

Nor did I know that both Ramanujan and Hardy had attempted suicide. In 1917 Ramanujan developed a mysterious illness, perhaps tuberculosis. It contributed to a deep depression during which he impulsively jumped in front of a London subway train. The engineer braked just in time. Ramanujan died three years later in India at age thirty-two.

Hardy, depressed early in 1947 after a heart attack, overdosed on barbiturates, but took so many that he vomited, fell, and merely banged his head on the sink. He died of heart failure in December of the same year.

In 1976 George Andrews, a mathematician at Pennsylvania State University, found in the library of Cambridge's Trinity College a batch of 130 scrap papers on which the ill Ramanujan had scribbled some six hundred new equations. Mathematicians are still plucking exotic flowers from what the physicist Freeman Dyson calls Ramanujan's Garden. In 1988, Robert Kanigel tells us, a computer search found three hundred technical papers with Ramanujan's name on their titles.

And his wife, Janaki, now ninety-one, is still living and, though they spent little time together, proud simply of having been married to a man whose mind was like no other in our century. She has been a widow for more than seventy years, which must be a record even in India.

CHAPTER THIRTY-SIX

HOW TO MAKE A PPO

The January 1990 issue of the *Journal of the Society for Psychical Research* (*JSPR*) published an English translation of an article by Bernhard Walti that had earlier appeared in a German periodical devoted to parapsychology. It described an alleged PPO (Permanent Paranormal Object) that had been produced by Silvio Meyer, a Swiss self-styled psychic. The object consists of two square frames, each about an inch on the sides, one made of paper, the other of aluminum foil. The two tiny frames are linked, with no sign that either had been tampered with in any way.

Silvio claimed that he cut a side of the paper frame, slid the foil frame through the slot, then held the cut between his thumb and finger for ten minutes. The cut paranormally healed. As John Beloff correctly perceived, if this had indeed occurred, and no way could be found for making such a PPO, it would be a stupendous milestone in the history of parapsychology.

In my regular column, "Notes of a Fringe Watcher" (*Skeptical Inquirer* 15 [Spring 1991]), I described this seemingly miraculous artifact and asked my readers if they could think of any easy way Silvio could have produced it without access to machinery for making paper or foil. Two readers, first John Geohegan, of Albuquerque, New Mexico, soon followed by a letter from P. M. deLaubenfels, of Corvallis, Oregon, described the same simple method.

It turns out that paper is extremely easy to make from paper, as many hobbyists know. I will describe the procedure for producing the PPO in words used by Geohegan.

First, obtain a piece of window screen, the finer the mesh the better. Cut a slot in one side. Into this slot push a frame of metal foil as shown in figure 1. The next step is to make a mixture of paper fibers and water. Cut a piece of writing paper into half-inch squares, boil them in 1 1/2 cups of water for half an hour, then beat the mixture with a blender or hand mixer until the squares disappear and you are left with a cloudy liquid.

───────────────

This article first appeared in the British *Journal of the Society for Psychical Research* (July 1991).

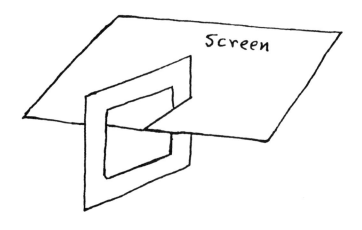

Figure 1

Put the piece of screen, with its inserted foil frame, on a dish towel, then spoon the pulpy mixture onto the screen to form a puddle that surrounds one side of the frame as shown in figure 2. With a spatula, press the mixture flat to force out the water. The purpose of the screen is to let the mixture dry quickly. A sheet of metal or heavy cardboard would do just as well, but the drying time would be much longer. After a few minutes, gently peel the wet paper from the screen and let it dry completely.

All that remains is to cut the square frame from the paper. Any irregularities can be smoothed out by pressing and rubbing with the back of a spoon.

Linking a foil frame with one cut from a dollar bill or a printed page of the *JSPR* would be a much more effective PPO. Geohegan suggests that two such frames be sent to Silvio with a request that he link them. You can be sure he will refuse.

ADDENDUM

John Beloff, England's most gullible parapsychologist and editor of the *JSPR*, has been hoping for decades that a psychic would create a PPO that would convince all skeptics of the reality of PK. He was sorely disappointed to learn how easily Silvio's PPO could be fabricated.

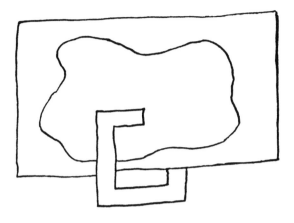

Figure 2

Parapsychologists seldom give up and admit error. Bernhard Walti, in a "Comment on Silvio's PPO," published in a German periodical in November 1991, cites my article as a reference. He concludes: "So far, however, no conventional solution of the Silvio PPO is at hand, despite some efforts by skeptics." Apparently he will doubt the technique I explained until he watches someone actually make such a PPO.

Duane Hill wrote to say that my suggestion about linking a foil frame with a frame cut from a dollar bill is not hard to do by a plating process called "electroforming." I doubt, though, if Silvio can obtain the necessary equipment.

CHAPTER THIRTY-SEVEN
ARCHEOLOGICAL CRANKERY

W e live at a time when science education in English-speaking countries is sinking, and interest in New Age, pseudoscience, and occultism is rapidly rising. Archeology has not been immune to these trends. Worthless books on cult archeology now sell almost as well as books on astrology, harmful diets, and the sex lives of the famous.

"Fantastic" is Stephen Williams's less pejorative synonym for crank. A distinguished anthropologist long associated with Harvard's Peabody Museum, Williams has written an entertaining history of fantastic archeology, richly illustrated, scrupulously documented, and a delight to read. Titled *Fantastic Archeology: The Wild Side of North American History*, the book was published in 1991 by the University of Pennsylvania Press.

Myths about advanced cultures on now submerged continents have fascinated the public ever since Plato wrote about Atlantis. Ignatius Donnelly's book *Atlantis* (1881) aroused widespread interest among gullible Americans. It far outsold his two other crank works, *Ragnarok*, which anticipated Immanuel Velikovsky's crazy cosmology, and a massive work purporting to translate ciphers hidden by Bacon in plays falsely credited to Shakespeare.

The Pacific also had its vanished continent, Lemuria or Mu, as popularized in absurd books by James Churchward. Williams debunks both myths, and traces their persistence in theosophical literature, in the dream delusions of Edgar Cayce, and in such recent potboilers as *Atlantis, the Eighth Continent,* by Charles Berlitz of Bermuda Triangle fame.

The Cardiff Giant was America's most bizarre hoax. George Hull had it fabricated out of gypsum and buried in New York, to be unearthed in 1869. P. T. Barnum tried to lease it. Turned down, Barnum had a copy made, a fake of a fake, which he exhibited as the original. Oliver Wendell Holmes, Sr., we learn, drilled a hole near its ear and marvelled at its interior anatomy. Emerson was enthralled. ("So much," writes Williams, "for Bostonian wisdom.") The original giant wandered here and there, finally

This review first appeared in London's *Times Literary Supplement* (October 18, 1991).

coming to rest in the Farmer's Museum, at Cooperstown, New York. Why did the fake generate so much public excitement? I have two conjectures: it supported the Bible's claim that there were giants in the old days, and viewers were titillated by its enormous petrified penis.

Constantin Rafinesque (1782–1840) is Williams's funniest charlatan. He was enormously prolific, writing books and papers on half a dozen sciences, a 300-page work on Ohio River fish, an autobiography, and a 248-page poem, "Instability." His most outlandish claim was that the Lenape Indians had migrated all the way from the Bering Straits to Delaware—a claim supported by hundreds of pictographs which he drew himself.

The Book of Mormon, with its pseudohistory about how the Ten Lost Tribes of Israel settled in America, does not escape Williams's attention. Joseph Smith claimed that angels wrote the sacred book in hieroglyphics on gold tablets, which Smith translated with the aid of two magic stones called the Urim and Thummim. Mormon archeologists later supported the Lost Tribes fantasy with a profusion of phony artifacts, some showing pictures of Noah's flood and the Tower of Babel.

Another popular myth that won't go away is that eastern America was first explored by Vikings. As Williams discloses, recent excavations in Newfoundland show that Vikings did indeed land on the continent about 1000 C.E., but never got farther south. In 1942, Philip Means's book *Newport Tower* argued that a stone tower in Newport, Rhode Island, had been built by Vikings in the twelfth century. Alas, excavations soon proved the tower to be a seventeenth-century structure.

Other preposterous myths about pre-Columbus settlers in America are defended in dozens of crank books, notably those by a retired Harvard biologist, Barry Fell. Fell is a superdiffusionist who actually believes that hundreds of thousands of years ago America was colonized by all sorts of Europeans, Asians, and Africans, including pygmies who settled in Tennessee. His best-seller, *America, B.C.* (1976), considered a joke by archeologists, was published, incredibly, by the *New York Times*. However, a *Times* reviewer called the book "ignorant nonsense." Williams devotes many pages to Fell's whopping errors. *Saga America* (1980), Fell's second book, was also published by the *New York Times.*

Fantastic Archeology swarms with pictures of bogus artifacts made to support myths of pre-Columbian settlements. Particularly amusing is the story of gravel found near a wharf in Boston. Pseudoarcheologists were agog when it was found that the gravel came from the River Thames. It turned out that it was ballast from ships which sailed empty to Boston, dumped the pebbles, then went back to England with timber.

It is not easy to believe, but two American archeologists, Stephen

Schwartz and Jeffrey Goodman, are now using ESP and pendulum dowsing over maps to locate sites for digs. Schwartz's major work, *The Alexandria Project* (1983), is about his efforts to locate the bones of Alexander the Great. ESP was provided by Hella Hammid, a psychic who earlier worked at Stanford Research International on the notorious "remote viewing" experiments of Harold Puthoff and Russell Targ.

Goodman's claims are even more preposterous. Ancestors of the American Indians, he maintains, did not come east across the Bering land-bridge. They went the other way, en route to France, where they vanquished the Neanderthals. The Garden of Eden was in California, where half a million years ago the first humans appeared. Their minds did not evolve, but arrived suddenly from "outside intervention" by a higher intelligence. From California they spread over the entire world.

"ESP," Goodman declares, "is replacing the spade as archeology's prime tool." He also believes in Atlantis, Lemuria, and crystal power. His first book, *Psychic Archeology*, was published by Putnams in 1976. His latest, *Genesis Mystery* (1983) was published—yes, once again—by the *New York Times*.

One of the most colorful myths about American Indians is that they were preceded by a wholly distinct race called the Mound Builders. Indians were considered too shiftless and ignorant to produce the elaborate artifacts found in the mounds. As usual, the myth was supported by endless streams of false artifacts, some so cleverly made that it took modern technology to prove them fakes. Williams skillfully summarizes the sad history of this myth, and the careers of its now forgotten mountebanks.

What is the true early history of North America? The first documented arrivals, we learn, were the Clovis Hunters, who came over the Bering land-bridge no later than 10,000 B.C.E. Their culture is found throughout the hemisphere. They are often called the Big Game Hunters, because they hunted mammoths and the now extinct bison.

A high mark in later Indian history (about the time of Christ) was the Hopewell culture of Ohio and Illinois. Williams has pictures of their highly developed arts and crafts, including panpipes with silver-plated mouthpieces, objects of copper, silver, and gold, and figures of persons and animals that look as if they were made yesterday. "Forget fantastic archeology," Williams concludes his admirable book, "this is the real fantasy."

CHAPTER THIRTY-EIGHT
JOSEPH CAMPBELL, "RACIST"

Although New Agers embraced Joseph John Campbell decades ago, it was not until after his death in 1987 that Bill Moyers's six television interviews turned him into a public superstar. His books on comparative mythology weigh down the New Age shelves at Walden and B. Dalton. Critical studies of his work are burgeoning, and now two ardent acolytes have produced a massive hagiography titled *A Fire in the Mind* (Doubleday, 1991).

The authors, Stephen and Robin Larsen, operate a growth potential institute on their farm near New Paltz, New York. Stephen, who teaches psychology at nearby Ulster County Community College, has written two previous books about myths, and Robin has edited a biography and anthology of the Swedish spiritualist and trance channeler Emmanuel Swedenborg. Stephen is also a student of Zen, Yoga, and karate, and has a private practice as a psychotherapist. Drawing heavily on Campbell's voluminous diaries and journals, and interviews with his wife and friends, the Larsens have written a comprehensive life of their mentor that will tell you almost everything you want to know,

Six feet tall, handsome, blue-eyed, Campbell played guard on the Dartmouth football team and captained the track team at Columbia, where he obtained his master's degree. A jazz buff, he played the piano and ukulele, and blew saxophone in dance bands. After several passionate romances, failed efforts to sell fiction (his early stories and one novel have not survived), and much wandering about the globe, Campbell settled down at Sarah Lawrence College in Bronxville, New York, where he taught literature for thirty-eight years. Most of his students idolized him. When he married one—Jean Erdman, who became a professional dancer—the women lowered the campus flag to half-mast.

Campbell burst onto the literary scene in 1944 with his *Skeleton Key to Finnegans Wake*, written with his friend Henry Morton Robinson. While working on the key, he and Robinson became inexplicably infuri-

This review first appeared in *Book World* (November 24, 1991). © 1996, Washington Post Book World Service/Washington Post Writers Group. Reprinted with permission.

ated by the extent to which Thornton Wilder had borrowed from *Finnegans Wake* in his play "The Skin of Our Teeth." In two *Saturday Review* articles they lashed Wilder for shameless plagiarism.

The Larsens give the impression that this vicious attack was justified, without mentioning that Joyce himself, in *Ulysses*, borrowed shamelessly from Homer. Like so many other authors, Wilder had playfully taken characters and episodes from an admired writer, as any student of *Finnegans Wake* would recognize, but Wilder's discreet silence only fanned the flames. Because of the plagiarism charge his play was passed over for the annual New York Critics' award, but it won Wilder his third Pulitzer Prize.

Campbell's most popular book, *The Hero With a Thousand Faces*, came out five years later. His magnum opus, the four-volume *Masks of God*, followed between 1959 and 1968. These and his other books, with their wide-ranging erudition and striking art, put Campbell alongside Mircea Eliade as the most admired experts on myth since Sir James Frazer, author of *The Golden Bough*.

Although their book is crammed with facts and quotations, the Larsens offer little insight into what Campbell privately believed. That he totally rejected the Roman Catholicism of his youth there is no doubt, but did he substitute any religious faith in its place? His favorite definition of mythology was "other people's religion," and his favorite definition of religion was "misunderstood mythology." He saw the great myths as Jungian archetypes, welling up from humanity's collective unconscious—lies on the outside, truth inside. What sort of truth? Myths obviously have poetic meaning, but do they suggest any truths beyond poetry?

It is said that Campbell made no value judgments about the superiority of one religion's myths over those of another. Not so. The Larsens quote a journal entry when Campbell was fifty-one: "Krishna is a much better teacher and model than Christ." In a lecture he poked fun at Mary's assumption into heaven by pointing out that had she traveled at the speed of light she would still be inside our galaxy.

Campbell's long flirtation with Hinduism is amply documented by the Larsens. He was a good friend and admirer of the theosophist Jeddu Krishnamurti. He was as fascinated as Shirley MacLaine by *kundalani*, the energy that slithers up and down the spine like a snake and concentrates inside the body's chakras. He walked on fire without damaging his feet. He was what the Larsens call "shell shocked" by the accuracy of a horoscope cast for him by the famous Evangeline Adams. He was a popular lecturer at Esalen, the pioneer New Age growth center where everybody believes almost anything on the paranormal scene. He taught New Age seminars, sharing platforms with such spiritualists as Elisabeth Kübler-Ross.

Campbell's often-repeated advice, "follow your bliss," is equivalent to the New Age "do your own thing," or "create your own reality." (How about a person, critics asked, whose bliss is to rape little children?) Yet in spite of his close associations with theosophists and New Agers, Campbell's basic metaphysical convictions remain hidden. When Bill Moyers asked if he believed in reincarnation, Campbell sidestepped by saying he believed in the metaphor of reincarnation. It is this mushiness that turns so many people off. We don't need myths to remind us that life is a quest, or that we battle dragons.

There is nothing "spiritual" about mythology unless it points toward transcendence. As far as we can learn from *A Fire in the Mind*, Campbell's mythic fires point to nothing beyond experience. It is surprising that he seems not to have admired George Santayana, the ex-Catholic myth-admiring atheist of whom it was said that he didn't believe in God, but he did believe that Mary was God's mother.

Campbell's darkest side was his anti-Semitism, forcefully detailed by Brendan Gill in the *New York Review of Books* (September 28, 1989). The Larsens dismiss it with a brief reference to "so-called bigotry." Campbell once said he moved to Bronxville to escape from Jews, and that the moon would be a good place to send them. He also objected to blacks entering Sarah Lawrence. He threatened to flunk, and once did, any student who engaged in leftist political action.

Similarly, Campbell's hatred of President Roosevelt prompted him to say there were three living Caesars: Hitler, Mussolini, and FDR. A great admirer of Thomas Mann, Campbell foolishly sent him a copy of a speech in which he urged artists and writers not to take sides in the unfortunate conflict between Hitler and Churchill. It drew a barbed response from Mann. Campbell's political opinions, wrote Gill, were to the right of William Buckley. "His glibness and his charisma," one of his students said in a letter to the *New York Review of Books*, "were a mask that concealed a narrow mind."

The Larsens have done a commendable job of assembling a thousand facts about the life of their hero with many faces. A balanced portrait of Campbell, covering his prejudices and inner beliefs, is still to come.

ADDENDUM

Book World published the following two letters, with my reply, in its December 29, 1991, issue:

While we appreciate your review of our book, *A Fire in the Mind: The Life of Joseph Campbell*, we feel there are certain factual inaccuracies and adverse assumptions in Martin Gardner's review. It is not difficult to discern that Gardner began—and concluded—his article with an animus that is not only anti-Campbell, but everything "New Age." But Campbell himself was hardly a "New-Age person." He was a scholar whose sources were primarily drawn from archaeology, psychology, philosophy, comparative religion, literature, and the arts.

Gardner attempts to document his belief that there must have been a sinister side to Campbell, taking as his own dark gospel the *New York Review of Books* article by Brendan Gill attacking Campbell and accusing him of anti-Semitism. We feel that Gill's article was constructed on willful misunderstanding, innuendo, and hearsay, and could easily have triggered a libel suit had Campbell been alive to defend himself.

There are inherent dangers in such journalistic gossip. For example, Gardner quotes Campbell as saying that he "moved to Bronxville to escape from Jews." But Campbell never moved to Bronxville because he never lived there (but he did teach at Sarah Lawrence in Bronxville for thirty-eight years, commuting from his Greenwich Village apartment).

The sad fact that Gardner could not have read our biography closely is illustrated by his accusation that "although the book is crammed with facts and quotations, the Larsens offer little insight into what Campbell privately believed." We were worried that our book was too full of verbatim citations from Campbell's private journals and correspondence.

We owe thanks to Gardner for the kind things he said about the research that underlies our work. We ourselves will be as pleased as Gardner to see that "balanced portrait of Campbell covering his prejudices and inner beliefs, still to come," because we firmly believe that if the biographer is fair-minded, he or she, too, will find under this man's personal rug not dirt, but gold.

Stephen and Robin Larsen, New Paltz, N.Y.

Martin Gardner's review of *A Fire in the Mind: The Life of Joseph Campbell*, by Stephen and Robin Larsen, was nothing short of a McCarthyistic attack on one of the greatest men of our time. Gardner begins by accusing Joseph Campbell of "inexplicably" attacking Thornton Wilder (fifty years ago) for outrageous plagiarism discovered in Wilder's play "The Skin of Our Teeth." While Gardner admits the truth of Campbell's claim that Wilder indeed plagiarized Joyce, his insinuation that Campbell was morally obligated to disclose other instances of purported plagiarism by other authors is utterly absurd.

Gardner also brings into question Campbell's religious life by faulting him for abandoning the "church" practices of Roman Catholicism. But Campbell's departure from the Catholic church was not an abandonment of the essential principles of Christianity, but a departure from the dogmatic doctrines that trouble many Catholics.

Lastly, Gardner's desire for sensationalism should earn him a job at the *National Enquirer*—for to insinuate that Campbell was a racist and anti-Semite is preposterous. A single thread does not make a suit and a statement or a line taken out of context does not validate a claim. Neither Campbell himself, nor his family and friends, ever claimed he was a saint—as he might have said, not to have sinned is not to have lived. And live he did—with an integrity achieved by few men of this century.

Terry Peay, Rockville

Martin Gardner Replies

Stephen and Robin Larsen accuse me of animus toward the New Age. They are right. "New Age" is a fuzzy catch-all term for a cluster of diverse ideas. The reason Campbell's books are so enthusiastically embraced by New Agers is mainly because of his lifelong friendship with Krishnamurti, his preference for Hinduism over Christianity, and his emphasis on creating your own reality.

There can be no doubt about Campbell's racism. A more detailed reference on this than Brendan Gill's attack is "Moyers's Myth-Deeds," by Sharon Churcher, in *Penthouse* magazine (April 1990). Gill's article provoked a controversy that impelled Roy Finch, for two decades a philosopher at Sarah Lawrence, to tell the *New York Times* that Campbell was convinced Western civilization was threatened by the decadence of "Christians, Communists, liberals, and Jews." When Campbell said in a lecture that it was natural for people to prey on "lower species of humans," a woman recalled: "I rose shaking from my chair and shouted, 'What about the six million who were gassed during World War II? . . . Mr. Campbell simply shrugged and said, 'That's your problem.'"

Churcher quotes a Sarah Lawrence alumna who told the *Village Voice* that when she informed Campbell she was Jewish and wanted to analyze the Old Testament, "he began to spew out this garbage about how the college was going Jewish and how he had moved to Bronxville to get away from the Jews." Perhaps he meant he had moved the locale of his teaching to Bronxville.

Of course I never said Campbell had no beliefs. Obviously he had thousands, including his beliefs in the inferiority of blacks, Jews, Christians, and liberal Democrats. The question I raised was about his deepest private beliefs. Did he share Krishnamurti's faith in reincarnation? Was he a theist, atheist, pantheist, or agnostic? You won't find the answers in the Larsens' hagiography.

As for Terry Peay, I urge him to calm down and read some of my supporting sources: Brendan Gill, in the *New York Review of Books* (September 28, 1989), and the letters it generated (November 9); Mary Lefkowitz in *American Scholar* (Summer 1990); John Wauck in the *National Review* (March 18, 1990); Sharon Churcher in *Penthouse* (April 1990) and the articles in the *New York Times* and the *Village Voice* to which she refers; and Mortimer Adler's strong attack on Campbell in *Truth in Religion* (1990) and in his review of *Fire in the Mind* in the *National Review* (February 17, 1992).

For Campbell's mean-spirited attack on Wilder, see Edmund Wilson's defense of Wilder in the *Nation* (January 30, 1943), and the discussion of this ridiculous charge in Malcolm Goldstein's *The Art of Thornton Wilder* (1965). Goldstein put it crisply when he wrote that Campbell was "unable to discriminate between the assimilation of a source and downright theft."

POSTSCRIPT

In addition to the references cited above, readers interested in Campbell's dark side should check Wendy Doniger's hatchet review of *A Fire in the Mind* (*New York Times Book Review*, February 2, 1992). Doniger is the Marcea Eliade professor in the University of Chicago Divinity School. She likens the book to the "authorized biography of a member of the royal family or a Hollywood star," with "banal and trivial events described in a bogus and quasi-spiritual diction." By avoiding any deep analysis of myths, Campbell "cooked up the TV dinner of mythology so that everything tastes the same" when obviously myths are *not* all the same in their meanings. Although Campbell was much admired and loved as the "hippie hero" of a New Age cult, "he was neither a scholar nor a gentleman."

Amy Taubin's article "Hit or Myth" in the *Village Voice* (December 12, 1989) is another valuable source. When Campbell's student Eva Feldman told Campbell she was Jewish, he became extremely agitated. Here is the full account of what Feldman said to Taubin: "He was sweating and pacing and running his fingers through his hair. He began to spew out this garbage, about how the college was going Jewish and how he had moved to Bronxville to get away from the Jews and here they were taking over. Every few sentences he'd break off and repeat 'I know I shouldn't be saying this, I know I shouldn't. . . .' He went down his class roster identifying the students who were Jewish. He said that the Jews had ruined twentieth-century culture and went through a list of Jewish artists." Feldman said that "it was horrifying. It was like watching someone have a fit or having them vomit uncontrollably all over you."

CHAPTER THIRTY-NINE

INFORMATION THEORY
AND THE UNIVERSE

Timothy Ferris's good, clean, poetic prose has raised him to the ranks of our nation's top science writers. The title of this, his seventh book, *The Mind's Sky* (Bantam, 1992), is a play on *The Mind's I*, edited by Douglas Hofstadter and Daniel Dennett, in turn a play on "the mind's eye." The title reflects Ferris's central theme, the interplay of mind and cosmos, or what John Dewey liked to call the interaction of an organism with its environment. Philosophers from the Greeks on have wrestled with this theme, but in recent years, because of the subjective aspect of QM (quantum mechanics), new books on the theme are being written by both philosophers and scientists.

"Each of us inhabits two equally mysterious universes," Ferris's book opens, "one outside the mind and the other within it." His symbol for this is an hourglass. The two bulbs are the two worlds. The flow of sand is the passage of information in both directions through the point where the two realms meet.

As one would expect from such a tall order, a wealth of relevant topics is considered. Ferris accepts the view that mind is a function of a material brain which harbors a variety of different kinds of intelligence. (A chapter is devoted to the intelligence of such great athletes as quarterback Joe Montana.) The author strongly supports the search for ETI (Extraterrestrial Intelligence). A chapter describes the latest work on VR (Virtual Reality), a new computer technique that puts you inside a three-dimensional world where you can walk about and move objects. Ferris gives a dramatic account of how he once tramped around a sim (simulation) of the surface of Mars.

Adopting a now fashionable point of view, Ferris sees information as a fundamental category. (Earlier philosophers called it knowledge.) Anything that can be quantified can be digitalized (as Leibniz recognized) by the "bits" of a binary code. Ferris repeats physicist John Wheeler's latest aphorism, "It from bit," in which "It" does double duty as IT, the acronym

This review first appeared in *Book World* (March 22, 1992). © 1996, Washington Post Book World Service/Washington Post Writers Group. Reprinted with permission.

for Information Theory, and "it" for any particular thing. Ferris is worried about how the growing information of science can be preserved in case humanity vanishes. He envisions a vast interstellar network of records, perhaps stored as VR programs, that the ETI can retrieve. We must, his book concludes, "grow a forest of knowing among the stars."

A chapter is devoted to "enlightenment," the mood in which a person is overwhelmed by a feeling of oneness with the cosmos or with God, and to NDEs (Near-Death Experiences). The late British philosopher A. J. Ayer is quoted on his bizarre NDE, even though afterward he remained an atheist.

Why do we laugh? Ferris rightly calls this "a mystery within the human brain as deep as anything we've found among the stars." As with most writers who struggle with this riddle, the author's jokes are funny but the mystery remains.

Ferris is good on the growing realization that catastrophes are essential to the process of evolution—the comet that may have felled the dinosaurs, for example, and Stephen Gould's "jump theory" of evolution. Such catastrophes suggest to Ferris a Manicheism in which evil is as essential as good, perhaps even destined to triumph. The destruction of the Amazon's rainforests gets another chapter, with excellent advice on what can be done to prevent this catastrophe.

Ferris grows more metaphysical near the end, when he takes up the bewildering paradoxes of QM. He approves of Wheeler's dictum: "No phenomenon is a phenomenon until it is an observed phenomenon." Of course, the observer can be an instrument, such as a bubble chamber or a recording device that "amplifies" quantum phenomena to the macroworld. The catch is that such records are larger quantum systems. According to QM, their wave functions do not "collapse" (do not become "real") until observed by a person. Alas, a person is also a quantum system, not really real until observed by another person, and so on into an awful infinite regress. Can the regress be stopped, as Bishop Berkeley argued, by a God who is not a quantum system and thus can make the entire universe real by observing it?

Ferris's marvelous history of cosmology, *Coming of Age in the Milky Way*, left no doubt that the Milky Way is "out there," not something conjured up by our minds. Nevertheless, he keeps reminding us, there is a sense in which the cosmos, *as we know it*, is a mental fabrication. "I don't mean that the universe doesn't exist," he hastens to add, "but merely that the concept of a 'universe' . . . must necessarily reside in the mind."

True, but isn't this a vacuous tautology? All ideas are in the mind, so this adds up to the great assertion that what is inside a mind is inside a mind. Obviously the universe in anyone's brain is a poor, flawed model of the universe outside—a universe which science only dimly comprehends, and with levels it will never comprehend. The deeper secrets of what Einstein called the Old One remain. In what sense is the mathematical structure of the universe mind independent? Does the moon exist when no one observes it? If not, will a mouse looking at the moon, as Einstein liked to ask, make the moon real?

Why does science, obviously a human endeavor, work so well? Why are simpler hypotheses the best bets? Can a digital computer become so complex that consciousness emerges? Are there moral laws binding on all sentient creatures? Is free will an illusion? Is there a God, and if so, what sort?

It is hard to see how information theory could ever shine a single beam of light into these dark corners.

CHAPTER FORTY
MATHEMATICAL BEAUTY
AND CERTAINTY

Creative mathematicians seldom write for outsiders, but when they do they usually do it well. Jerry King, a professor at Lehigh University, Pennsylvania, is no exception. His informal, nontechnical book *The Art of Mathematics* (Plenum, 1992), as the title implies, is organized around what Bertrand Russell called the "supreme beauty" of mathematics—a beauty "capable of a stern perfection such as only the greatest art can show."

King sharpens C. P. Snow's famous distinction between the two cultures by making it a distinction between an M-culture (those who know mathematics) and an N-culture (those who don't). Widespread ignorance of mathematics, he is convinced, springs mainly from incompetent instructors of the young, often people who actively dislike what they teach. King recalls amusing ways in which he was damaged by such teachers until one fine day, almost by accident, he took a course in which the beauty of calculus struck him like the light that felled Saul on his way to Damascus.

King's tour of his topic begins with the counting numbers, then takes the reader painlessly through their generalizations to the rationals, the reals, through imaginary and complex numbers, and into the wonders of elementary geometry. He is good at conveying the supreme importance of the concept of limit, and how it underlies both branches of calculus. A drawing depicts the differential and integral calculus as two sides of a great arch, each a mirror image of the other, held together by a capstone that is the fundamental theorem of calculus. There is a long chapter on the philosophy of aesthetics, and another on the reluctance of a mathematical aristocracy to reform mathematical teaching.

King has nothing to say about recent developments such as computer science, fractals, chaos theory, or topology with its spinoffs of graph and knot theory. To go into these trends, however, would have defeated his main purpose—to introduce low-level mathematics to readers who have learned to hate the subject.

This review first appeared in *Nature* (July 2, 1992). Reprinted by permission from *Nature* 358, p. 28. Copyright © 1992 Macmillan Magazines Ltd.

King avoids the trap of thinking that the discipline is infected by the uncertainty of science. Pure mathematics, he makes clear, "lives" inside formal systems. Given a system's assumptions, theorems are not only unassailable, they are the only kind of certainty we mortals have. King's answer to Pilate's question is: "Truth is what you find at the end of a correct chain of arguments."

The author quotes Einstein: "The reason why mathematics enjoys special esteem, above all other sciences, is that its laws are absolutely certain and indisputable, while those of all other sciences are to some extent debatable." Two plus two cannot be anything but four, but when one applies this tautology to the world one has to invoke what the philosopher Rudolf Carnap called "correspondence rules." These are assumptions such as that a pebble, a cow, or a star is taken as 1. If such equivalence is not assumed, then $2 + 2 = 4$ is violated by, for example, the fact that two drops of water added to two drops makes one big drop. Nothing could be simpler than this obvious distinction between pure and applied, yet some philosophers and mathematicians, frightened by the word "truth," seem unable to grasp it.

King shares physicist Eugene Wigner's puzzlement over the "unreasonable effectiveness" of mathematics. This puzzlement puzzles me. Not only is the Universe mathematically structured, it is made entirely of mathematics. Matter consists of fields and their particles, which are not made of anything except equations. What is so mysterious about the application of these equations to a Universe from which our minds, in turn made of mathematics, originally extracted them? If mathematical patterns are not discovered, but are entirely human creations like poetry and music, then their powerful effectiveness in science and technology is indeed what Wigner called an undeserved miracle.

King is particularly fond of the poetry of Robert Frost. His poems "stay with you because of their simplicity: you come back to them for their depth. . . . Frost brought poetry to the multitudes; let's now bring them mathematics." The Frosts of mathematics have yet to appear, but King is "certain as sunrise" that they will some day revolutionize mathematical teaching.

The author has a romantic vision of himself as "an aging gunfighter, walking alone the mean streets of academe." His fire is aimed at a conservative elite too self-absorbed in their specialized research to be much concerned about the public's growing mathematical illiteracy. The dull "cinder-block textbooks" get "clunkier." Although their diagrams are splattered with color, somehow the splendor of ideas behind the diagrams remains as invisible as the textbook authors. Meanwhile the M- and N-cultures "fly apart like galaxies on opposite sides of an expanding universe."

CHAPTER FORTY-ONE
MORE SPECULATIONS
OF FREEMAN DYSON

Freeman Dyson, leading wise man at Princeton's Institute for Advanced Study, is always worth listening to, whether you are a physicist reading one of his technical papers or a layman reading one of his popular books. *From Eros to Gaia* (Pantheon, 1992), a selection of his writings, opens with a fragment from an unfinished science-fiction novel about a collision between the Moon and the asteroid Eros. Dyson wrote it when he was nine. It is here to prove that he wanted to be a writer long before he decided to become a physicist.

The book ends with a plea to preserve Gaia, James Lovelock's poetic name for Mother Earth, or run the risk of ending the human adventure. Between Eros and Gaia we have the pleasure of learning Dyson's opinions about a wide diversity of topics: ecology, government funding of science, "White Oliphants" (disastrous accelerator projects built by Mark Oliphant), the vicissitudes of space flight, new methods of craft propulsion, strategic bombing, cosmic rays, quantum fields, and much more. There are entertaining sketches of persons Dyson admires: Michael Pupin, Robert Oppenheimer, Richard Feynman, Paul Dirac, Philip Morrison, George Kennan, and Helen Dukas, the faithful keeper of Einstein's papers.

Unlike most of his colleagues, Dyson is a pantheist convinced that the human adventure has a transcendent purpose, albeit one totally beyond our grasp. It is this strong sense of mystery about existence that makes it impossible for Dyson to share the dreary opinion of Stephen Hawking and others that physics is about to discover everything. We see only the shadows in Plato's cave. The more powerful coming telescopes and particle accelerators, Dyson believes, are sure to reveal unexpected horizons. "There is no illusion more dangerous," he writes, "than the belief that the progress of science is predictable."

One of the most surprising aspects of science is the eerie way mathematical structures, discovered with no thought of how they might apply to nature or technology, will suddenly turn out to be enormously useful.

This review first appeared in *Book World* (July 5, 1992). © 1996, Washington Post Book World Service/Washington Post Writers Group. Reprinted with permission.

In a chapter defending unfashionable research by mavericks, Dyson speaks of the recent discovery of a bizarre structure in the class of "sporadic groups." It has been dubbed "the Monster" because it requires fifty-four digits to express its number of elements, and because it describes the symmetry of how hyperspheres can be close-packed in a space of 196,883 dimensions. Smaller sporadic groups have already found applications in designing error-correcting codes, but is there anything in the universe that the Monster models?

"We should always be prepared for surprises," Dyson writes. "I have a sneaking hope, a hope unsupported by any facts or any evidence, that sometime in the twenty-first century physicists will stumble upon the Monster group, built in some unsuspected way into the structure of the universe. This is only a wild speculation. The only argument I can produce in its favor is a theological one. We have strong evidence that the creator of the universe loves symmetry, and if he loves symmetry, what lovelier symmetry could he find than the symmetry of the Monster?"

To me the book's most interesting chapter is about Paul Dirac, England's great architect of quantum mechanics. There are, Dyson tells us, two ways to do physics. The bottom-up style starts with empirical results, then invents laws and theories to explain them. The top-down style pays little attention to experiments. Instead of deducing laws and theories from facts, one starts with a gut feeling about nature, akin to religious faith, then constructs a broad, elegant theory from which laws of nature can be deduced. Like Newton and Einstein, Dirac was a superb top-downer. Dyson quotes from one of Dirac's marvelous lectures:

"We don't really know what the basic equations of physics are, but they have to have great mathematical beauty. . . . Mathematical beauty transcends . . . personal factors. It is the same in all countries and at all periods of time. . . . In fact one can feel so strongly about these things that when an experimental result turns up which is not in agreement with one's beliefs, one may perhaps make the prediction that the experimental result is wrong. . . ."

Exactly this happened to Einstein's relativity, and to several of Dirac's major conjectures. For a while, a flurry of experiments seemed to contradict both scientists, but it soon turned out that the experiments were flawed. Someone once asked Einstein how he would feel if relativity were ever refuted. He replied, only half in jest, that he would feel sorry for the Lord.

One of the great achievements of modern quantum theory has been quantum electrodynamics, developed by Feynman and Julian Schwinger from earlier work by Dirac. Its ability to predict quantum effects is spectacular, but essential to the theory is a sneaky trick called renormalization that gets rid of unwanted infinites. Dyson once asked Dirac for his opinion of this development. "I might have thought that the new ideas were correct," Dirac replied, "if they had not been so ugly." At present, nature seems to prefer ugly renormalization methods, but Dyson wisely adds that quantum electrodynamics is not a closed system. New perspectives may make the ugly tricks superfluous.

The latest example of top-down physics is the theory of superstrings, in which pointlike particles such as electrons and quarks are actually inconceivably tiny closed loops whose vibrations generate the particle's properties. So far, not only does superstring theory lack an empirical basis, defenders cannot even imagine how it could be confirmed. An extreme example of Diracian top-down Platonism, it is supported solely by what Dyson calls its "incomparable beauty."

"We must admire the courage and skill of the superstring fraternity," Dyson comments, "even if we do not share their faith. Perhaps Nature will in the end smile upon their efforts, as she smiled upon Dirac's electron."

CHAPTER FORTY-TWO

RICHARD FEYNMAN, MAGICIAN

There have been two earlier books about the remarkable life of Richard Feynman, but they were little more than anecdotes based on conversations with Feynman and his friends. The stories were amusing because Feynman was, in words that James Gleick takes from physicist Freeman Dyson, "half genius and half buffoon." Not until now have we been given a full account of Feynman's extraordinary career and no less extraordinary personality.

Genius: The Life and Science of Richard Feynman (Pantheon, 1992) is a splendidly written, scrupulously documented biography of one of the most creative and influential of modern physicists. James Gleick, a former *New York Times* reporter still in his thirties, never met Feynman, but he seems to have read every relevant book, every paper and personal letter and to have talked to everyone who ever knew Feynman. It was Gleick's previous book, *Chaos: The Making of a New Science*, that established his reputation as a science writer. Although not a scientist himself, he somehow managed to acquire enough knowledge of modern mathematics and physics to explain chaos theory, and now he provides a readable, accurate account of Feynman's great contributions to quantum mechanics.

Gleick cites the mathematician Mark Kac's useful distinction between two kinds of genius: the ordinary and the magicians. "An ordinary genius is a fellow that you and I would be just as good as, if we were only many times better. There is no mystery as to how his mind works. . . . It is different with the magicians . . . the working of their minds is for all intents and purposes incomprehensible. Even after we understand what they have done, the process by which they have done it is completely dark."

Edison was an ordinary genius. Newton, Einstein, and Feynman were magicians. As a boy, Richard loved to solve mathematical puzzles. As an adult, he saw the universe as a monstrous conglomeration of difficult puz-

---

This review first appeared in the Raleigh, N.C., *News and Observer*, October 25, 1992.

zles—perhaps unified by a single Theory of Everything, perhaps not—to be tackled for the sheer fun of solving. His greatest achievements were cracking problems in quantum electrodynamics, the study of how relativity applies to electromagnetism. For this work he shared the 1965 Nobel prize with Julian Schwinger and Shin'ichiro Tomonaga.

To calculate a particle's path, Feynman devised a bizarre technique called "sum over histories." It assumes that a particle can take any possible path. As he explained it to Freeman Dyson, "The electron does anything it likes. It just goes in any direction at any speed, forward or backward in time, however it likes, and then you add up the amplitudes and it gives you the wave function." In other words, it gives the particle's most probable path.

In this view a photon of light can bounce off a mirror at any possible angle. Because there are billions of photons in a light beam, almost all of them take the most probable path, one that minimizes their time to go from here to there. Billions of electrons are in the beam that scans a television screen. They can hit the screen anywhere, but their most probable paths are toward the pixel (point on the screen) at which the beam is aimed.

Physicists at first thought Feynman's idea of sum over histories crazy, a view Feynman himself never abandoned. In his book *Q.E.D.* (the acronym for Quantum Electrodynamics), you will find him calling it crazy, peculiar, absurd, strange, magical, absolutely ridiculous, and wild and wonderful. "I don't understand it," he confessed. "Nobody does." Indeed, Feynman looked upon all of quantum mechanics as crazy magic.

Another of Feynman's contributions to quantum mechanics was what are now called Feynman graphs—ways of diagramming particle interactions with little zigzag arrows. The graphs are equivalent to algebraic methods, but more efficient to use. In a Feynman graph a positron is an electron moving backward in time. The graphs were not based on a new theory so much as on what Gleick calls a shift in vision, a novel but useful way to describe quantum events.

Feynman's longtime rival, Julian Schwinger, refused to use Feynman graphs. He thought them too ugly. Gleick quotes Murray Gell-Mann, the discoverer of quarks, as saying that he once spent a semester in Schwinger's house. He searched it carefully for traces of Feynman graphs without finding any—but one room, he cryptically added, was locked.

All the familiar anecdotes and legends about Feynman are retold in Gleick's book in colorful detail: his expertise on the bongo drums, his exploits at Los Alamos as a lock picker and safecracker, his thousand-dollar prize (which he paid) for a working motor smaller than a $\frac{1}{64}$-inch cube, his endless practical jokes, his fantastic speed in mental calculation, his classification of 4-F after flippant responses to an army psychiatrist, his co-invention of hexaflexagons—weird paper strips colored and folded into hexagonal forms that change color when flexed.

Feynman's one great romance was with his first wife, Arline Greenbaum. Because she had tuberculosis, they did not kiss on the lips when they married. After Arline's death in an Albuquerque sanitarium, Feynman became an uninhibited, at times cruel, womanizer. Gleick spares no details. He dated undergraduates, paid prostitutes, and slept with the wives of friends. The affairs often ended bitterly.

Feynman's second marriage was to Mary Louise Ball, a Kansas woman he had met in a cafeteria while teaching at Cornell. When Cal Tech hired him (it was rumored that the university needed someone capable of conversing with Gell-Mann), she pursued him to Pasadena. The marriage ended in divorce four years later. Mary told the court she couldn't abide the sound of bongo drums, and said Richard was less interested in her than in doing calculus in his head. Feynman's last marriage, to Gweneth Howard, from Yorkshire, England, was happier. They raised a son and an adopted daughter.

Feynman was born in 1918 in Far Rockaway, New York. His parents were atheists, and he shared their view until his death in 1988 from stomach cancer. He made a scene at his father's burial by angrily accusing the officiating rabbi of hypocrisy in his graveside tribute. After Feynman's own death a heartrending letter (Gleick gives it in full) was found that Feynman had written to Arline two years after she died. It recalls many happy things they had done together, then closes:

> My darling wife, I do adore you. I love my wife. My wife is dead.
> Please excuse my not mailing this—but I don't know your new address.

CHAPTER FORTY-THREE

IS THE SECOND COMING COMING?

For Christians who think the Bible is without error, verses in which Jesus predicts his early return are not easy to explain. In Matthew 24, Mark 13, and Luke 21, after describing a darkening of the sun and moon, and stars falling, Jesus adds: "this generation shall not pass" until he comes to earth once more.

Did Jesus mean the generation of his listeners? That he did is surely clear by his remark, in the same three gospels (Matthew 16, Mark 9, and Luke 9), "There be some standing here which shall not taste of death till they see the Son of man coming in his Kingdom."

When Jesus' generation ended with no sign of his return, believers were obliged to concoct ingenious ways to escape the obvious intent of his words. The most fantastic explanation was that Jesus' generation had, in fact, not entirely passed away. Because he mocked Jesus when the Lord was carrying the cross, the so-called Wandering Jew was doomed to live on until Judgment Day. The most bizarre way out was the notion that the disciple John was sleeping underground in a state of suspended animation.

Some Bible scholars slyly reasoned that "this generation" referred to those who at some far future time would witness the "signs" immediately preceding the Second Coming. (Seventh-day Adventists identified the falling stars with the great meteoric shower of 1833, but after a century had passed they quietly dropped this from their literature.) Others decided that the Second Advent occurred when Jesus was transfigured. Augustine identified Christ's return with the Holy Spirit's coming at Pentecost, distinguishing this from a final judgment at the end of history. Augustine's way out soon became the Roman church's dominant view. It explains why Catholic priests today are not thundering about Armageddon.

Because no century of the Christian era has been free of believers insisting fervently that the Second Coming was just around the corner, one might suppose that today's evangelists would be uncomfortable about warning their flock to prepare for the Rapture—being lifted into the

This review first appeared in *Book World* (November 8, 1992). © 1996, Washington Post Book World Service/Washington Post Writers Group. Reprinted with permission.

clouds to meet Jesus. But few fundamentalists have any sense of history, although they have finally learned the folly of specifying the year of the Lord's return.

Excellent books have been written about the sad history of biblical prophecy, and the mysterious significance of 666, the number of the Antichrist, but not until now has anyone covered in such vast detail the eschatologies of America's present believers. Paul Boyer, a historian at the University of Wisconsin, takes his book's title, *When Time Shall Be No More*, from the old hymn that begins, "When the trumpet of the Lord shall sound, and time shall be no more." His book, published by Harvard University Press (1992), is a splendid, rigorously documented treatise, as up to date as the morning newspaper.

All the famous televangelists are covered: Billy Graham, Jimmy Swaggart, Jerry Falwell, Pat Robertson, Oral Roberts, Jack Van Impe, and dozens of others whose knowledge of modern biblical criticism can be scribbled on a file card. You will learn the doctrines of our nation's leading Adventist movements: Shakerism, Mormonism, Seventh-day Adventism, Jehovah's Witnesses, and Herbert Armstrong's comic Worldwide Church of God. A 1983 Gallup poll, Boyer discloses, reported that 63 percent of Americans had "no doubts" about the Lord's soon return.

Mainline denominations continue to decline while evangelical churches, preaching the Rapture and eternal hell for the unsaved, are on the upswing. In small Madison, Wisconsin, Boyer counted more than fifty such churches, and seven evangelical bookstores. "All America, not one region," he writes, "is a Bible Belt." Fifty percent of college graduates expect Jesus to be here any day now. We are, says Boyer, almost unique in the Western world in combining high educational levels with high levels of bibliolatry.

Historians differ on the extent to which the year 1000 sparked Second Coming mania, but there is no doubt that the approach of 2000 is having this effect. Hal Lindsey's *Late Great Planet Earth*, Boyer reminds us, by 1990 had sold twenty-eight million copies, and no less a skeptic than Orson Welles narrated its movie version. Lindsey has since repeated his gory warnings in half a dozen other profitable volumes. For a while, such potboilers were issued only by small fundamentalist houses west of the Hudson, but it wasn't long until greedy New York publishers discovered the gold. Bantam took over Lindsey's preposterous best-seller. ABC acquired Word Books. Harper and Row bought Zondervan for $57 million.

Hollywood also leaped into the fray with movies such as *The Omen, Damien-Omen II, The Final Conflict, The Seventh Sign, The Rapture,* and many others. Rock and pop songs about the Apocalypse continue to proliferate. Bumper stickers read, "Beam Me Up, Lord." Boyer reproduces a photograph of a watch that has on its face, "One Hour Nearer the Lord's Return."

Boyer is good on covering the extent to which today's believers have latched onto nuclear war as the means by which God will precipitate the final holocaust. Political bigwigs are not immune to such fears. Somehow Ronald Reagan managed to combine his unscriptural faith in astrology with anticipations of Armageddon. You'll find his simple-minded pronouncements in Boyer's book. Who knows what professed born-againers such as George Bush and Dan Quayle think about the Antichrist and Armageddon? Marilyn Quayle, however, is on record as having been a devotee of Col. Robert Thieme, Jr., a Houston Bible-thumper. Lindsey's *The Road to Holocaust* is dedicated to Thieme.

Caspar Weinberger once said he believed the world would end "by an act of God, I hope—but every day I think time is running out." Interior Secretary James Watts justified his soft stand on the environment by saying he didn't "know how many future generations we can count on before the Lord returns." Surgeon General C. Everett Koop is another "premillennialist"—one who believes the Second Advent will precede, not follow, the millennium.

No book provides more comprehensive information about the awesome degree to which biblical literalism and prophetic fervor have invaded the hearts and minds of Americans, rich and poor, educated and ignorant. It will not alter the convictions of a single believer. Others who read the book can laugh and weep.

Matthew 24:29 says the darkening of the sun and moon, and the falling of stars, will precede the Second Coming of Christ. Early Seventh-day Adventists took these prophecies to be fulfilled by the "dark day" in New England, May 19, 1780, and the great meteoric shower of November 13, 1833. The illustration is from J. H. Waggoner's *From Eden to Eden*, published by the Adventist's Pacific Press in 1888. Today's Adventists no longer refer to either event as signs of the immanence of the Second Coming.

"The Falling of the Stars." From J. H. Waggoner, *From Eden to Eden* (1888).

CHAPTER FORTY-FOUR

DO HUMANS
SPONTANEOUSLY COMBUST?

Here we go again—another worthless book pandering to public obsession with the paranormal. The authors of *Spontaneous Human Combustion* (Robert Hale, 1992), Jenny Randles and Peter Hough, have separately and in tandem perpetrated previous books about UFOs, crop circles, witchcraft, and similar wonders. In this book they do their best to persuade readers that there have been hundreds, perhaps thousands, of cases of people bursting into flames from causes science cannot fathom.

The simplest explanation of most such burnings is that victims fall asleep, often while intoxicated, and set fire to their clothes with a cigarette, cigar, or pipe. If elderly, fat, and dehydrated, and given sufficient time, almost all of the body can be reduced to ashes. Because the media love to sensationalize, sometimes to lie, the myth of spontaneous human combustion continues to thrive.

Not a single chemist or physicist of repute is cited in this shameful book, and for an obvious reason. None believes that a human body can spontaneously catch fire. Virtually all the periodicals cited in the book are not scientific journals but obscure fringe magazines devoted to the paranormal.

The authors discuss a variety of ways in which a body might ignite apart from contact with such things as burning cigarettes and fireplaces. Perhaps ball lightning enters a room to smite the victim. Static electricity? (The authors call this a "shocking suggestion.") Forcefields from high tension wires? Psychic curses from enemies? Poltergeists? "Kundalini fire," an energy that Yogis claim pervades a person's astral body? One "researcher" thinks the body may contain a subatomic particle—he calls it a "pyrotron"—that undergoes a chain reaction unknown to physicists.

The authors take seriously what they call a "phosphinic fart." That expelled gas is highly inflammable is easily demonstrated. Could it be, the authors wonder, that such gas might float up through clothing to be fired by a cigarette?

This review first appeared in *Nature* (November 26, 1992). Reprinted by permission from *Nature* 360, p. 283. Copyright © 1992 Macmillan Magazines Ltd.

The sole merits of this preposterous book are that it catalogues more than a hundred alleged cases of spontaneous human combustion, cites earlier books even worse than this one, and briefly considers cases of the phenomenon in fiction. The earliest example is in Charles Brockton Brown's novel *Wieland.* Others include Captain Marryat's *Jacob Faithful,* Herman Melville's *Redburn,* and Emile Zola's *Le Docteur Pascal.* The most famous instance is the spontaneous human combustion of a drunken Mr. Krook in Charles Dickens's *Bleak House.* Dickens was soundly trounced by George Henry Lewes, George Eliot's live-in lover, for treating spontaneous human combustion as a fact. (See *Blackwood's Edinburgh Magazine* 89 [April 1861].) Their debate was notable among the many controversies about the subject that raged in nineteenth-century England.

The jacket of *Spontaneous Human Combustion* shows a grisly photograph of the remains of Mary Reeser, a plump sixty-seven-year-old resident of St. Petersburg, Florida, who burned to death in 1951. The authors devote a chapter to this most famous of all modern cases. When Mrs. Reeser caught fire, she had not eaten dinner, was wearing a flammable nightgown, had taken two Seconal tablets, and was smoking a cigarette. When her son kissed her goodnight before leaving, she said she intended to take two more sleeping pills. Not until the following morning were her ashes found. The well-stuffed chair in which she sat was also consumed. The authors cannot imagine why the house did not burn down, ignoring the fact that the floor was concrete and a ceiling beam was burning when firemen arrived.

The Federal Bureau of Investigation's laboratory report on the case, based on many similar investigations, stated: "Once the body starts to burn there is enough fat and other inflammable substances to permit varying amounts of destruction to take place. Sometimes this destruction by burning will proceed to a degree which results in almost complete combustion of the body." Yet the authors strive valiantly to avoid the obvious and to convince readers that something strange and inexplicable had felled Mrs. Reeser.

Why are cases of alleged spontaneous human combustion so much rarer today than in past centuries? Because reporting is more accurate and forensic methods have improved. In 1982 the U.S. press had a field day when a Chicago woman was said to have burst into flames while walking along a street. When a medical examiner investigated, he found that the woman had been dead for twelve hours, and her clothes doused with gasoline.

On their last page the authors conclude that spontaneous human combustion is "triggered by forces that are just as puzzling to us as electricity was to Leonardo da Vinci. Yet, like electricity, it is probably a natural—not supernatural—energy dormant in our midst. If we can learn to tap into it, to harness its raw power and perhaps control its anger, then who knows what advantages it might bring to our children?"

Elsewhere, indulging in another pun, the authors call the "mystery" a "burning question" for modern science. It is not a burning question. It is not even a question. Not a single textbook on forensic medicine written this century considers the phenomenon a possible cause of death. The only burning question is how today's cynical publishers can maintain a clear conscience when they flood the market with absurd potboilers solely for the purpose of extracting money from an ill-informed, gullible public.

ADDENDUM

Of recent writings about SHC (spontaneous human combustion) I will cite a few references of special interest.

One of the most naive articles defending SHC appeared, in of all magazines, *Science Digest* (October 1981). Larry E. Arnold called his article "Human Fireballs." The editors say he is working on a book titled *Ablaze! The Incredible Mystery of Spontaneous Human Combustion*. As far as I know, it has not been published.

Michael Harrison's *Fire from Heaven* (Methuen, 1977) is even worse than the book I reviewed. Harrison links SHC to all sorts of paranormal phenomena. That poltergeists are responsible in some cases, he says, "is now beyond question." A prolific British author, Harrison is an expert on Sherlock Holmes, about whom he has written or edited several books. An expert on science he is not.

Two articles highly recommended are:

Joe Nickell and John Fischer, "Incredible Cremations," in the *Skeptical Inquirer* (Summer 1987). See also the letters section of the Winter 1987–88 issue.

Warren S. Walker, "Lost Liquor Lore: The Blue Flame of Intemperance," in the *Journal of Popular Culture* 16 (1987): 17–25. Walker stresses how America's temperance movement promoted myths about SHC being caused by heavy boozing.

CHAPTER FORTY-FIVE

WILL SCIENCE
DISCOVER EVERYTHING?

Dreams of a Final Theory (Pantheon, 1993) is an unusually well written and informative account of the search for nature's final laws. Its author, Steven Weinberg, is one of the world's most creative theoretical physicists. In 1979 he shared a Nobel prize with Pakistani Abdus Salam and his former high school chum Sheldon Glashow for unifying two fundamental forces of nature—the weak force and electromagnetism.

In our cold universe those two forces are distinct, but when the universe was very much hotter they were almost certainly one and the same. No one yet knows why, as the universe froze, the beautiful symmetry of the electroweak force broke in half. The most likely theory is that the break was caused by a field known as the Higgs field.

Wether or not a Higgs field, with its quantized particle, actually exists may soon be answered if the Superconducting Super Collider (SSC) is built south of Dallas. This fifty-three-mile oval tunnel, to cost at least $8 billion, would be the world's most powerful particle accelerator.... Weinberg makes strong arguments for the SSC's cost effectiveness, and they are summarized in his final chapter.

Although philosophy may have played a positive role in the work of Einstein, Heisenberg, and others, it has, in Weinberg's opinion, done more harm to science than good. Particularly baleful, he argues, was an early, crude version of positivism that prevented many eminent physicists from regarding unobservable entities as "real." The most flagrant example was the refusal of the Austrian physicist Ernst Mach, who had so strong an influence on Einstein, to admit the reality of atoms or to accept the unobservable fields of general relativity.

Despite his negative view of philosophy, Weinberg devotes more attention to metaphysics than most of his colleagues. Like almost all physicists he is a hard-nosed realist, with little use for sociologists of science and New Age thinkers and writers who deny there is a structured world "out there," independent of human observation. "The experience of

This review first appeared in *Book World* (January 31, 1993). © 1996, Washington Post Book World Service/Washington Post Writers Group. Reprinted with permission.

listening to a discussion of quantum field theory or weak interactions in a seminar room in Tsukuba or Bombay," he writes, "gives me a powerful impression that the laws of physics have an existence of their own."

The fact that for the past hundred years not a single fundamental theory of physics has been refuted suggests strongly to Weinberg that science is moving closer to objective truth, that its progress is not like changes in the fashions of dress. "A party of mountain climbers may argue over the best path to the peak, and these arguments may be conditioned by the history and social structure of the expedition, but in the end either they find a good path to the peak or they do not, and when they get there they know it."

Another source of antagonism toward science is the appalling growth of pseudosciences promoted by those who, in Weinberg's happy phrase, have "holistics in their heads." Why do scientists spend so little time trying to counter such nonsense? Weinberg's answer is straightforward:

> Suppose that someone today reported evidence that there are seven golden cities somewhere in modern Texas. Would you open-mindedly recommend mounting an expedition to search every corner of the state between the Red River and the Rio Grande to look for these cities? I think you would make the judgment that we already know so much about Texas, so much of it has been explored and settled, that it is simply not worthwhile to look for mysterious golden cities. In the same way, our discovery of the connected and convergent pattern of scientific explanations has done the very great service of teaching us that there is no room in nature for astrology or telekinesis or creationism or other superstitions.

Earlier physicists predicted prematurely that all the basic laws of science were about to become known. Weinberg is convinced, along with Stephen Hawking, that the spectacular progress of particle theory has made such a prediction more reasonable now than before. Obviously, if "dreams of a final theory" come true science will not end. There will be countless future discoveries—understanding how galaxies form, how evolution works, the nature of mind, and so on. There will be awesome technical inventions to be made and a monstrous universe to explore. But Weinberg hopes and believes that we will soon know all the fundamental laws—laws that cannot be explained by more basic ones. The final TOE (Theory of Everything) will be a thing of fantastic beauty and rigidity, "like a piece of fine porcelain that cannot be warped without shattering."

Physicists appear to Weinberg like early geographical explorers, filled with wonder about unknown regions. Their wonder vanished when the entire earth became known and there was nothing left to find north or south of the poles. This analogy can be turned around. Beyond the poles are all the wonders of a vast, dimly comprehensible universe. Weinberg himself speculates that our world may be only a bubble in an infinite sea of bubbles, each an entire universe with its own unique laws. Many physicists think the universe has infinite levels of structure, with enormous surprises ahead that no living scientist can even imagine. They suspect that the TOE is attached to an as yet invisible foot, in turn attached to who knows what?

Perhaps it is no accident that physicists who see a big TOE protruding around the corner, the way fundamentalists see signs of the Second Coming, are reluctant to attribute the universe to the work of a transcendentally Great Mathematician. Weinberg finds Einstein's God of Spinoza, like the pale god of liberal Christians, too "vague" to be relevant. He prefers that the word *God* be restricted to a deity concerned about human history. Like many other atheists, his main reason for rejecting such a God is the existence of irrational evil. He doesn't quote Marlene Dietrich, but she put it crisply: "If there is a supreme being, he must be crazy." Weinberg sees no sign in nature of a higher power interested even slightly in the lives of you and me. In this sense, as he said before in his popular book *The First Three Minutes,* the universe seems pointless.

Like Bertrand Russell and other eminent secular humanist thinkers, Weinberg admits that atheism is a cold, sad way to view existence. However, he concludes in his chapter "What About God?" even though atheism "is only a thin substitute for the consolations of religion, it is not entirely without satisfactions of its own."

ADDENDUM

Much to the dismay of physicists, Congress has cut off all funds for the SSC (Superconducting Super Collider), and there are no signs they will soon be restored.

Of many reviews of Weinberg's book, particularly significant is one by Roger Penrose in the *New York Review of Books* (October 21, 1993). Penrose is convinced that if the SSC is ever built, it will not get us much closer to any sort of final theory. "Perhaps what it may tell us will shock those who most strongly support the continuation of the SSC project. Perhaps the symmetry of the current electroweak theory is *not* fundamental, and there is no proper Higgs particle. I would myself hope that this is the case."

CHAPTER FORTY-SIX
TUNNELS OF THE MIND

Cognitive psychologists study how we think and make decisions. In recent decades they have devised a vast array of confusing questions that most people answer incorrectly because of their poor grasp of logic and probability theory. The correct answers are so counterintuitive that they arouse strong emotions of disbelief comparable to those produced by familiar optical illusions.

Massimo Piattelli-Palmarini, a cognitive psychologist at the Massachusetts Institute of Technology, has written a delightful informal survey of what are known as "cognitive illusions." His book (Wiley, 1995) is titled *Inevitable Illusions: How Mistakes of Reason Rule Our Minds.* Such illusions arise, he says, because of curious blind spots, or mental tunnels, in our minds. Moreover, these tunnels often seriously distort our thinking in such areas as law, politics, economics, and medical statistics.

The author's example of what he calls a "super tunnel" is a notorious brain teaser involving elementary probability. It generated such a storm of controversy when Marilyn vos Savant published it in her *Parade* magazine column that the *New York Times* (July 21, 1991) reported the fuss on its front page. We can model the problem with three playing cards, one of which is an ace. The operator of the game shuffles the cards and places them face down. You put your finger on a card. The probability you have chosen the ace clearly is $\frac{1}{3}$.

Suppose the operator, who knows where the ace is, removes a card that is not the ace. Two cards remain. Most people believe that the probability your finger is on the ace has now risen to $\frac{1}{2}$. Wrong! It remains $\frac{1}{3}$. Even more amazing is the fact that if you shift your finger to the other card, the chance it is the ace doubles to $\frac{2}{3}$. Savant was bombarded with thousands of letters, some from leading mathematicians, objecting to her correct answer.

Piattelli-Palmarini has a raft of other instances where intuitions lead one astray. Which is larger, the set of all seven-letter words ending with

---

This review first appeared in *Nature* (March 2, 1995). Reprinted by permission from *Nature* 374, p. 25. Copyright © 1995 Macmillan Magazines Ltd.

"ing" or the set of all such words with "i" in the fifth position? Obviously the second set is larger because it includes the first, yet on actual tests most people guess the other way.

Consider this statement:

> Steve is very shy and withdrawn, invariably helpful, but with little interest in people or in the world of reality. A meek and tidy soul, he has a need for order and structure, and a passion for detail.

Which is more likely, that Steve is a librarian or a farmer? Most people pick librarian. Their blind spot is letting a librarian stereotype override the fact that there are far more farmers than librarians.

This neglect of background statistics is involved in other classics of cognitive research. A laboratory test is 79 percent accurate in detecting a certain disease. The disease is known to affect only 1 percent of the population. If you test positive, what is the probability you have the disease? The correct answer, which the author says can be established by Bayes's theorem (to which he devotes an informative chapter) is 8 percent! Our intuition, we are told, is faulty because we have failed to consider the background information.

Are the cognitive psychologists right on this one? Let's raise the accuracy of the test to 100 percent. Surely the background information is now totally irrelevant. Why would it become relevant if the test were, say, 99 percent accurate?

The most tireless researchers on cognitive illusions are Amos Tversky, at Stanford University, and Daniel Kahneman, at Princeton. Is Piattelli-Palmarini right in saying their discoveries are so revolutionary that they deserve the Nobel prize in economics? Or should we agree with their leading detractor, the German psychologist Gerd Gigerenzer? He and others argue that the tricky problems posed by cognitive-illusion researchers represent rare, carefully contrived instances where intuitions are indeed unsound, but that their work on such illusions is making mountains out of molehills.

Whatever the case, *Inevitable Illusions* is the best popular book yet in this peculiar field. It will be of as much interest to recreational mathematicians as to psychologists and general readers.

ADDENDUM

Some notion of how vague nouns are can be gained from studies reported by Piattelli-Palmarini showing that most people say a sparrow is more "typical" of a bird than a toucan or a penguin. They also report on tests that 7 is more typical of an odd number than, say 51, and 4 is more typical of an even number than, say, 196. An apple is more typical of a fruit than a coconut, a truck is more typical of a vehicle than an elevator, and so on. Obviously such statements merely reflect the way words are commonly used, yet no less than seven cognitive psychologists have published research along these lines!

I don't want readers to think I doubted the paradox about drug testing. Indeed, I gave a variation of this paradox as Problem 26 in my *Riddles of the Sphinx*. Brian A. Kennedy, vice president and treasurer of Blue Cross-Blue Shield of Illinois, explained the situation very clearly in the following letter:

> I was delighted by your "cognitive illusions" review of the Piattelli-Palmarini book.
>
> Were you yourself playfully practicing a little cognitive sleight of hand? You *appeared* to hesitate—using two question marks in a three-sentence paragraph that cries out for periods.
>
> You correctly point out that if the accuracy of a test is 100 percent, then "the background information is now totally irrelevant." However, you then ask, "why would it become relevant if the test was, say, 99 percent accurate?"
>
> Here is why. Let the population be 10,000, of whom 1 percent have a disease. So 100 persons are sick, and 9,900 persons are well.
>
> If the test is 100 percent accurate, then by definition the test will identify 100 percent of the above 100 as sick, i.e., 100 persons; and the test will identify zero percent of the above 9,900 as sick, i.e., zero persons. If this test says that you are sick, believe it.
>
> However, if the test is 99 percent accurate, then by definition the test will identify 99 percent of the 100 as sick, i.e., 99 persons; and the test will identify 1 percent of the 9,900 as sick, i.e., another 99 persons. If this test says that you are sick, then you are one of either 99 sick people or 99 well people.
>
> The blind spot is to fixate on the seemingly minuscule 1 percent reduction (from the full 100 percent, to a still massive 99 percent). Actually, of course, a mere 1 percent of a large number can be (and is here) nonnegligible.
>
> With "background statistics" (conditional probabilities—Bayes's theorem), it is sound practice to tabulate the calculated numbers into rows and columns, with cross-footed subtotals that sum to the population's grand total (here, 10,000). This low but solid methodology automatically protects the researcher. It gives the blind spot no place to hide.